Volunteers in the
Texas Revolution

THE NEW ORLEANS GREYS

Gary Brown

Republic of Texas Press

Library of Congress Cataloging in Publication Data

Brown, Gary, 1945-.
   Volunteers in the Texas Revolution: the New Orleans Greys / by Gary Brown.
      p.   cm.
   Includes index.
   ISBN 1-55622-675-6
   1. Texas--History--Revolution, 1835-1836. 2. Mercenary troops--
Texas--History--19th century. 3. New Orleans (La.)--History,
Military--19th century. I. Title.
   F390.B883   1999
   976.4'03--dc21   98-31802
                                                CIP

ISBN 1-55622-675-6
10 9 8 7 6 5 4 3 2 1
9812

All inquiries for volume purchases of this book should be addressed to
Wordware Publishing, Inc., at 2320 Los Rios Blvd., Plano, Texas 75074.
Telephone inquiries may be made by calling:
(972) 423-0090

Table of Contents
(With Biographical Sketch at Beginning of Each Chapter)

This book is dedicated to
Dr. Donald F. Powell,
A professor and a friend
And
Devin J. Brown,
My son and a friend

Preface

For a state that brags about and promotes itself on largeness, the Texas Revolution is an anomaly. A relatively few Anglo settlers aided by outside adventurers revolted and wrestled a very large section of land away from Mexico and, in the process, created legends seemingly larger than life—William Barret Travis, James Bowie, David Crockett, Sam Houston, and Stephen F. Austin.

But as a military conflict, it lasted only seven months and consisted of eight battles. The siege of the Alamo lasted just thirteen days and the Alamo battle itself was concluded in barely one hour. Even the decisive Battle of San Jacinto, securing Texas' independence from Mexico, was brief—an estimated eighteen minutes.

By military standards, there was really no "Texas" army. More often than not, settlers merely picked up their weapons and marched toward the Mexicans. Volunteers did come to Texas but, for the most part, they were more like citizen militias than military units.

Military uniforms were almost nonexistent. Weapons consisted of whatever the volunteer reported with. At Gonzales, Sam Houston found that many of the volunteers had reported without arms and he had none to supply. Unit discipline was seldom defined, much less enforced. Officers were promoted (and demoted) by popular vote of the men.

Some of the volunteers came for free land. Others, especially the established settlers who generally opposed secession from Mexico, reluctantly took up arms to defend what they perceived as their homes. A few may have even volunteered for the cause of constitutional freedoms. A considerable number of U.S. Army members could be found in Texas—whether they were officially or unofficially "deserters" remains open to debate. Land speculators and lawyers in the United States could hardly wait for the Texans to break away from Mexico and Mexican laws of canonization.

A large number of volunteers, however, came to Texas and the promise of conflict here out of a sense of adventure. The supposedly threatened liberties being taken away from the Constitution of 1824 made for good campfire discussions, but "the promise of a good scrape with the Mexicans" was the primary attraction for many of the volunteers, especially the younger ones. And wars couldn't be fought very well without strong, brave, and idealistic young men.

Such a group came to Texas in 1835. They were an exception to most of the military standards of the Texas army at that time. As a unit, they were born in a New Orleans coffee arcade on October 13, 1835. Only 175 days later, they had been destroyed as a military unit and only a handful lived to learn of the victory at San Jacinto.

During that 175 days they were the premier Texan military unit in the rebellion. They wore uniforms. They carried similar weapons. And they fought.

They led the charge into Bexar during the battle for San Antonio and claimed that settlement for Texas—street by street, house by house, and in the end, hand to hand with the Mexican army.

Later they would again fight hand to hand in defending the Alamo, and they were one of the few volunteer units with members participating in San Patricio, Agua Dulce, and Refugio.

At Coleto, after effectively engaging far better equipped and supplied Mexican foot soldiers and cavalry, they were forced against their will to surrender. One week later, at Goliad, they were among the first to be marched out unarmed and massacred.

It was a short, violent 175-day unit history. Somehow, at least three of them were found among the rolls after the battle and victory at San Jacinto.

Bexar, the Alamo, San Patricio, Agua Dulce, Refugio, Coleto, Goliad, and San Jacinto . . . Had their battle standard survived, it would have been the most decorated unit herald of the Texas Revolution.

But, in the end, even their flag was gone. Known incorrectly as the Alamo flag, their banner is located yet today in the museum of the Castle of Chapultepec in Mexico City—Santa Anna's "proof" of U.S. involvement in the Texas Revolution.

There are scattered around Texas some monuments for members of this group, but they are all memorials. Almost all died—few were properly buried. At the Alamo and Goliad their bodies were partially burned and left for the vultures and wolves before being finally interred in mass graves.

Their unit history is one of bravery, courage, and fighting skill. It was also one of poor leadership, internal political division, and terrible logistics and supply. But they were for the most part strong, brave, and idealistic young men.

These young men carried ideals—no matter how misplaced—into the revolution. They were ruthless in battle yet compassionate in victory. While they lived, they were formidable. When they died, they left a legacy of valor and courage.

They were known as the New Orleans Greys.

Chapter 1

Bank's Arcade

New Orleans Harbor, October 13, 1835: A group of slaves dressed in gray work uniforms struggled to wrench the cannon up the ramp onto the deck of the schooner *Columbus.* "A big one," Robert Musselman thought to himself as he studied the artillery piece from the sidewalk bench in front of the tavern. "Must be at least an eighteen-pounder," he figured as he signaled for another mug.

Musselman was no stranger to artillery, although this massive gun was far larger than anything he'd seen in Florida. Taking another drink, he continued to ponder. Slaves, land, and fighting—seemed that his whole life was beginning to revolve around these three issues.

Florida had been a tour in hell. He'd hated the swamps and the Indians. His army tour of duty was over and he'd discharged to get away from it all, but here he was again, in New Orleans, and he was about to start it all over only this time in Texas.

Land had been the issue, or at least the excuse, for Americans moving into Spanish Florida to settle. Initially the Spanish government had encouraged white settlers, but they inevitably clashed with the Seminoles—largely over the Indian practice of harboring runaway slaves.

Although the October air was cool on the New Orleans dock, the slaves Musselman was studying were sweating as they continued to hoist the cannon and other military equipment aboard the schooner.

"Slavery's going to destroy this country," he thought as he took another swig and wiped his mouth with the back of his hand. He'd seen the effects of slavery back in Shelby County, Ohio, where he'd been born thirty years earlier. The issue was just as divisive in Pennsylvania where he'd lived before joining the army. In Florida, it had caused two wars with the Seminole Indians and now, in Mexico, the cycle was starting all over again.

"Yeah, a cycle," he thought to himself, "just like in Florida. Only this time instead of Indians, it was Mexicans, but the issues were the same—slavery and land."

Slavery had never been a personal issue for Robert Musselman although the desire for land now was. He'd planned to move back East after military duty, but the death of his father while he was in Florida had changed all that. Now he had nothing to go back to, and his father had left no inheritance, so he'd discharged the army and headed to New Orleans.

He'd known immediately after arrival that New Orleans was too expensive for him and that he'd probably never be able to save enough money to buy a place here. But as he'd started thinking about it, he'd also become more aware of the current hot political topic being discussed everywhere around the city. That topic was the northernmost province of Mexico called Texas.

Trouble had been brewing there for a long time. Same as Florida, it had been American settlers moving into a new territory: first with permission, then in defiance. And like in Florida, the institution of slavery was a significant part of the problem.

Constitutional freedoms being retracted by the current Centralist government in Mexico was being blamed by the rumormongers around New Orleans for the current problems in Texas. But Musselman knew that it was more complicated than that. Slavery was prohibited in Mexico, and the early settlers had for the most part complied, but now there was an unrestrained flood of Anglo immigrants crossing the Sabine River into Texas from the American south, and many were openly bringing their slaves into the territory.

More disturbing, Musselman thought to himself, were the land speculators who had moved into Texas and cared nothing about restoring constitutional guarantees of personal freedoms. These unscrupulous entrepreneurs cared only about getting rich developing land grants, and the only way they could succeed was to convince the whites in Texas to break away from Mexico completely—secede and create their own country.

By now the massive cannon had disappeared over the gangplank onto the deck, but the slaves continued to carry boxes of military supplies and foodstuffs onto the ship. With nothing else to do, Musselman signaled the waitress for another drink and continued to ponder the decision he was about to make.

Worse than the Texas land speculators, he figured, were the Jacksonian Democrats who were officially "neutral" but secretly encouraging the breakaway Texas movement. Again, freedom was the stated reason for support, but Musselman suspected that what was really at issue was an independent Texas that could be annexed into the United States as a slave state and tilt the delicate balance between slave and free states in the U.S. Congress.

The United States was headed for division or civil war over the slavery issue. Musselman had seen how divisive the issue was while he was in the army—a northern soldier stationed in the Deep South.

He paid for the fresh drink, and his thoughts turned to his personal interest in Texas: free land. All over New Orleans, placards and newspaper headlines were proclaiming free land for homesteading once Texas was freed of Santa Anna and the corrupt Centralist Mexican government. Headrights, they were called, and they were guarantees of free land for any man willing to go to Texas and help overthrow the Mexicans.

The various newspapers around New Orleans trumpeted the abuses of Santa Anna and the bounty to be claimed in Texas. The problem, according to the reports, would be getting to Texas before the revolution was over. It seemed nobody expected the Mexicans to put up much of a fight.

Musselman had never been to Texas, but he suspected otherwise. As part of Jackson's Indian Removal Act, he'd been sent into the Florida swamps for what was to be a simple job of resettling a bunch of "uncivilized savages." It had been a mistaken assumption, he recalled bitterly, when the Seminoles had ambushed the army soldiers as they entered unfamiliar, hostile territory and defeated them time after time in a type of warfare for which he and his fellow soldiers had not been prepared to fight.

It appeared to him that in Texas, the land speculators had succeeded, since the Anglo Texans had started a rebellion recently and were now assembling at some old mission city in northern Mexico called San Antonio de Bexar. There seemed to be too many similarities to Florida for him to believe this would be a simple military exercise.

And so, with his family gone and his ties to the East severed, Robert Mussleman had decided like so many others to go to Texas for free land. But first he'd have to do some more soldiering—a task he didn't particularly care for.

For the past several weeks he'd listened in taverns, coffee arcades, on work gangs, and to dockside conversations by young men who were planning to also go to Texas, maybe skirmish a bit with the Mexicans, then lay claim to large tracts of free land and become wealthy.

But he could also tell by listening to their conversations that these young men—usually in their twenties—were not trained soldiers. He had no reservations that these big, raw-boned, and boisterous boys could fight. However he had seen hundreds of these same kids die in the Florida swamps facing Seminole Indians who had inferior weapons and equipment but who were maintaining a sense of identity with the territory they were protecting. Intuition and military experience told him that the situation might be similar in Mexico.

Darkness was settling on the docks now and he finished his drink. The activity on the schooner in front of him had slowed considerably, but under the low glow of torches, a steady line of slaves continued to enter and depart the gangplank loading supplies.

He walked to the corner of Gravier Street and looked up at the clock on the tower of the nearby Cathedral of St. Louis. The meeting tonight at Bank's Arcade was scheduled for eight o'clock and it was half past seven, so he started walking the three blocks up to 336 Magazine Street between Gravier and Natchez Streets.

Gravier Street was busy this evening, but the mass of men seemed to be, like him, gravitating toward the three-story red-bricked arcade building that was well known as a Texas recruiting center. Placards around the city had advertised this meeting for several days, and Mussleman knew that it would likely be filled with young, would-be mercenaries looking for adventure and fortune in northern Mexico.

He stepped into the street and started working his way up to the arcade. As he grew closer, the crowd of men grew larger until, as the bells of the cathedral chimed eight o'clock, the mass forced its way into the entrances of the arcade.

Musselman worked his way into the main hall and inched up toward the makeshift stage where he knew the speakers would be located. This was not his first trip to Bank's Arcade to attend one of these meetings. Thomas Banks, owner of the building, was well known for his support of the rebels in Texas, and the arcade had for some time now served as a focal point for recruitment.

Before, however, he had attended meetings out of curiosity. Tonight his desire to settle down on his own land brought him here with the intent to sign up.

The main hall quickly became packed with men standing shoulder to shoulder, and the noise from their conversations was deafening. Shortly after eight o'clock the first of several speakers stepped onto the platform and gestured with his arms for some time before the roar of the crowd ceased and he could address the group.

Several speakers gave short, impassioned pleas for men to sign up and go to Texas—usually with the call to "fight Mexican tyranny" or "overthrow the corrupt Centralist regime of Santa Anna." Musselman secretly wondered to himself what personal stakes these entrepreneurs had in an independent or U.S.-annexed Texas. "Hell," he thought to himself, "they probably haven't ever even been to Texas themselves."

Finally, a speaker he recognized took the stage. As a young boy in Ohio, he had heard stories of William H. Christy, an Indian fighter who had distinguished himself against Tecumseh at Fort Meigs in 1813. Much later, while he was searching for Seminoles in the Florida swamps himself, he had come to truly respect Christy's bravery earlier under similar circumstances.

Since Musselman had arrived in New Orleans, the name of William Christy had figured prominently in the political conversations around the arcades and taverns. Christy had served with Andrew Jackson at the Battle of New Orleans and discharged from the army to remain in the city and become involved in local politics.

After passing the bar exam, Christy had practiced law and served as a city alderman. Tonight, he was speaking to the group as the chairman and treasurer of one of the many committees to raise men and money for Texas.

Musselman genuinely admired Christy's record of bravery against the Indians over thirty years earlier. He did not, however, extend that respect to William Christy the politician who was addressing the arcade tonight.

He knew that Christy had, in fact, been to Texas. He had even been imprisoned in Mexico for going to Texas earlier and assisting the Long Expedition attempting to overthrow the Mexican government.

For that reason he suspected Christy might be one of those unscrupulous land speculators who had everything to gain and nothing to lose in the secessionist movement in Texas. Musselman knew that if he were to sign up for military service in Texas, he wouldn't be guaranteed free land, and if things went wrong, he might end up like Christy in a Mexican prison or even killed as a pirate. He and others like him tonight had little to gain and much to lose.

When Christy finished his call for volunteers, he introduced another speaker. Again, Musselman was familiar with the name of the speaker—Adolphus Sterne—but knew little about him except that, like Christy, Sterne had been involved in Texas politics for some time now.

Sterne and Christy, according to local gossip, had studied law together in New Orleans in the period right after the Battle of New Orleans, only Sterne had left Louisiana for Texas where he became a land agent and judge in the east Texas settlement of Nacogdoches.

As the German made his way to the speaker's platform, Musselman recalled that the Texas agent had, like Christy, been imprisoned for attempting to overthrow the Mexican authorities—this time in the Freedonian Rebellion in east Texas. His Masonic affiliations, attorney connections, and probably his friendship with William Christy, had secured his release, and he was now acting as a recruiting agent—supposedly financing much of his activity with his own money.

By now the crowd in the arcade was becoming restless and tired of political oratory. Sterne managed to silence the crowd one more time, then gave a short but impassioned plea for men to volunteer for military service in Texas. Although Musselman didn't think he liked or trusted this land agent, he was interested in what the German had to say because this was the man who could offer him free land in Texas if he enlisted.

Sterne briefly explained how if Texas obtained independence from Mexico, military veterans would be offered large tracts of land through what was called a headright program. To Musselman, that was a very large "if," and he noticed how the discussion about restoring individual freedoms under the Mexican Constitution of 1824 had virtually disappeared from the oratory this night. Tonight all discussion centered not on reform, but on secession.

Sterne's rallying speech was short, and throughout his talk various men in business clothing called out offers of financial support, in effect pledging monies if the meeting succeeded in organizing a military unit.

To these pledges, Sterne made a public statement of appreciation but stressed that what Texas really needed was men—men ready to fight the Mexicans. In conclusion, he personally offered a free rifle to the first fifty volunteers who would sign up.

At first there was silence in the hall, then a tall frontiersman stepped up—someone later said he was from Kentucky—and asked where he needed to sign his name. Then pandemonium broke out throughout the arcade as men milled around debating whether to enlist. Musselman had worked his way into a good spot to hear the speakers but couldn't get into a line to qualify for a free rifle.

Resigned to enlisting and returning to military duty, he was still in no hurry to make his commitment. Wandering around the hall, he noticed that most of the observers had left the building after Sterne's speech, but the recruitment call seemed to have been successful. He estimated that over one hundred men were lining up to enlist. He was about to join them.

Two lines quickly formed, leading to speculation among the men that two companies were being organized. Musselman got into one line and, waiting his turn, observed the men around him with whom he would be traveling to Texas as a military mercenary.

It seemed to him that about a third of the men were foreigners while the rest were Americans about equally split between northerners and southerners. They were a young group and, at age thirty, he felt older than most. If their youthful bravado could be believed, they represented a diverse background of occupations. Ominously, he observed, few seemed to have any military experience.

Finally he reached the enlistment table, and with no comment and only a nod of his head to the clerk sitting there, he picked up the pen, dipped it into the ink, and signed his name.

"Congratulations," the clerk told him, "you are now a New Orleans Grey."

CЗCЗCЗ𝕾𝕌𝕾𝕌𝕾𝕌

*T*he Sabine River, or *Rios de Sabinas*, flows for 555 miles. It has at various times separated New Spain from New France, divided New Spain into provinces, delineated New Spain from the United States, and provided a border between Mexico and the United States.

Such was the case in 1835 when the Sabine served as the boundary between Louisiana and a Mexican republic in turmoil. In the autumn season of that year New Orleans was a recruiting center for volunteer groups enlisting to go to Texas.

Bank's Arcade was a three-story building with a barroom, a glass-roofed courtyard, and an auction mart. The rooms on the second and third floors were used for the secret meetings of the plotters; recruiting for filibustering campaigns was carried on openly over clinking glasses in the barroom; and in the spacious courtyard and auction mart were held the mass meetings.[1]

The night of October 13, 1835, Thomas Banks used the occasion and the arcade to promote the organization of the New Orleans Greys.

William Christy, often called the Lafayette of Texas, presided. He told his audience that news of the struggle in Texas had aroused the cities of Nashville, Macon, Huntsville, Mobile, New York, Cincinnati, Louisville, and Nachitoches. He described how funds were being raised and men organized for military aid. "Shall we let these distant cities outstrip us, when we are so much nearer both geographically and in understanding of the situation?" he demanded.[2]

Upon hearing this challenge, an unnamed merchant stepped forward and contributed fifty dollars. Before the meeting was finished, an estimated seven to ten thousand dollars had been pledged.

Following Christy, Sterne addressed the group. Adolphus Sterne, despite his twenty-four years of age, was a veteran of the political intrigue in both Texas and New Orleans. Well connected in both regions through family connections, he was alcalde—a Mexican political office combining the duties of mayor and judge—of Nacogdoches. He had sworn Sam Houston as a Mexican citizen, and his Catholic wife was godmother at Houston's baptism into Catholicism as required by Mexican law.

It is estimated that when the meeting was over at least one hundred twenty men had volunteered for service. In the excitement two companies were formed in different areas of the auction mart, not by design but because two different men had assumed the role of commander and began enlisting volunteers. The New Orleans Greys had been born.

After the initial recruitment, events moved quickly. Plans were made for one unit to travel north by boat to Alexandria, then march across the Sabine River to Nacogdoches where Sterne promised to supply them with horses. They would then cross the Texas prairie to Bexar, otherwise known as San Antonio, where the rebels were laying siege to the Mexican army in the colonial hamlet and old Alamo mission.

The other company would sail by ship from New Orleans to the Texas port of Velasco and then march overland to join the first company at Bexar. This ship was the schooner *Columbus* that Robert Musselman had watched being readied even before the recruitment meeting.

But the immediate order of business was organization and supply. The arcade had on the second floor an armory belonging to a group known as the Washington Guards. Probably some of the additional weaponry issued that night came from that armory, and certainly many of the volunteers who enlisted already possessed the weapons of their choice. Later reports from that meeting indicate that the standard weapons included "rifles, pistols, swords and large knives." The large knives referred to the mass-produced replicas of the already legendary "Bowie knife."

Previous companies had been named "greys," and many subsequent volunteer units would also adopt that name— creating a great deal of confusion in interpreting muster rolls and rosters. The spelling of the unit name would variously be recorded as "grays" and "greys." The New Orleans Greys would, in the future, merge and assume other "greys" titles: San Antonio Greys, Cooke's Greys, and the Mobile Greys.

But the two companies organized in New Orleans that October 13 evening were *the* Greys. Their name was derived from the distinctive gray uniforms they were issued. A great deal of debate has centered on the uniforms: The popular historical view has been that they were surplus U.S. military uniforms—possibly 1825 army fatigue jackets—a theory supported by reports that Texas Indians who first encountered the group believed they were witnessing the American army inside Texas.

More recently, however, some historians have pointed out that the uniforms also closely resembled the gray wool/cotton fustian uniforms commonly worn that time of the year on the New Orleans ship docks by laborers and in some cases, by slaves. There are several accounts of such interwoven cotton and wool material being used as slave's clothing.[3]

One Grey, Herman Ehrenberg, referred to the uniforms as "grey, for-service-in-the-prairie-fitting uniforms, which we found ready-made in the numerous magazines of the city." At least two illustrations suggest that the uniforms had military-style drop-flap pants and wraparound jackets.[4]

Historians Amelia W. Williams and Eugene C. Barker state in their edited edition of Sam Houston's writings that "the only kind of clothing that could be secured in sufficient quantity to outfit these men was a kind of homespun of gray color, called *jeans*. Suits made of this cloth were somewhat comparable to the ordinary workman's suit that may be bought ready-made in most department stores today."[5] Since they were procured from "numerous" magazines throughout the city, they were probably similar but not completely "uniform" in appearance.

The distinctive black forage caps were almost certainly of military issue—probably the M1825 or M1833 forage cap. Similar caps, however, also were worn by laborers and many seamen of that period. Made of sealskin, they had flaps in the back that folded up into the band or could be dropped to protect the neck against the elements.

In the confusion during enlistment, two groups formed, giving the erroneous impression that two units were being created. As it developed, the successful recruitment effort resulted in the two groups being designated as companies. Neither company was given a numerical designation, however the unit to first reach San Antonio is often erroneously referred to as the First Company.

Also confusing is the fact that, just prior to the storming and occupation of San Antonio, one unit captain was promoted to the rank of major and William G. Cooke was selected as the new captain—resulting in the company being referred to as "Cooke's Greys" and leading some historians to report that there were actually three companies of the New Orleans Greys.

If muster rolls were recorded that evening at Bank's Arcade, there appears to be no existing record of them. Two decades later, in 1855, a fire at the Louisiana Adjutant General's Office destroyed many original rolls possibly including those of the Greys. As a result, there are numerous spelling inconsistencies, and dates often do not match up correctly (even the date of the meeting at Bank's Arcade is disputed— some sources claim the date was October 11).

The company arriving at Velasco on October 25 recorded a handwritten muster roll that is on file at the Alamo library operated by the Daughters of the Republic of Texas. The copy, however, is so poorly handwritten that many of the names are almost illegible, and as a result, subsequent lists often show names spelled in various styles.

As historian Karl Baker wrote in 1937:

> . . .the sources are scattered fragments
> which must be hunted out and pieced together,
> bit by bit. In the process dates shift, names
> change their spelling, numbers refuse to yield
> their proper totals. This attempt to reconstruct
> the story, to fit all the discoverable facts into
> their right places in the pattern, is to be taken
> as an attempt only—an invitation to future
> inquirers to amend and complete.[6]

Sixty years after Baker made this observation, subsequent research has made the accounting of the New Orleans Greys rosters even more difficult.

The Texas General Land Office in Austin also has available three sets of roll books for Greys titled Muster roll, "New Orleans Greys Capt. Wm. G. Cooke, in the Army before Bexar 1835"[7]; Muster roll, "Captain Thomas H. Breece's Co. Texas Volunteers, in the Army before Bexar 1835"[8]; and Muster roll Captain Petus "Company. New Orleans Greys."[9] Since Pettus' (another example of alternative spelling) unit was a later union of members of the original two companies, it provides no information about the original volunteers.

By cross-referencing the General Land Office rosters with the Velasco muster roll and names of the rolls at the Alamo and Goliad, it is possible to re-create company rosters that correlate with early reports of unit numbers for the two companies. As with Baker's observation in 1937, this is an attempt only, an invitation for future inquirers to amend and complete.

When tabulating these figures, it appears that one company totaled between 53 and 56 members and the other company enlisted between 64 and 67 volunteers at the arcade that evening.

Much of the problem in re-creating unit rosters can be attributed to spelling inconsistencies, but it was also common to find, during the Texas revolution, fathers and sons sharing the same given as well as family names and also cases in which brothers become confused on different rolls.[10]

An example of this would be Blaz Phillipe Despallier, who enlisted as a Grey and participated in the siege of Bexar but afterwards became sick and returned to Louisiana. His younger brother, Charles, also volunteered for service in Texas but not as a Grey. After Blaz Phillipe had returned to Louisiana, Charles participated in clearing the *jacales* near the Alamo walls, under heavy fire, during the siege and then served as a courier—returning to the Alamo for the final time with the Gonzales Ranging Company of Mounted Volunteers and dying in the battle on March 6, 1836. The name "

Despallier" appears on Breece's New Orleans Greys muster roll and on the death list of the Alamo—yet the Alamo defender was not a Grey.

Another example would be Andrew Greer, a Tennessee volunteer. His brother, Thomas, also came to Texas but did not join the Greys—serving, instead, as an artillerymen at the Battle of San Jacinto, manning one of the Twin Sisters cannon as a member of Lt. Col. James Neill's artillery corps.

George Nelson was a volunteer that night whose younger brother, Edward, joined him during the siege and occupation of Bexar and died with him inside the Alamo but never joined the Greys.

The name "New Orleans" Greys has given the erroneous impression that the two companies were comprised of local, or at least Louisiana, men. In a way this was true, but only in the sense that New Orleans was probably the most diverse, multicultural urban center in the United States in 1835.

The common method of recording identification during that period was to list volunteers by home state. This, however, could also be misleading since many of the volunteers were transitory hunters, trappers, Indian fighters, or roving businessmen and tended to list their current address—or perhaps their last semi-permanent location—as their home state. Others, trying to leave elements of their pasts behind, may have purposefully listed false home states to confuse enemies, creditors, or angry wives.

Much has been written about the character and backgrounds of the Texas soldiers during the revolution. They have been characterized as the social and economic outcasts from the United States looking for quick fortune or escaping the American criminal justice system. Paul D. Lack, in his book *The Texas Revolutionary Experience,* cites one particularly harsh characterization:

"... generally collected from the very dregs
of cities and towns, where they had obtained a
scanty living by pelf and petty gambling. They
are the most miserable wretches that the world
ever produced."[11]

Lack also points out, however, that "early volunteers from
the United States also took pains to disassociate themselves
from mere mercenary impulses."[12]

Since the Greys were among the first of the volunteer
units, their ranks probably contained a few "outlaws" but, for
the most part, consisted of men who would have been considered of "good character" for that period.

Charles Clark is an example of the confusion caused by
using state citizenship as identifying criteria. A Charles Clark
enlisted with the New Orleans Greys and is listed as a native
of Louisiana who served at Bexar and was later killed at
Goliad. Another Charles (A.) Clark was also born in Louisiana but traveled to Texas from New York. Alamo records
show that a Charles Clark from Missouri traveled to New
York then to New Orleans where he joined the Greys and
died in the Alamo. In fact, Charles (Henry) Clark did die at
the Alamo but was not a Grey.

By cross-referencing, a list of names with "alleged" home
state citizenships can be developed for the Greys and
includes eighteen states as well as members from England,
Ireland, Germany (sometimes listed as Upper Saxony),
Wales, Scotland, Upper Canada, and Nova Scotia. Thus the
Greys were truly neither "New Orlean" nor "Louisianian" nor
even completely "American."

Most of the names on the rosters have little information
available. Youth seems to be one recurring factor when
reviewing the names, so most of the volunteers probably had
not had the opportunity to create business skills beyond
those that required mobility—as evidenced in the wide background of declared home states. Some volunteers, however,

had established business and personal histories prior to that October 13 evening at the arcade.

Robert C. Morris of New Orleans was a military man—having served several years in the Louisiana Guards prior to Greys enlistment. He, like Robert Mussleman, represented the few Greys who had formal military backgrounds. John Cook was an experienced artilleryman with service as a British marine. Most volunteers, however, appear to have had little or no prior military experience.

William Gordon Cooke was a druggist from Virginia. Michael Cronican had apprenticed as a newspaperman in Massachusetts and was a skilled printer. Stephen Dennison, an Englishman, was a painter and glasscutter by trade.

There were at least two medical doctors with the Greys—one assigned to each company. William Howell had been a doctor in New York before traveling to New Orleans. Albert Moses Levy, born in the Netherlands but a naturalized citizen and graduate of medical school at the University of Pennsylvania, was a surgeon attached to the other company of the Greys. Levy is listed on the rosters as Surgeon while Howell is recorded simply as "Pvt." At least one of the Greys, William Hunter, was a lawyer and also served as a private.[13]

Francis Johnson had been born in Virginia and educated in Tennessee as a surveyor. At age thirty-two, he was one of the older Greys, but before reporting to New Orleans he had worked as a grocer, miller, constable, miner, and militiaman as well as a surveyor. Thomas Saltus Lubbock, at age seventeen, was working in a New Orleans cotton warehouse when he enlisted.

Julian Harby came to New Orleans from Charleston, South Carolina, where his father had previously introduced and established beginnings of Reform Judaism in Charleston and the United States. His uncle, Levi, was also traveling to Texas to join in the revolution to serve in the Texas navy. Levi was a veteran of naval battles in the War of 1812 and against the Mediterranean Barbary pirates. He had returned to the United States and had fought in the Seminole Indian Wars in Florida and in the independence movement in Bolivia. His interest in joining the Texas revolution had greatly influenced Julian as he signed up with the New Orleans Greys that night.

Thomas William Ward, a young Irishman who would later be seriously wounded at Bexar, had immigrated to Quebec and then to New Orleans where he was studying engineering and architecture. Herman Ehrenberg, listed as a German, had studied writing and engineering at the University of Jena.

It is Ehrenberg as a writer who leaves the best known account of the New Orleans Greys in the form of a personal diary. Signing up with what would become known as Breece's Company in New Orleans, he records his experiences from the siege and occupation of Bexar, joining Grant's Matamoros Expedition, and finally ending up at Goliad where he participated in the Battle of Coleto and miraculously escaping after being wounded in the Palm Sunday massacre.

Because he survived the Goliad massacre, his account is one of the few available that was written by a Grey. In escaping and swimming the San Antonio River that Sunday morning, he lost his original diary. A few years later, back in Germany, he rewrote the account and published it as *Texas und Seine Revolution* in 1843. The next year it was reissued as *Der Freiheitskampf in Texas im Jahre 1836* and yet again in 1845 as *Fahrten und Schicksale eines Deutschen in Texas.*

There are several problems with relying upon Ehrenberg for information about the Greys. The account was rewritten from memory after the fact and, as the titles suggest, the diary was written in German. In 1935 Charlotte Churchill translated and published an abridged version of the diary titled *With Milam and Fannin: The Adventures of a German Boy in Texas.* The translation, however, was written on an intermediate school level, and the book reads like a young adult novel rather than a war diary. In 1997 a more scholarly translation by Peter Mollenhauer was published.[14]

Also, Ehrenberg was very self-promoting and opinionated—traits not uncommonly found in participants, especially the military leaders and politicians, of the Texas revolution. For a writer, however, these traits tend to cast doubts on credibility. Ehrenberg's review of Fannin, in particular, was so vehement as to cause some historians to question his ability as a writer to maintain objectivity.

But Ehrenberg does help illustrate the varied backgrounds of those volunteers who signed the muster rolls that evening at Bank's Arcade.

Enlistment into the two companies appears to have been random. The American volunteers seemed to have joined without regard to the geographical differences that were already dividing the country.

The Greys volunteers who were American did not divide into two North/South groups, as would their sons three decades later in the Civil War. Southern volunteers, including those from Kentucky, slightly outnumbered northern recruits while Europeans accounted for at least thirty-nine soldiers, or approximately one-third of the combined rosters.

Northern recruits did tend to favor enlistment in Morris's company while southern enlistees were almost evenly divided between the two companies.

Of all the states with three or more enlistees, all except Maine had men in both companies. Louisiana, the state with the most volunteers, was evenly divided between the two companies.

The European volunteers, however, tended to enlist mostly in what would become known as Breece's company, whose rolls included English, Irish, and Germans. Except for the Germans, variously also listed as from Prussia and Upper Saxony, all of the other European Greys were from the British Isles, Ireland, or Canada—so language was probably not a consideration in enlistment. Language may, however, explain why all the Germans were enrolled in Breece's company.

The New Orleans Greys enlisting that autumn evening at Bank's Arcade did truly encompass the broad spectrum of America and even part of Europe as they made adjustments to their new gray uniforms and became acquainted with their new comrades. Very quickly, one company embarked up the Mississippi River toward Alexandria and Nacogoches. Within two days, the other company left by ship for Velasco.

On two separate fronts, the 555-mile Sabine River, or *Rios de Sabinas*, was being challenged once again. On the west bank awaited the Mexican republic with its northern province known as Texas. From several reports attributed to members of the Greys as they left New Orleans, there was great anticipation of adventure, fighting, and glory. Exotic places with names like La Bahia, Goliad, Bexar, the Alamo, and Velasco awaited them to the west. Earlier, the Spanish, then the French, then the Mexicans, and finally the Anglo immigrants to the territory had learned the hard way that these exotic sounding places were also hotbeds of political turmoil, intrigue, deceit, and betrayal.

But to the young New Orleans Greys that October in 1835, the waters of the Sabine River couldn't arrive fast enough.

---

1   Herbert Asbury, *The French Quarter—An Informal History of the New Orleans Underworld* (New York: Alfred A. Knopf, 1936), pp. 172-3.

2   Bess Carroll, "Help for Texans," October 17, 1935, in an unlisted San Antonio newspaper and part of the Daughters of the Texas Revolution Alamo library archives.

3   Accounts of slave clothing that resembles those uniforms worn by the Greys can be found in Killion, Ronald and Waller, Charles, *Slavery Time When I Was Chillun Down on Master's Plantation—Interviews with Georgia Slaves* (Savannah: The Beehive Press, 1973).

4   Illustrations of the Greys uniforms can be found in color plates by Paul Hannon displayed in Philip Haythornthwaite, *The Alamo and the War of Texan Independence 1835-36* (London: Osprey Publishing, 1986) and a sketch by Gary S. Zaboly in Stephen L. Hardin, *Texian Iliad—A Military History of the Texas Revolution* (Austin: University of Texas Press, 1994), pg. 124. Both illustrations indicate the uniforms had military-style drop-flap pants and wraparound jackets.

5   Amelia W. Williams, and Eugene C. Barker, *The Writings of Sam Houston 1813-1863, Vol. I* (Austin: Jenkins Publishing Company, 1970), pg. 343.

6   Karl Wilson Baker, "Trailing the New Orleans Greys," *Southwest Review, Vol. XXII,* April 1937, No. 3, pg. 216.

7   Texas General Land Office, [A3; T1 p43-45], [A1].

8   Texas General Land Office, [A1], [A2, Section C], [A3; T1 p45-46].

9   Texas General Land Office, [A2, Section C], [A3; T1 p37].

10 The *New Handbook of Texas in Six Volumes* (Austin: The Texas State Historical Association, 1996) offers short biographical sketches of a few of the Greys and their ancestors. The majority of unit members, however, were interred in mass burials and their family and personal histories lost forever.

11 Quoted in Paul D. Lack, *The Texas Revolutionary Experience—A Political and Social History 1835-1836* (College Station: Texas A&M University Press, 1992), pg. 141.

12 *Ibid.,* pg. 111.

13 Clarence Wharton, *Remember Goliad* (Glorieta, New Mexico: The Rio Grande Press, Inc., 1968), pg. 51.

14 There are at least three English translations of Ehrenberg's diary. Dr. Peter Mollenhauer's 1993 translation will be used to reference Ehrenberg's writings in this book. His translation can be found in the Natalie Ornish book *Ehrenberg: Goliad Survivor, Old West Explorer* (Dallas: Texas Heritage Press, 1997).

Chapter 2

By Sea with Morris

Velasco Beach, October 23, 1835: Robert C. Morris swatted the flies hovering around his face. The beach was deserted now and his fellow Greys were scattered—some hanging around the encampment and others lounging in the grog shops located at the mouth of the Brazos River.

Morris had come to this isolated beach area to watch the waves break on the sandbars and to organize his thoughts. He had a lot to think about.

Velasco was only three days by sea from New Orleans, but the tiny settlement made it seem as if he'd traveled back a hundred years in time. He welcomed any opportunity to get away from it and, like the other Greys, was anxious to move out and go to San Antonio de Bexar where the fighting was going to occur—if it wasn't already over by now.

The settlement—if you could call it that—consisted of two ramshackle sheds that served as stores and a hotel so filthy and smelly that the Greys had preferred to camp away from it on the beach. Some of the men, especially the younger volunteers, idled their time in the half dozen grog shops, which consisted of open-air shelters serving homemade corn liquor to the local population of Anglo immigrants, Indians, and Mexicans.

As if the incessant flies, mosquitoes, and other insects were not bad enough, the humidity was oppressive and the locals completely untrustworthy. To them, the Greys represented a rare opportunity to make money, but Morris had to admit to himself that for a hastily organized unit of young men, the Greys had conducted themselves well.

He had made a conscious effort to get to know each one of the men since that night when the company had been organized at Bank's Arcade ten days earlier. All of his personal campaigning during the sea voyage had paid off last night when the men had elected him the unit captain.

Like everyone else in the Greys, he'd enlisted as a private, but that commitment had represented to him only the first step in developing a position in the new political order evolving inside Texas this very moment.

He looked back over his shoulder at the pathetic village of Velasco and its equally dismal twin community across the Brazos—Quintana. At least the late afternoon coastal breeze was blowing southwesterly and keeping the stench of the combined garbage and sewage of the settlements away from him.

The area was quiet now and there was almost no movement discernable. It was hard to imagine any type of new political order evolving here. Morris knew that the real political action was occurring in faraway places like San Felipe de Austin, Washington-on-the-Brazos, Bexar, and Goliad by participants who had been in Texas far longer than his twenty-four hours. But he would soon be in the midst of the intrigue—and opportunities—and this disgusting coastal hamlet was the necessary first step.

Morris had connections in Texas but not the means to use them yet. His election as unit captain of the New Orleans Greys had been the first of several well-planned steps to get him in a position to be involved in the real Texas opportunities. Now he had to get the unit to Bexar in time to participate in the attack on that city and removal of all Mexican military forces from Texas. Then the real conquest would start and then his connections would work for him.

Staring into the gulf and watching the waves break in front of him, he took comfort in the fact that at this very moment personal letters of reference were being forwarded to Stephen F. Austin and Sam Houston.

His old New Orleans friend William Christy had offered to personally write Sam Houston on his behalf, and it had been Christy who had directed him toward Velasco and its even more important contacts: Thomas Freeman McKinney and Samuel May Williams.

McKinney would be a useful future contact when Texas was independent. Fluent in Spanish, McKinney had traveled extensively in Chihuahua and worked with Christy in New Orleans some five years ago. He was now senior partner in the McKinney, Williams and Company that was underwriting much of the Greys expenses here at Velasco and providing river transport for their first leg of the journey to San Antonio de Bexar.

The Greys had taken to Thomas McKinney immediately. He was, in their young eyes, the kind of man to have on their side. It was McKinney who, only a month earlier, had boarded one of his own schooners and captured the Mexican ship *Correo de Mexico* that had been pirating Texas-bound supplies. He was a fighter and his name was well known throughout the Texas settlements.

His partner, Samuel Williams, represented to Morris an even more valuable future contact. Williams' association with New Orleans dated back to 1819 when he had known Christy and Sterne there. While Morris viewed McKinney as a fighter and adventurer, he saw Williams as a shrewd land speculator.

Shortly after meeting Christy in New Orleans, Williams had come to Texas under an alias, then applied for and received legal title to a league of land from Stephen Austin in the 1820—using his real name. By 1833 he was involved in Texas intrigue and had been involved in a failed land scheme to claim Galveston Island and one year later formed the partnership with McKinney that resulted in the establishment of the twin port entry points on the Brazos River.

Within a year, Velasco and Quintana had become major supply points for the coastal Texas settlers, and the McKinney, Williams and Company now owned three steamships, which linked the Anglo settlements in Texas with New Orleans commerce. One of those steamers, the *Laura*, was expected to arrive tonight and depart up the Brazos River with the Greys tomorrow for the town of Brazoria.

But in the meantime, Morris continued to stroll the beach and force his thoughts back to Samuel Williams and the real objective in Texas.

Before the Greys had departed New Orleans, Christy had explained to Morris about Williams' involvement in Texas and Mexican politics. After the 1835 Galveston land scheme had been thwarted, Williams had traveled to the Coahuila capital in Monclova with several other U.S. entrepreneurs.

They had visited the Mexican provincial legislature as official "observers" and guests of the secretary of the legislature, a former Scotsman named James Grant who was heavily involved in internal Mexican politics, land speculation, and intrigue.

Through Grant, the "observers" fraudulently obtained between 1,500 and 1,600 leagues of Mexican land in Texas to develop for Anglo settlements and sell with part of the revenues being used to finance the Mexican Federalists in their opposition to Santa Anna and his Centralists. Coincidentally, the province of Coahuila was, like Texas, wanting to secede from Mexico and start an independent republic.

Not surprisingly, Santa Anna took exception to this and quickly moved his army into Coahuila and occupied the legislature in Monclova, causing Grant, Williams, and the other American speculators to flee northward into Texas. Williams had returned to Velasco and his profitable port and river businesses. Grant was at this moment on his way to Bexar to assist in the overthrow of the Mexican forces garrisoned there under Santa Anna's brother-in-law, General Martin Perfecto de Cos.

Morris had sought out Williams as soon as the Greys had disembarked from the *Columbus*. With William Christy as their mutual acquaintance, Morris had quickly impressed Williams with his knowledge of Mexican politics, and the two had talked at length about the events currently developing.

There was no mention of constitutional reform. Reversion to the constitutional freedoms of 1824 would validate the illegality of the massive land grants that Williams, Grant and the other speculators at Monclova had received earlier that year. Only secession and the establishment of an independent republic in Texas would allow them to recover their lost land grants.

And anybody who joined their cause now would also get in on the incalculable riches to be gained through controlling land in a free Texas. Robert C. Morris intended to be one of those insiders. But first he had to lead a company of New Orleans volunteers to Bexar and establish himself.

Again, he swatted at the flies around his face.

CЗCЗCЗ80 80 80

*T*he two groups of Greys left New Orleans within two days of each other. Both units left New Orleans by ship—one unit going north on the Mississippi and Red Rivers and the other unit going south on the Mississippi toward the open seas and the Texas coast.

Immediately after formation of the groups, supplies and armaments were procured, and three blocks south of Bank's Arcade, on the New Orleans wharf, slave laborers continued loading ordnance, including an eighteen-pounder cannon, munitions, food provisions, and military supplies, aboard the schooner *Columbus*.

The Greys volunteers embarked on October 17, 1835, becoming, on that date, the first volunteer unit to join the Texas army. News had recently reached New Orleans of the skirmish at Gonzales between Texas militiamen and the Mexican army, but that conflict had involved Anglo settlers— technically Mexican citizens themselves. Other volunteers probably filtered individually into Texas before this unit of Greys arrived, but these men aboard the *Columbus* were the first volunteer *unit* to join the Texas revolution.

Sailing the Gulf Coast waters near Texas in 1835 was a dangerous occupation, and the ship captains of that period faced bad weather in the form of "blue northers" that developed seemingly with no warning, uncharted waters with destructive sandbars, hostile (even cannibalistic) Indians on shore, privateers and pirates, and finally the constant threat of Mexican warships. The profession produced many colorful characters during these years, however little is known about the skipper of the *Columbus* on that voyage. He is listed simply as Captain Leidsdorf, and it was reported that he "had a good vessel under his feet, good whisky under his belt, and the cargo was something that would make history on the highroads of the gulf."[1]

After boarding on October 17, the Greys found themselves at anchor for two days across the river from the French Quarter at a small city named Algiers. From Algiers, steamers towed the schooners and other sailing ships down the Mississippi—a passage that usually required about twelve hours.

Despite sediment deposits and rerouting, the Mississippi has historically divided into three major distributaries—the South Pass, the Southwest Pass, and Pass a l'Outre, with the Southwest Pass being the deepest and carrying the largest volume of river traffic. It was from the Southwest Pass that most of the vessels embarked Louisiana for the Texas coast and that the *Columbus* was cast loose at Balize on October 19 to sail past the mouth of the Sabine and into the northern province of Mexico called Texas.

Sailing times varied depending upon weather, tides, cargo, and Mexican naval activity in the gulf. Despite its cache of military supplies, the *Columbus* made the journey in a very quick three days, arriving at Velasco on the mouth of the Brazos River on October 22.[2]

It was after disembarking at Velasco that the Greys held their election of officers—choosing Captain Robert C. Morris as commander. It appears that the Greys anticipated a short fight and quick victory as the officers elected on the beach that day were specifically appointed for three months starting on October 26.[3]

Morris arrived in Texas with excellent credentials and was one of the very few Greys who had a military background. In a letter of introduction to Stephen F. Austin dated October 20, 1835, a J.W. Collins stated that Morris had been "a fellow soldier with me in the Louisiana Guards for 5 or 6 years" and recommended him as "a Soldier & Tactician." The day following, William H. Christy (the Bank's Arcade recruiter) addressed a similar letter to Sam Houston, and on October 29 Archibald Hotchkiss described his friend Morris to Houston as "a young man of firmness and a man who will not disgrace the grays."[4]

Morris' immediate second-in-command was First Lieutenant William G. Cooke, a twenty-seven-year-old druggist from Fredericksburg, Virginia. Charles Bannister, a Louisiana native, was voted second lieutenant.

Albert Morris Levy, the thirty-five-year-old Dutch-born surgeon from Richmond, Virginia, was appointed as the unit surgeon. Levy's wife, Maria, had died a few months earlier, and Levy had left his three-year-old daughter with his younger sister and traveled to New Orleans to be with his older brother.[5] Having graduated from the University of Pennsylvania medical school only three years earlier, Levy was a relatively inexperienced physician but a valuable asset to Morris' company.

Mandaret Wood was appointed commissary officer. Little is known about his background—one source lists him as a Pennsylvania native, but most rosters do not list even a home state.

Nathaniel B. Brister, a Virginian, was the first sergeant; H.L. Smith, no citizenship listed, was the second sergeant; George Stephens and Edward Wrentmire, two Englishmen, were appointed third and fourth sergeants.

Completing the noncommissioned officer roster were First Corporal Richard Ross of Illinois, Second Corporal Joseph P. Riddle from Pennsylvania, and Third Corporal Lewis F. Amelung of Louisiana. Irishman J.L. Hall was fourth corporal and would soon be promoted to second lieutenant.

At least two other Greys boarded the *Columbus* with letters of personal reference to Texas leaders. One, dated October 15, while the Greys were still in New Orleans, introduced one of the volunteers to Stephen Austin's brother-in-law, James F. Perry, in San Felipe:

> I take pleasure in introducing to you the bearer, Mr Stiff who visits your Country, as a volunteer in defence of your wrights—
>
> I feel every assurance in saying that you will find encased in his delicate frame, a mind fully adequate to bear up through trials which would crush others of superior phisical force, and a spirit worthy of being honorably employed in your contest against the usurpers of power, the perfidious advocates of central government.— Mr Stiff's pecuniary circumstances renders it perfectly unnecessary that he should visit your country in quest of fortune, and I think I may say, without detriment to the motives of others, that you are indebted for his aid, to those more generous and extended feelings, which are inherent in the bosoms of all true Americans

Any attention which the turmoils of war will
permit you to show him, will be gratefully
acknowledged by

A.R. McNair[6]

This unusual reference to Thomas R. Stiff, a native Virginian, as "delicate" would indicate that the volunteer was sickly
or physically challenged. If so, Stiff would in the future show in
combat that McNair was correct—he could "bear up through
trials which would crush others of superior phisical force."

Another Grey, one of several with a newspaper background, had a letter written to Stephen F. Austin on October
20, the day after the *Columbus* had left New Orleans. A copy
was also forwarded to Sidney Callender aboard the ship, but
it is not known if he ever received his copy. In it, Austin was
informed that:

The Bearer Mr Sidney S Callender is one of
the Young men who have volunteered to aid the
people of Texas in defending their rights—He is
a practical printer and was for sometime Editor
of the Lafayette Gazette—Sympathizing in your
Cause he has determined to make Texas his
adopted Country and to fight in her defence. . . .

L.R. Kenney[7]

Another Grey aboard the *Columbus* was a young runaway
who, unknown to all except possibly one other Grey, had
impressive contacts back in New Orleans. He carried no personal resume of introduction or reference, but some six
weeks later, in a letter that speaks passionately of the worry
of a mother for her wayward young son, the following correspondence was sent to Sam Houston:

New Orleans 2nd Decr 1835
Dear General [Houston]
A nephew of Mrs. Christy by the name of
Vincent A. Drouillard, smuggled himself off in
the first company of volunteers which went by

31

sea under the charge or command of a Mr. Hall
to your aid, you once knew his mother at my
house, he is brave, fond of a roving life,
devoted to a Gun and to performing any executive business, will be very useful, he writes a
pretty good hand, has been brought up to the
Apothecary business & might possibly be useful
in this Department of the Army for he under-
stands his business well, if you can find him out
& do anything for him, you will do much
towards soothing the anxious cares of a mother
whom you know is a lady of the first family and
standing.

We are entirely without advices from you,
what does this mean?

> Yours in great haste
> Wm Christy

11th January 1836
This was returned to me.
W.C.[8]

It appears from this letter that, in the bustle and activity
of the organizing rally at Bank's Arcade, Christy's own
nephew managed to sneak inside and anonymously register
as a New Orleans Grey. His letter suggests that young Drouillard had a reputation for the "roving life" and, in an indirect
way asks Houston to help extend consideration to him.

This letter never reached Houston because Christy noted
some six weeks after it was written that the correspondence
had been returned to him. Christy also on December 2 ends
his letter stating, "We are completely without advices from
you," suggesting that the organizers in New Orleans had
been out of contact with Houston for some time—something
understandable considering the events taking place in Texas
at that time.

The "Mr. Hall" under whose charge Drouillard enlisted almost certainly had to have been J.L. Hall, the Irish fourth corporal who was the only Grey with that last name in Morris' company aboard the *Columbus*. There are no further references to any connection Hall might have had with either Christy or Drouillard.

From Charleston, South Carolina, Julian Harby had traveled to New Orleans to join the Greys. Twenty years old, he was the son of Isaac Harby, who had passed away seven years earlier and was considered by many to have been the founder of Reform Judaism in the United States and largely responsible for the economic and cultural rise of Charleston in the early 1800s.

Having established their staff roster, the Greys spent a brief period at Velasco shooting game, stocking provisions, and generally getting their "land legs" under them again. Some of the traveling provisions they obtained were from the dock at which the *Columbus* had landed—the McKinney and Williams and Company wharf.

In a letter dated November 15 from Quintana, McKinney and Williams notified Dr. Branch T. Archer, a close associate of Sam Houston:

> Dear Sir
> I have forwarded a number of the arms which were purchased to be delivered to you. . . . We also gave the New Orleans grays some muskets I hope this will be approved by you as the muskets were for the defence of the country & they seemed to be needed at that time in that way & as it was impossible to ask for permission to do so we have been compeled by the force of circumstances to use our own discretion many things. . . .[9]

Thomas F. McKinney and Samuel M. Williams had founded the company the year before and prior to the revolution had three steamers, the *Laura,* the *Yellow Stone,* and the *Lafitte,* linking the Brazos plantations with the New Orleans export trade. During the revolution the provisional government used the vessels for conveying troops and supplies.[10]

From Velasco, the Greys boarded the *Laura* for the twenty-five-mile trip up the Brazos River to the small town of Brazoria. Compared to the speedy schooner *Columbus,* the *Laura* must have seemed slow and cramped during the short journey. Only four months old, the small craft had been constructed in Louisville specifically for McKinney and Williams to use on the Brazos.

Eighty-five feet long and sixteen and a half feet wide, she drew five and a half feet and could carry sixty-five tons of cargo. Two months earlier she had been involved in the capture of a Mexican cruiser that had been seizing United States vessels calling at Texas ports.[11]

The 840-mile-long watershed with its three major branches was named *Brazos de Dios* (the arms of God) by the Spanish by 1721. Indians called it *Tokonohono* while a French explorer named it *La Maligne* (malignant).

Of the three waterways accessible to the colony, the Brazos offered the best shipping entrance. The Colorado River was constantly blocked by debris and emptied into shallow Matagorda Bay instead of the gulf. Galveston Bay had an oyster shell reef stretching across the bay that permitted only boats drawing less than five feet to ascend to the San Jacinto River. The *Laura* drew five and a half feet and was fully loaded, so the Greys embarked up the Brazos to begin their inland journey to San Antonio.

Ehrenberg had earlier reported, "We also received from the Texan committee several cannon that were to make the journey on board the ship with us."[12] Although he didn't specify which unit transported the pieces, the ship referred to was almost certainly the *Columbus* since the other group (to which Ehrenberg was attached) would be marching considerably further overland.

Nearly two months later, during the storming of Bexar, the Texans had three artillery pieces including a captured six-pounder, so it is thought the Greys must have brought two guns.[13]

One of the cannon loaded aboard the *Columbus* that didn't arrive in Bexar in time to impact the conduct of the fighting was the eighteen-pounder that would later play a prominent part in the siege and battle for the Alamo. The Greys had arrived in Texas with the huge cannon but without any ball ammunition for the gun.[14]

Left behind in Velasco, the cannon was placed on the schooner *San Felipe,* which McKinney had used to capture the *Correo de Mexico,* and shipped to Matagorda where it was nearly lost in a shipwreck on Matagorda Peninsula. At a cost of $136, McKinney and Williams had the cannon and other goods salvaged.[15]

From Columbia, William Hall wrote Stephen Austin that he was attempting to locate the gun and escort it to San Antonio. In his November 23 letter he told Austin:

> I arrived in Brazoria on the 13th Inst. And found that the heavy piece of cannon . . . was lost inside the Matagorda Bay. The guns was however saved and landed on bird Island . . . I left on the 18th calculated on joining the cannon at Matagorda or on the road on My way I met Mr Patton directly from Matagorda who told me that the Schooner William Robbins had sailed on the 13th Inst—from that place with the Intention of taking the Cannon on board and bringing it round to the Brazos I have therefore delayed and have sent expresses to both places—and so soon as I can learn at what

> point the cannon can be found I will use every
> exertion to get her to Bexar—the weather has
> been excessively bad and the roads are very
> muddy. . . .[16]

Soon afterward, a company of artillery led by Captain Thomas K. Pearson was dispatched to transport the gun from Dimitt's Landing to San Antonio. Jakie Pruett and Everett B. Cole Sr., in their book *Goliad Massacre*, list Pearson as an artillery officer with the New Orleans Greys,[17] but Morris' muster roll taken at Velasco does not list any Grey by that name.

A "Mr. Johnson of the New Orleans Greys" is listed as accompanying the party transporting the gun.[18] Morris' Velasco roster does indicate a Private Francis Johnson from Maine (not to be confused with Virginia Colonel Francis White Johnson), so this would probably be the Grey left behind to escort the gun to San Antonio.

Following the battle for Bexar, there would be several references to a twelve-pounder used by the Texans. Ehrenberg refers to the piece several times during the storming of Bexar, and author Thomas Lindley claims that the twelve-pound "gunade" from the *Columbus* was taken to Bexar as a result of leaving the eighteen-pounder behind at Velasco.[19]

At the Alamo complex today several Spanish and English cannon of the period are positioned for display in the cavalry courtyard including a carronade listed as a veteran of the Alamo. Its inscription reads:

> This cannon was used in the Battle of the Alamo,
> probably on the west wall. It was made inoperable
> by General Santa Anna
> before he left for San Jacinto.
> This type of cannon was made in Carron,
> Scotland in the 1790s.

The piece has been referred to as an "insurance gun" often carried by merchant ships to meet insurance requirements, and while the gun on display at the Alamo compound has trunnions, it is considered too long to be a true carronade. Although the Carron Company did make a carronade with trunnions instead of the traditional naval lug mounting, this cannon is an American-made gun and probably the twelve-pounder gunnade.[20]

Transporting at least two cannon, the Greys left Velasco on a 25-mile uneventful river journey, disembarking at the small town of Brazoria where "a tremendous welcome" awaited them. According to one report, "flowers were strewn at the feet of the newly arrived soldiers, and they were entertained at the home of Mrs. Jane Long—the widow of already legendary Texan filibusterer General James Long. Later they were tendered a public banquet by the citizens of Brazoria."[21]

One of the Greys, however, recalled the reception in terms more characteristic of young soldiers marching off to war: "Speeches were made and sumptuous dinners prepared for us, and by the time we had emptied some dozen baskets of champagne, we had in our imagination conquered all Mexico."[22]

The local newspaper, the *Texas Republican*, reported the Greys arrival at Brazoria and noted a minor item which the Greys brought along with them was a spirited little song entitled "New Yankee Doodle Dandy." Two of the nine stanzas run as follows:

> St. Anna did a notion take
>   That he must rule the land sir,
> The church and he forthwith agree
>   To publish the command sir.

Chorus:
> In Mexico none shall be free,
>   The people are too blind to see,

> They cannot share the liberty
> Of Yankee Doodle Dandy

> The Texians say they won't receive
> The *central plan* at all sir,
> And nobly go to meet the foe,
> With powder and with ball, sir.[23]

For two days the Greys remained in Brazoria enjoying the attention and hospitality of the local citizens there. This was something they would experience again in a few days at Victoria and, unknown to them, something that was also being experienced by the other company of the Greys to the north through Alexandria and Nachitoches in Louisiana and in San Augustine, Nacogdoches, and Bastrop in Texas.

Prior to their entry into combat, both companies of Greys were always offered gifts, food, and munitions by the Anglo settlements they visited. Once they became involved in the war, contact was limited with Anglo civilians; but this period of travel to Bexar—for both companies—was characterized by festive welcomes, cannon salutes, and brass bands.

During this pre-combat period, the Anglo settlers were usually more than willing to offer free food, provisions, and even horses to the Greys. Once the fighting had begun and most Texan civilians were heading east with Sam Houston in the famous "Runaway Scrape," the Texas soldiers had to help themselves to food and provisions along their routes. Soldiers regularly suffering from commissary shortages were frequently left to their own devices. In desperation the government authorized impressment of whatever the army required.[24]

All too often, however, this "impressment" turned into petty larceny. The Greys, later involved in virtually every battle of the revolution, certainly were faced with the need to impress civilian goods: horses around Goliad being a good example.

At Brazoria, there was no need for impressment. The settlers there were more than happy to share their provisions with these volunteers from the United States. After two days, however, the Greys resumed their journey toward San Antonio.

From Brazoria, the Greys were no longer marines but, instead, infantrymen and as such earned the centuries-old right of footsoldiers to complain about their lot:

> . . . now, indeed were to commence our troubles and hardships. We had to travel on foot, with our rifles on our shoulders, knapsacks on our backs, provisions sufficient for several days, canteens, powder horns and equipment. Leaving Brazoria late in the evening, we encamped upon the banks of the river San Banard [Bernard] where we were initiated into the duties of soldiers; a guard was detailed for the night, though there was not an enemy within 100 mi., but we were now soldiers, and it was necessary that we should be disciplined.[25]

The journey from Brazoria to San Antonio would be approximately two hundred fifty miles. It began with a forced march a short distance north to Columbia, then the group moved westward following an established minor trace and across the San Bernard River and Grand Caney to the Colorado River and Cayce's Crossing.

Continuing in a westerly direction, they crossed the Navidad River into the settlement of Victoria on the bank of the Rio San Marcos. At Victoria, the Greys were again greeted by "another ovation, presided over by 'those two noble ladies, Mrs. Margaret C. and Miss Susan Linn'."[26]

The ovation referred to was a banquet prepared for the Greys by John Joseph Linn, the alcalde of Guadalupe Victoria. Less than a month earlier Linn had been appointed quartermaster of the Texas army and was in the process of provisioning the garrison at nearby Goliad when the Greys arrived at his home. The Mrs. Margaret C. Linn referred to was the alcalde's wife, who later organized the women of Victoria in her home during the war to mold bullets for the soldiers.

It was also at Victoria that the Greys received their first horses—although the experience was less than successful. As one Grey later recalled, "At Victoria, a small Mexican town on the Guadalupe river, part of the company were supplied with mustangs, or wild horses, which only the most expert were able to ride."[27]

And so the Greys continued on toward San Antonio with only a few of the volunteers actually mounted as horsemen. For the most part, they were still an infantry company, and as such, they continued across the Coleto Creek where, before they would reach San Antonio and the siege of the Mexican army there, the Greys would make one more stop—at an old Spanish mission and presidio named *La Bahia* (The Bay) at the old Mexican town of Goliad.

They could not have known the importance this seemingly insignificant little body of water would have for many of them in four short months. In crossing it, they probably didn't even pay attention to its shallow waters. But the very name of Coleto would soon be associated with an infamous act of barbarism, and the New Orleans Greys would be the foremost victims.

They arrived at La Bahia too late to be of any assistance in attacking and occupying the stronghold, for the Texans had taken the fort a few days before. The unit bivouacked at Goliad only long enough to procure some more horses, and again, the results were less than satisfactory. As one unnamed Grey later recalled:

> At La Bahia we were supplied with horses,
> some of them beautiful creatures from snowy
> white to jet black, but about as devilish and

wicked as they well could be; pitching, snorting, biting, kicking, stampeding and doing various other mustang manoeuvers [sic]. We had no little difficulty in conquering them. Being mounted we took up the line of march for the main army, about 30 leagues off, which was lying before San Antonio waiting for reinforcements to attack the place, it being well fortified and strongly garrisoned. On our march we had opportunities of discovering that a mustang was no fool; some of these sagacious animals took up the preposterous idea that we had no business on their backs and accordingly took the liberty of relieving themselves of their loads, which was no very hard matter; and the first thing we knew, without our consent of course, several of us found ourselves most unceremoniously brought in violent contact with the ground and upon looking up had the satisfaction of beholding our horses flying over the prairie as if the devil was after them, with saddle under their bellies, lariats dragging behind, our traps strewed along the prairie in the most inestimable confusion. Away would go some half dozen in pursuit of the animals which were soon recaptured, saddled and mounted and under way, with the mutterings and curses of the unfortunate riders and the laughter of our more fortunate companions. The weather had been very cold, as it was the middle of November, and to add to our discomfort it had been rainy, pouring down sometimes in torrents, so that we looked like "drowned rats," wet, cold and hungry, and we were in no pleasant mood.[28]

As poor quality as the horses might have been, they had been impressed without payment but with a written promise of future reimbursement. The owner was understandably indignant while at the same time diplomatic in trying to recoup his losses from the leaders in San Felipe:

> To The Honorable the Council of the Provisional
> Government of Texas
> ... I had my Horses taken from me by an order
> of Capt Dimitt contrary to my will and valued
> at less than they originally cost he only giving
> me the accompaning document in payment
> which amount I hope that the council of the
> people will pay me as I am entirely out of
> funds, and unable to procede to New Orleans
> my place of residence, although the amount is
> considerabely less than the actuel cost I will be
> for ever thankful for the liquidation of this
> claim trusting to the particular situation of the
> petitioner he refrains from any further observa-
> tion and Remain their Truly Humble Servant
> At Felipe de Austin   Bartholome Pajes
> Decr 2 1835[29]

As proof of his claim, Pajes submitted the following document signed by Dimitt:

> Fortress of Goliad Nov. 18th 1835
> Pressed into the public service, in pursuance
> of my order, Fifty one horses, or riding animals;
> the same being part of a caballade, on the way
> from the interior of his country to the United
> States of the north, and said to belong to one
> Bartolome Pajes; thirty one of whish, were
> taken for the use of the New Orleans, "Volun-
> teer Greys;" ... at an average of Seventeen
> Dollars the animal the original documents

relating to these proceedings being on file in
my possession.[30]

During their brief stay at Goliad and La Bahia, horses
weren't the only things the Greys impressed that were contested. On November 27, 1835, after the Greys had left
Goliad, Dimitt was forced to call a Goliad court of inquiry to
investigate the right of possession and ownership of several
boxes of manufactured tobacco. The tobacco in question had
been earlier stolen by two sailors, recovered, and stored in
the old mission at the nearby Irish colony of Refugio.

The claim inferred that Dimitt had sent one of his soldiers to impress the tobacco and part of a barrel of whiskey
and return with it to Goliad "for the use of the Volunteers,
and particularly for that of the Volunteer Greys from New
Orleans. . . ."[31]

Testimony and depositions in the case failed to determine
if any of the tobacco actually left Goliad with the Greys, since
the majority of it remained in the fort during the course of
the inquiry after they had departed.

And so, as the Greys left Goliad for San Antonio, some
were still on foot and others attempting to ride seventeen-
dollar horses. The complaint that they were "drowned rats,"
wet, cold and hungry, and "in no pleasant mood" indicates
that the Greys were pretty much representative of infantrymen throughout the ages: "laughter of our more fortunate
companions" one moment and "in no pleasant mood" the
next. The naivete and romantic thoughts of war were about
to end for these young volunteers, however, for it was on this
last leg of their journey to San Antonio that the first known
combat casualty of a New Orleans Grey was to occur.

Leaving La Bahia, the Greys started northward to San
Antonio. There were two minor traces they might have
taken. One followed the northern bank of the San Antonio
River until it connected with the Camino de Medio and
entered San Antonio through Casablanca.

The other route, and the one the Greys probably traveled, followed the south bank of the San Antonio River all the way into San Antonio and passed through at least three Tejano ranches: La Mora Rancho, Les Chayapines Rancho, and the Seguin Rancho.

Charles W. Connor, a private from Pennsylvania, had been in poor health since leaving New Orleans. Feverish and shaking, he had been advised to remain at Goliad but had refused. As the Greys neared San Antonio, his condition worsened due to the cold, rainy weather, and he was dispatched ahead of the group to a Tejano ranch near San Antonio where he could rest and get out of the weather until the company arrived.

Advancing alone, disoriented with fever, and unfamiliar with the territory, he became lost in heavy fog and took the wrong road. Exhausted, he stopped and attempted to start a fire but failed and, instead, wrapped himself in a blanket and went to sleep beneath a tree.

When the Greys reached the Tejano ranch later that night, they figured Connor had either camped nearby or gone on the short distance and joined the Texan army at San Antonio. As they were to find the next morning, this was not the case:

> The night was hideous and dark; bright and vivid flashes of lightening darted across the sky; the thunder pealed in the heavens and rain poured down in torrents; and Conner's [sic] stiffened corpse lay exposed to the pelting storm. Alas! He heeded it not; he had been cowardly murdered. The next morning his body was discovered along the roadside with three musket balls in his breast, and in his bosom were deep marks—bayonet wounds. He had been found by a party of Mexican soldiers who killed him, stripped his body and divided their

ill gotten spoils . . . Placing the body upon a baggage wagon, covering it with our cloaks, we marched on to the army, which was but a few miles distant where we gave to the unfortunate Conner a Christian and a soldier's burial.[32]

Thomas Stiff also later commented on the murder when he wrote:

. . . The day previous to our arrival at the Mill Mr. [blank] separated from the company, and expected to join them that Evening at the Seilow but unfortunately took the wrong road, and proceeded on until he came within Two or four miles of the Town, where he stoped and Kindled a fire and waited for the balance of the Company, I suppose he met with some of the Mexican spies, as we found him dead, having received two shots passing through his body—entering on his left side. His horse and Pistols were missing—also his coat.[33]

On this same day, November 7, another Grey became a casualty—this time a prisoner. Johann George Andreas Voss (often referred to as "Vose") was a German from Hamburg who had joined Morris' unit in New Orleans. According to Stiff:

Mr. Vose was on the same day taken prisoner in the following manner,—was left at the camp on the Seilow, alone, when he started from the Camp he took the left-hand rode and instead of going to the Texian Camp; found him self standing by the walls of the Alamo! Where he found that he was in the wrong pugh he then enquired of Genl. Cos where Austins Colony was, Cos answered that perhaps he was mistaken, that it was Austins Camp he was looking for, he said not, that he was a poor

> man looking for work, and would work for him
> (Cos) as soon as any body else if he could get
> paid for it, Cos asked him if he was a member of
> any Ch. He said yes, a Catholic, Cos then asked
> him if he could. make Cigars, yes, he then
> was–taken by order of Cos and Lodged in the
> Calaboose to follow the above business....[34]

So Voss, if not good at directions, was at least quick of mind under pressure and no doubt, stressing his heavy German accent, played the role of confused traveler when questioned by General Cos. Being from Hamburg, he probably wasn't Catholic but was quick enough to realize it might save his life if he claimed so. He did live but could not avoid becoming a prisoner of the Mexicans.

The Greys arrived at San Antonio during the first week of November 1835, missing two men, and discovered that the siege of Bexar was still in progress and that they had not missed the impending attack on the city. What they also found, however, was a Texan army that was quickly falling apart and in danger of disbanding completely.

The Greys, with their distinctive uniforms and new weapons, added an element of professionalism to the Texan army and bolstered morale immeasurably. Later, several Texan leaders including Stephen F. Austin would credit the Greys' arrival with preventing the collapse of the army and, therefore, the revolution itself.

---

1   Bess Carroll, "Help from U.S.," November 21, 1935, in an unlisted San Antonio newspaper and part of the Daughters of the Texas Revolution Alamo library archives.

2   Frederick C. Chabot, *The Alamo Mission Fortress and Shrine* (Copyright Frederick C. Chabot, San Antonio, Texas, 1941, 3. Edition: No publisher listed), pg. 55. A copy is located at the Daughters of the Republic of Texas Alamo library. The appendix is based upon a manuscript by Pearson Newcomb, "High Water Marks of Texas History," quoting an unnamed Grey. No additional citation is listed.

3   "List of the New Orleans Greys," Archives of the Adjutant General's Office (Louisiana), copy supplied by the Daughters of the Texas Revolution Alamo library archives.

4   Thomas W. Cutrier, "Morris, Robert C." *New Handbook of Texas.*

5   Natalie Ornish, "Levy, Albert Moses" *New Handbook of Texas.*

6   John H. Jenkins, Ed., *The Papers of the Texas Revolution 1835-1836 in Ten Volumes* (Austin: Presidial Press, 1973), Vol. 2, pp. 135-6.

7   *Ibid.,* pg. 172.

8   *Ibid.,* Vol. 3, pg. 74.

9   *Ibid.,* Vol. 2, pp. 422-3.

10 Curtis Bishop, "McKinney, Williams and Company" *New Handbook of Texas.*

11 Margaret Swett Hensen, *"Laura" New Handbook of Texas.*

12 Ornish, *Ehrenberg,* pg. 88.

13 Mike Koury, "Cannon for Texas Artillery in the Revolution and the Republic," *Military History of Texas and the Southwest,* Volume X, No. 2, 1972, pg. 134.

14 Thomas Ricks Lindley, "Alamo Artillery—Number, Type, Caliber and Concussion," *The Alamo Journal,* Issue #82, July 1992, pg. 6.

15 *Ibid.*

16 Jenkins, *The Papers of the Texas Revolution,* Vol. 2, pp. 493-4.

17 Jakie Pruett and Everett B.Cole, *Goliad Massacre* (Austin: Eakin Press, 1985), pg. 25.

18 Lindley, pg. 6.

19 *Ibid.,* pg. 7.

20 *Ibid.,* pg. 5.

21 Chabot, Appendix #1, pg. 55.

22 *Ibid.*

23 James A. Creighton, *A Narrative History of Brazoria County, Texas* (Waco: Texian Press, 1975), Published by the Brazoria County Historical Commission, pg. 111.

24 Paul Lack, *The Texas Revolutionary Experience,* pg. 147.

25 Chabot, pg. 56.

26 Karle Wilson Baker, "Trailing the New Orleans Greys," pg. 217.

27 Chabot, pg. 56.

28 *Ibid.,* pp. 56-7.

29 Jenkins, Vol. 3, pg. 80.

30 *Ibid.,* pp. 80-1.

31   *Ibid.*, pp. 27-33.
32   Chabot, pp. 57-8.
33   Jenkins, Vol. 3, pp. 388-9.
34   *Ibid.*, pg. 389.

Chapter 3

Overland with Breece

West Bank of the Sabine River, Texas, Early November, **1835:** Captain Thomas Breece would rather fight Mexicans or march all the way to San Antonio on foot than do what was expected of him right now. Why couldn't John Baugh, the young Virginian who was his first lieutenant, do this? Or George Washington Main—another Virginian who was a lieutenant and much better at words and speeches?

Not that he didn't feel honored to be a captain of the New Orleans Greys. His position wasn't appointed—the Greys had voted him into the officership based upon their impression of him during the trip up from New Orleans. It was a vote of confidence.

And that confidence was, he hoped, based upon their trusting his ability to lead them in combat. But this was different, and now, standing in loose formation behind him, they were expecting him to lead them in something he wasn't comfortable doing.

He had to give a speech, and it terrified him.

Looking out at the small group of civilians assembled in front of him in a semicircle, he searched their faces for signs of emotion. They were an interesting group, he thought. Certainly different from the civilians the Greys had come into contact with in Louisiana.

These Texans—Anglos, some called them—looked rougher, tougher, and hardier than any he remembered in Louisiana.

But he also knew that these people had come from east of the Sabine, and their haggard appearance was the result of hard living in this Texan wilderness. And their eyes reflected fear.

These people were among the few legitimate white Texans in this area. Most had come here legally under the Spanish land grants, pledged allegiance to Mexico City, and converted, on paper at least, to Catholicism. Some of the younger ones were second generation Texans—having been born on this soil.

And today they were under siege. The men in the group looked back at him with resolute stares. He knew they were tough men and would be formidable in a fight, but they wouldn't be going west with the Greys to fight the Mexicans. They would stay behind and guard against Indian raids on their settlements and cabins—a responsibility as important and potentially deadly as the challenge in Bexar.

But if the revolution in Gonzales and at Bexar were to fail, the Mexican army would be coming here eventually. And when they arrived, there would be no differentiation between these legitimate white settlers and the flood of illegal émigrés crossing the Sabine in violation of the 1820 Laws of Canonization.

These people knew that the Centralist government in Mexico was determined to start collecting tariffs in this region—something they had been excused from previously through Mexican governmental laxity and geographical distances. Such a tax collection would have dramatic effect on their meager livelihoods and homesteads.

The women looked as haggard as the men. They, too, knew that if the Indians, wild animals, unpredictable weather, smugglers, or lawyers and land speculators didn't destroy them, the Mexican army very well might. Their future wasn't secure, and their actions as they awaited Breece's speech indicated their concern. It was obvious to him that they hoped he would be able to give them reassurances.

Even the young women directly in front of him had that harried look. Despite the hardships of frontier life, these women—still girls really—were attractive by any Eastern standards. The rigors of hard work and the lack of "city" grooming aids failed to mask their natural, youthful beauty. But their eyes, too, showed fear.

It was this small group of young women who had just handed the pole staff with its banner to Lieutenant Main, who was standing at attention to his right.

Military formalities and regiment would never be a strong suit of the New Orleans Greys. Breece had figured that out quickly. Still, they had been uncomplainingly cooperative when he had asked them to stand in formation to receive a donated unit banner from this group.

Probably, his fellow Greys had also been touched by the expression of gratitude these settlers had shown them. True, communities in Louisiana had turned out to greet them and had showered them with food and lodging, but it had somehow been different.

These Texan Anglos assembled in front of him saw the Greys not just as a mercenary force entering Texas to overthrow a corrupt dictatorial Mexican government under Santa Anna. They saw the Greys, and others who were beginning to cross over on Gaines Ferry from Louisiana to join the revolution, as possibly the only thing that might make the revolution succeed and save their homes and property from the Mexican Centralists. And the gratitude they were extending to the Greys this morning was sincere.

Stiffly and in good military fashion, he hoped, he did an abrupt right face turn that placed him directly beside Lt. Main who was also standing at attention with the rough-hewn flagstaff tucked against his right side.

Breece made a deliberate show of looking up at the banner and studying it. It was, he had to admit to himself, beautiful. This group of rustic frontier people with their crude possessions had created a unit banner worthy of those representing the traditional, established U.S. Army units to the east.

With a yellow border, it had a distinctive military look. Centered in the flag was the inscription: "First Company of Texan Volunteers From New Orleans." An eagle carried in its beak a streamer on which appeared the words: "God & Liberty." The flag itself was made of a beautiful pale blue silk.

Captain Breece did a sharp left face turn and returned to attention in front of the group of civilians. Clearing his throat before beginning to speak, he glanced once more at the collection of impoverished settlers in front of him.

Not one, he noted to himself, wore anything that remotely resembled the quality of silk.

"Citizens of Texas," he began, "this company of New Orleans Greys accepts with honor the unit banner you have offered us. I pledge to you, on behalf of each man beside and behind me today, that we will offer ourselves to assure that the inscription of "God and Liberty" will be honored. With the blessings of the Almighty, the New Orleans Greys present this banner and ourselves to the Mexicans in order that freedom and independence will be assured for yourselves and all other tyranny-hating Texans.

"May the Mexican Army come to recognize this banner and associate it with what we stand for here today."

Neither Captain Thomas Breece, Lieutenants George Washington Main and John L. Baugh, the rest of the New Orleans Greys, nor the group of settlers assembled on the bank of the Sabine River that morning could have known how true these last words would soon be.

CRCRCRROROR

*T*wo days before Morris' company left New Orleans by ship, the other unit of Greys also left the Crescent City by boat but not by way of the Gulf.

Boarding the steamer *Washita*, Breece's company headed north up the Mississippi River, then west on the Red River toward Alexandria. There are no records indicating why the two units departed for Texas by such diverse paths.

Although primitive, there were in 1835 established routes to Texas from New Orleans. Those with money usually took the quicker and more comfortable sea route through the Gulf. Those with large wagons or without funds took the free overland route.

Money was probably not a consideration in the decision for Breece to lead his company on the overland route. The Bank's Arcade meeting had raised pledges between seven and ten thousand dollars to outfit the Greys.

Records indicate that Morris' unit, with its supplies and cannon, were crowded on the schooner *Columbus*, and it is not known if another schooner was available that was large enough for Breece's company.

The most probable reason that Breece's unit entered Texas overland was that they would be traveling through Nacogdoches—home of Bank's Arcade organizer Adolphus Sterne. The German had been involved in Texas intrigue earlier and had participated in the 1826 Fredonia Rebellion attempting to secede from Mexico. When he was arrested and imprisoned, his Masonic connections in New Orleans had managed to arrange his parole on the condition he never take up arms against Mexico again.

Now, less than a decade later, he was organizing and outfitting the Greys and was once again one of the strongest proponents for Texas secession. At Bank's Arcade he had promised new rifles to the first fifty volunteers, and in Nacogdoches he had pledged horses and additional equipment for the unit. Horses are the most likely explanation that

Breece led his unit of the Greys overland into Texas. Throughout their short unit history, horses—or the lack of—would be a constant problem.

Morris' group, after entering Texas from the south, had attempted to appropriate unbroken mustangs from Mexican civilians with disastrous results. Breece, on the other hand, was being made an offer of outfitted, and broken, horses that the Greys desperately needed.

As a result, his group left New Orleans with a planned stop at Nacogdoches. It is along this journey that Ehrenberg's diary provides a good description of the Greys' travels. Other accounts, notably Duval's *Early Times in Texas*[1] and Dr. Jack Shackleford's reminiscences as physician and captain of the Alabama Red Rovers, provide us with more detailed descriptions of the military aspects of the revolution—particularly at Coleto and Goliad. But Ehrenberg's account gives us a surveyor's perspective of the new land these soldiers were entering, and it also gives us insight about the men who comprised Breece's company.

A great deal of mystery surrounds Ehrenberg prior to his joining the Greys. Various reports indicate he was born in Mariewerder (Prussia), Thuringia (Germany), or Steuden (Prussia) between 1816 and 1818. He may have been the son of William von Ehrenberg, a royal official of Prussia, or the son of Johann and Sophie Ehrenberg. He is often reported as being Jewish, however the birth of a Herman Vollrath Ehrenberg was registered at the Lutheran church in Steuden on October 17, 1816.

The Texas General Land Office archives contain a letter, written in English and dated September 16, 1881, in which a Carl Friedrich Albert Ehrenberg swears before the Royal Prussian Court of Justice at Marienburg that he is the brother of Herman Vollrath Ehrenberg.

The letter, which was also filed in Travis County, State of Texas, contains the following information about the New Orleans Grey:

> Herman Vollrath Ehrenberg, born October
> 17th, 1816 at Steuden, near Halle o/y in Prussia,
> is the very same H. Ehrenberg, who fought under
> Col. Fannin in the war of independence against
> Mexico between the years 1830 and 1840.[2]

This document appears to confirm that Herman Ehrenberg was probably the youngest Grey, having joined the unit at Bank's Arcade less than a week before his nineteenth birthday.

He had attended school at the University of Jena and immigrated to America by way of Canada at a young age, possibly because of involvement in liberal student movements at the university. He immigrated to New York a year before traveling to New Orleans and joining the Greys.

Leaving the Mississippi River, Ehrenberg and the other Greys journeyed west on the Red River aboard the *Washita*. The Red River extended from the Tucumcari Indian settlement in what is now New Mexico and ambled southeast forming a border between Texas and Indian territory on the north before turning across Louisiana and joining the Mississippi River at the northern boundary of the Florida parishes.

Following the Louisiana Purchase, the United States sent the Freeman-Custis Expedition in 1806 to explore the Red River and refute Spanish border claims. Some two decades before the Greys, the steamboat *Enterprise* had traversed the river to Alexandria. In 1835 river navigation extended past Alexandria to Nachitoches where a massive log raft prohibited further travel northward.

At Alexandria the Greys were greeted with the same festive salutes as were Morris' men to the south when they arrived at their first Anglo settlement. They probably visited the trading post located on land owned by Alexander Fulton, who had platted the village of Alexandria in 1805. Following a short stay, they again boarded the *Wichita* for the fifty-mile trip to Nachitoches.

While at Alexandria they were joined by a local volunteer named Blaz Phillipe Despallier. The Despallier family was well known, though somewhat ill reputedly, throughout the Rapides Parish of Louisiana, and at least three of the brothers were involved in Texas' events during 1835-36.

Blaz Phillipe would participate in the upcoming battle for Bexar with the Greys but would become ill and return to Louisiana prior to the fall of the Alamo.[3] After his return to Alexandria, his younger brother Charles traveled to Texas and arrived at the Alamo during the siege and was commended by Travis for his actions in burning the Mexican huts constructed outside the Alamo walls, which were providing cover for the Mexican army.

Charles also acted as a courier for the besieged Texans in the Alamo and relayed Travis' request for reinforcements to the settlement of Gonzales, returning with the Gonzales Ranging Company of Mounted Volunteers on March 1, 1836, and dying in the Alamo on March 6. He was not a New Orleans Grey.

Another Despellier brother, Matthew, joined David Crockett and others at Nachitoches in 1836 on their way to the Alamo. Matthew had a particularly bad reputation, and according to one report by a gambler named Greene, "He was a villainous bully. He drew on me at Alexandria, in 1833, but I was expecting it, and shot him with a derringer. I hurried away, supposing he was killed. . . . I am not sure whether it was Matt, or his equally bad brother, who was killed by ex-governor Wells."[4]

Since Charles Despellier is documented as having died in the Alamo, the other "equally bad brother" referred to by Greene might have been New Orleans Grey Blaz Phillipe or yet another unlisted brother from the family.

Blaz Phillipe, the son of a Natchitoches Frenchman named Bernardo Martin Despallier and his wife Maria Caudida Grande, came from a Louisiana family already historically embroiled in Texas intrigue. His father had received a military appointment from the Louisiana governor in 1794 and moved from New Orleans to Nacogdoches. He was expelled from Texas by the royal Spanish government for illegal trade with Natchitoches and Louisiana and was active in the movement to separate Texas from Spain in 1813. His mother's family is thought to have been involved with the Gutierrez forces with at least one uncle captured and executed.

It was at this stage of the river journey that Thomas H. Breece, a native of Louisiana, was officially elected unit captain. Directly under his command were First Lieutenant John J. Baugh, a thirty-two-year-old Virginian, and Second Lieutenant William Blazeby, a forty-year-old Englishman who had come to New Orleans from New York before joining the Greys.

Several sources, including the *New Handbook of Texas*, list George Washington Main as one of Breece's lieutenants, however the Texas General Land Office muster rolls do not indicate this.[5] Main, also a Virginian, did later serve as a second lieutenant in the Alamo after the siege and battle for Bexar.

Unit sergeants included twenty-five-year-old New Yorker John Jones; a Pennsylvanian listed simply as "McNally"; a thirty-one-year-old volunteer from Ohio named Robert Musselman; and George Andrews, whose background does not list state or national citizenship.

Of the four sergeants, Musselman probably had the only military background, having served in the U.S. Army during the Seminole Indian War. While he was on active duty in Florida, his father died, leaving little or no inheritance. Born in Ohio, his family had moved to Pennsylvania, and instead of returning to New England after his discharge from the army, he chose to travel to New Orleans where he had joined the Greys.[6]

Nachitoches had been established as a settlement at the confluence of the Red and Cane Rivers, and from here the Greys began marching east along *El Camino Real* (The King's Highway) towards Gaine's Ferry and the Sabine River. Before they left the settlement they were again toasted by the local citizens and given a wagonload of provisions, and according to Ehrenberg, "when we walked through the streets, we were invited to friendly meals from all sides."[7] They stayed at Nachitoches for two days before starting the march eastward.

Before they left, however, another recruit was added to their roster. Nicholas Kelly, an Irishman who was working in Nachitoches as a newspaperman, joined the group as quartermaster with the following letter of reference:

> Alexandria, [La.] Oct 30th 1835
> ... There passed up the river on board the
> Steam Boat Oachita on the 28th inst a company
> of sixty men bound for your country said to
> belong to Captain Stern who was Nachitoches—
> I thought It my duty to do my part as far as I
> could and get a man and put him in the com-
> pany I fitted him out with a uniform and good
> rifle 25 lb of good powder and as much lead as
> he could cary—Blanket Butcher Knife &c I gave
> him a letter to you he came to me recom-
> mended by our Editor, who is a gentleman and
> that he was a journeyman in his office at the
> rate of $110 per month and that he was very
> sorry to lose him—this is the character of the
> man I have sent to your country to fight....
> Your friend & obt Servt
> Thos Hooper[8]

They encountered heavily forested but gently rolling hills, and the forced march was probably not too difficult. One obstacle, however, stood between them and the Sabine River border of Texas: the U.S. Army outpost at Fort Jesup. When the Louisiana Purchase Treaty of 1803 failed to define clearly the western boundary of Louisiana, which was also the western border of the country at that time, the United States claimed eastern Texas and Spain claimed western Louisiana.

In a compromise, both nations established a "Neutral Ground" in which the laws of neither nation were enforced. Soldiers and settlers were kept out, and as a result, outlaws, bandits, cutthroats, and every other known fugitive from justice moved into the region and created a lawless territory from which they could operate.

On various occasions both the Spanish and American authorities had sent short-term expeditionary forces into the Neutral Ground, but it was not until after the territorial boundary was finally fixed at the Sabine River by the Florida Purchase Treaty of 1819, that the United States truly gained control, legally and militarily, of the territory.

To achieve this, the United States Army built Fort Jesup in 1822. Lieutenant Colonel Zachary Taylor established and commanded the garrison, which was originally called Cantonment Jesup in honor of Taylor's good friend Brigadier General Thomas Sidney Jesup. Taylor's troops managed to establish law and order in the Neutral Ground, and Fort Jesup remained an important military post for nearly twenty-five years.

In 1835, however, the United States was officially "neutral" with regards to the insurrection in northern Mexico, and the post commandant was ordered not to let the volunteer militia groups pass through the fort on their way to Texas.

The Greys, on their second day out of Nachitoches, had to avoid the fort and, as a result, were forced off the Camino Real to the south for some distance until they could camp safely to the west between the fort and the Sabine River.

On the next day they reached the Sabine where the Camino Real entered Texas at Gaine's Ferry. The ferry had been established some forty years earlier, in 1795, and was purchased by James Gaines in 1819. When the Greys crossed that autumn of 1835 Gaines also operated an inn, mercantile store, and postal office on the Texas side.

At that time, the ferry was the established entry point into Texas from the United States. It is estimated that, during its operation, the ferry brought four-fifths of the colonists across from the U.S.

Ehrenberg reports that the neighboring plantation settlers on the Texas side met them at the ferry landing and that "The tender hand of a Texas woman gave us in the name of all beauties of the land a splendid blue silk flag on which the following inscription appeared: 'To the first company of Texan Volunteers from New Orleans'. We kissed the soil of the new homeland, received the holy ordnance of citizenship, and Captain Breece expressed in so many ways to the ladies our abundant gratitude."[9]

It was this flag that would some five months later become famous, or infamous, as the "Alamo flag" captured by Santa Anna and exhibited in Mexico City as proof of U.S. involvement in the Texas succession. But that day on the Mexican side of the Sabine River, the flag was just one more gift bestowed on the Greys by grateful Texas settlers along their way to San Antonio.

Continuing to follow the Camino Real, which in Texas was often referred to as the Old San Antonio Road, the Greys marched another two days to the Anglo settlement of San Augustine where they were met outside the community by the local militia and escorted into town with a marching band. To the Greys, the slow, methodic beat of the local drummer sounded melancholy and depressing. Showing him how to do it, the Greys' own drummer (whom Ehrenberg referred to as "a wily Creole") broke into a furious beat of "Beer in the Mug."[10]

They spent the night in San Augustine with the local citizens again offering them food and lodging, and the next day they left, anticipating a two-day march to Nacogdoches where Adolphus Sterne was waiting for them with horses and other provisions. Cold weather and heavy frost, however, slowed the march, and on the evening of the second day, most of the Greys found themselves scattered along the road, lodging in any available cabins or camping in the forests unaware they were within less than ten miles of Nacogdoches.

The next day they mustered in the town around the wood-framed house of Adolphus Sterne. The house was both the social and the political center of activity in Nacogdoches. Sam Houston had boarded with the Sternes when he first arrived in Texas and was baptized into the Catholic Church in the front parlor of the house with Mrs. Sterne serving as his godmother.

The majority of the Greys bivouacked directly in front of the house, and they were honored with a "Feast of Liberty" in the orchard where they were camped. Bear, beef, mutton, turkeys, raccoon, and other specialties were served on a table a hundred and fifty feet long. With glasses of Rhine wine from Sterne's cellar, toasts were made and speeches delivered.

Sterne had been particularly pleased to find several Germans among the ranks of the Greys, and during the toasts, two of these expatriates presented speeches. Peter Mattern toasted the "Republic of Texas" while another German, Henry Courtman, pledged "the last drop of his blood for 'the new republic'."[11]

Courtman's toast was particularly prophetic: Four months later he would in fact be among the Greys to die in the

Alamo. Ehrenberg listed him as one of the Greys massacred at Goliad, but the Courtman killed there was George Courtman, Henry's brother. The other German toaster at the feast, Peter Mattern, would become a massacre victim at Goliad.

That night the Greys drank "eighty dollars worth of the champagne in addition to drinks more usual to the wilderness."[12] The scene is very similar to that of the other unit of Greys to the south, toasting champagne in the coastal settlement of Brazoria in which "we had in our imagination conquered all Mexico."

After three days at Nacogdoches camped around Sterne's house the soldiers received all of the promised horses, and on the following day the mounted Greys departed for San Antonio. At this point, both companies of the Greys had, as the situation warranted, been marines, infantrymen, cavalrymen, and—since Morris' unit was drawing cannon—they would in the future also be artillerymen. These were clearly the kind of versatile soldiers that Houston and Austin needed in Texas, but the fact remained that almost none of the young Greys had had previous military experience.

As they would soon prove, they could—and would—fight, but as a cohesive military unit they were never specialists in warfare. As marines, they disembarked ship at every opportunity; as infantrymen they fought best when breaking ranks and fighting hand to hand; as cavalrymen they were never the equal of the renowned Mexican cavalry lancers; and as artillerymen they were almost certainly apprentices learning their deadly trade through rushed practice drills and battle exposure. In just four short months after these two companies of Greys entered the revolution, a free and independent Republic of Texas could look back and remember that these volunteers had literally been universal soldiers.

The Greys' presence in Nacogdoches also provided an unexpected reward for the Anglo settlers living there. Although the white Texans living there maintained an uneasy peace with the local Indians in the area, there was always an underlying threat of violence. Many Anglos living in east Texas suspected that what peace did exist between the two cultures was based largely upon the Indians' fear of U.S. Army troops making punishing raids across the Sabine River to avenge Indian deprivations.

The appearance of Breece's men in their gray uniforms had a sobering effect on the many Indians visiting Nacogdoches at that time:

> The appearance of Breese's company at Nacogdoches had a fine effect on the Cherokee Indians, a large number of whom were then in town. Their fine uniform caps and coats attracted the notice of the chief Bolles. He inquired if they were *Jackson's* men. "Certainly they are," said Sterne. "How many more?" asked Bolles. Sterne told him to count the hairs on his head, and he would know. In twenty minutes the Indians had all left the town![13]

But upon leaving Nacogdoches that November day, the Greys were no doubt grateful to be on horseback for the remaining trip to San Antonio. Moving southwest from Nacogdoches, they crossed the Angelina River and continued along the Camino Real, crossing the Neches River at William's Ferry.

From William's Ferry, they traveled past Brown's Fort, Master's Fort, and Clapp's Blockhouse before reaching the Trinity River and Robbin's Ferry, which had been established in 1821 by Joel Leaky and was named for ferryman and owner Nathaniel Robbins.

Here, the Greys passed through Trinidad, also known as Spanish Bluff, near what today is known as Madisonville. Just west of Trinidad the Greys left the Camino Real, traveling southwest on the La Bahia Road through Plasterville and Zubar's Farm to Fantharp. They then crossed Robinson's Ferry and entered the new colony of Washington-on-the Brazos.

Why they chose to leave the Camino Real is a mystery. The La Bahia Road did not offer a shortcut nor would it have been an easier or faster route, and there was no mention of any Mexican soldiers patrolling the Camino Real.

Fearful of arriving in San Antonio too late to participate in the battle, they had been pushing hard, and Ehrenberg reports that upon arriving at Washington-on-the-Brazos the forced marches had so exhausted men and beasts that they required a rest for a few days.

From Washington-on-the-Brazos, the Greys traveled west across the prairie of Tamaulipas on a minor trace north of the La Bahia Road through Cole's Settlement, also called Independence, southwest to the Kerr Settlement, then directly west to a point identified as the Spanish Mail Exchange on the Camino Real just northeast of the established Anglo community of Bastrop—a settlement also referred to as Mina.

At Bastrop the Greys were again greeted with food and offers of lodging but chose instead to camp out in the streets where large fires had been lit in their honor. Bastrop would be their last contact with Anglo settlers until they reached San Antonio.

Four days west of Bastrop, the Greys were camping in a grove of live oak trees covered with Spanish moss when they noticed dark clouds ahead of them. Thinking the smoke might be the result of the fighting for San Antonio, they vowed to press forward the next morning. During the night, however, they were startled to learn that the smoke had been a raging prairie fire that was surging toward them. Helpless, they gathered the horses inside the "oasis" of live oaks and watched as the fire burned itself out at the edge of their grove.

The next day required a forced march across the blackened and charred wasteland that had previously been prairie grass. Exhausted and parched, they reached the Cibolo Creek, watered their horses, and continued on to the Salado

River where they learned that they were only six miles from San Antonio.

Just as Morris' unit had sustained its first military casualty as it came within sight of San Antonio, Breece's company also made its first contact with the Mexican army and recorded its first casualties after reaching this final leg of their journey.

A Grey named Nelson became lost on the road and had his horse shot from beneath him after being wounded in the side. He managed to avoid the Mexicans by hiding in a pond under the cover of darkness and was found the next day by fellow Greys who rescued him.[14]

Ehrenberg states that Nelson was an Englishman, however Breece's muster roll lists only George Nelson, a thirty-one-year-old volunteer from South Carolina. The *New Handbook of Texas* reports George Nelson was wounded during the siege of Bexar,[15] suggesting the Carolinian may have been the Grey to whom Ehrenberg was referring.

At the same time, another Grey became lost and disoriented on the trail and was surrounded by Mexican soldiers. Captured, he was taken to the Alamo, tried, and sentenced to death.[16] Joining George Voss from Morris' unit, he became the second Grey prisoner of war. Ehrenberg refers to him only as "a wily Creole from Louisiana." The muster rolls show the following names for enlisted men claiming Louisiana: Clark, Despallier, Fitzgerald, Garrett, Griffin, and Spohn.

Later, after the battle, Ehrenberg refers to Joseph H. Spohn (also sometimes spelled Spawn) as "a Creole from Louisiana."[17] There is no mention of the death sentence being carried out, so it is likely the soldier—probably the drummer Spohn—was released by the Mexicans or freed by the Greys after the storming of Bexar and the Alamo where he would continue on with the Greys and play a crucial role in the events following the battles at Bexar and Coleto.

After these two incidents with the Mexicans, the rest of the Greys reached the Salado where they camped overnight. The next day, thought to be November 21, 1835, they were escorted through the woods into Bexar where they joined the Texas army and quickly found Morris' company of their fellow Greys who had arrived a fortnight earlier.

The New Orleans Greys were once again united only a mile from Bexar, the Alamo, and the Mexican army. Their paths had been radically different but they were once again a united military group ready for the coming fight. Bloodied—with one dead, one wounded, and two captured—they were still a unit of young, inexperienced military recruits full of revolutionary fervor.

That was about to change.

---

1   John C. Duval, *Early Times in Texas* (Lincoln: University of Nebraska Press, 1936).

2   Texas General Land Office Archives files.

3   Bill Groneman, "Despallier, Charles," *New Handbook of Texas*.

4   *Biographical and Historical Memoirs of Northwest Louisiana* (Chicago: John Morris Co., 1890), pg. 309.

5   Texas General Land Office Archives, [A2, Section C][list][tran][note].

6   Bill Groneman, "Mussleman, Robert," *New Handbook of Texas*.

7   Ornish, *Ehrenberg*, pg. 89.

8   Jenkins, *The Papers of the Texas Revolution,* Vol. 2, pg. 270.

9   Ornish, *Ehrenberg*, pp. 89-90.

10 *Ibid.*, pg. 90.

11 Baker, "Trailing the New Orleans Greys," pg. 221.

12 *Ibid.*, pg. 223.

13 Henderson King Yoakum, *History of Texas From its First Settlement in 1655 to its Annexation to the United States in 1846 in Two Volumes* (New York: Redfield, 1855), Vol. 2, pg. 23.

14 Ornish, *Ehrenberg*, pp. 127-8.

15 Groneman, "Nelson, George," *New Handbook of Texas*.

16 Ornish, *Ehrenberg.*, pg. 129.

17 *Ibid.*, pg. 167.

Chapter 4

Siege of Bexar

Volunteer Texan Encampment, San Antonio de Bexar, Texas, December 1, 1835: Albert Moses Levy sat huddled on the makeshift stool near the campfire and pondered the bleak scene in the field before him. He sipped from his cup of coffee—steaming this morning because the temperatures were near freezing.

He found Texas depressing. From the filthy coastal towns of Quintana and Velasco to the crude living conditions of the Anglo settlers at Columbia and Victoria, he had missed the more gentle and cultured New England countryside. The Mexicans were even worse, he had decided, the way they had subsisted at Goliad. He had hoped San Antonio de Bexar—by virtue of being a Spanish and Mexican provincial trading center—would have some semblance of culture and bearing.

Maybe it did, but neither he nor any of the other Greys had had the opportunity to enter the town to find out. From their encampment about a mile away, the small village with its church tower and mission compound was still a mystery.

Another of the Greys named Ehrenberg had recently remarked that the old Spanish missions outside the town reminded him of castles in his native Germany. Taking another sip of coffee, Dr. Levy had found nothing in Texas that had reminded him of his native Holland. Certainly nothing comparable to the beauty and grace of his boyhood hometown of Amsterdam.

In his depression, he missed Amsterdam and he missed New England. But most of all he missed his wife, Maria, and their daughter. Dead less than a year now, Maria's memory was never far from his thoughts, and the pain and depression were, if anything, worsening each day. His daughter, Rachel, was now living with his sister in Richmond, and he daily thought of her also. He had sent some letters to his sister through McKinney and Williams back in Velasco but had no way of knowing if they had even left Texas for New Orleans and Richmond.

The sound of two almost simultaneous explosions rolled across the gently sloping hill where he sat, and he recognized them as Texan artillery. Within seconds, three rounds were fired back from the old Alamo compound followed by another from the San Fernando church tower. The Mexicans were responding quickly this morning.

The doctor, like the other Greys in the encampment, barely paid any attention to the artillery duel. It would go on intermittently throughout the day with little damage on either side. So far, this had been pretty much a bloodless war—good from a medical doctor's viewpoint.

As unit surgeon with Morris' company of the New Orleans Greys, Levy had really only been called upon to treat minor ailments and injuries—saddle sores and a few broken bones. Lately, the skirmishes between the Mexicans and Texans had resulted in some gunshot wounds, but the pathetic firepower of the Mexican soldiers had resulted in few serious injuries. He'd lost count of the Texans he'd treated for bruises caused by Mexican bullets.

He took another sip of coffee and glanced over at the old Alamo mission. It looked the same as it had earlier in the morning, so he figured the two cannon shot had missed their mark.

It was beginning to look as if the siege of the old city was going to disband any day now. He wondered what he would do then. He could always go back to stay with his brother

Lewis in New Orleans or his sister, at least temporarily, in Richmond. God, how he wanted to see his daughter again! But he'd come to Texas to obtain land and start a new life and a new medical practice. To start a new life without his Maria. And now, even this dream was falling apart in front of him here in Bexar.

He glanced around the Greys' camp. Except for the officers, Levy felt he had little in common with any of the other volunteers. For the most part, in his surgeon's eyes, he saw them as slovenly, uncouth, and filthy soldiers.

Their personal hygiene was atrocious. For the most part they seldom bathed, washed their clothes, or even prepared their food in a sanitary manner. The smallest of scratches or cuts on them became infected because of the lack of cleanliness.

Not that he could help much in his position as a doctor. He had brought his own personal medical kit with the expensive surgical tools he'd purchased in Pennsylvania. But medical supplies were nonexistent here in the Texan camp. They had received some supplies from the captured stock at Goliad earlier in the month, but there had been no medicine, soap, or bandages. His personal supply of medicine, limited to start with, was now depleted. Even his supply of laudanum, which he was saving to treat his own melancholy, was almost gone now.

Treatment for infection had been limited to bloodletting for over a week now, and there was no camphor for colic. His supply of calomel subchloride of mercury and quinine had been exhausted on the journey from Velasco. Corn liquor, never in short supply, was being used to kill pain and to disinfect open wounds. Without new bandages, he had been collecting spiderwebs each morning but only to treat the worst of the open wounds.

Any field dressings had to be reused until they became rags. Sanitation consisted of boiling used bandages. The men simply wouldn't listen to his advice about thoroughly cooking the meat and washing their hands and knives, nor would they bother boiling the water they retrieved from the San Antonio River—a new medical remedy being advocated at a medical school in Kentucky.

Not only were the men sick, but the whole camp atmosphere had an unhealthy air about it. With corn disappearing during the winter months, their diets had consisted almost entirely of unsalted beef, which the men "appropriated" from the local Mexican ranchers and slaughtered in the nearby barren cornfield. Initially the offal had not created a problem, but the siege had been carrying on for six weeks now, and the carrion and intestinal remains were rotting and creating a stench. He and the other officers had repeatedly warned the men about shooting the vultures for fun. Now the hideous creatures were their best source of cleaning and removing the unhealthy cattle remains.

Hearing movement to his right, he glanced over to see one of the Greys, who had just crawled out of his tent, stumble barefooted on the nearly frozen dirt to the area behind his tent and relieve himself on the ground. From the grunts and groans of the soldier, Levy could guess that he was suffering from the hangover effects of the liquor the night before—an almost epidemic condition among these bored, frustrated volunteers now.

Dr. Levy watched the man stumble back into his tent and thought about how little he had in common with most of the men who had volunteered for the New Orleans Greys. While he'd never felt he was an integral part of them—and wasn't sure he ever wanted to be—he also recognized that they accepted him mostly because of their need for his medical skills and knowledge.

Shortly after Morris had led his company of Greys to Bexar, Levy had set up a temporary shelter to use as an aid station. When Breece's company arrived a couple of weeks later, Levy invited their doctor, William Howell, to join him, and the two men had worked well together.

But Howell was more like the other men in the Greys, and Levy hadn't been able to establish any kind of bond—professional or personal—with the backwoods physician from Massachusetts. Levy suspected Howell's training had been typical of most doctors in America's rural areas. Many of these doctors had no medical training but had just read some books or maybe watched another doctor a few times and then decided to try their luck. Their medical practice usually consisted of steam baths, herbal remedies, and bloodletting or "purging."

He thought back to his days as a medical student in Pennsylvania and his graduation in 1832—the same year Rachel had been born. Those had been happy days. He had his medical degree, a wonderful wife, and a beautiful baby daughter. Today, he was treating saddle sores and diarrhea in this godforsaken place, Maria was dead, and he couldn't even send his love to his daughter from this isolated spot in Mexico.

And his depression was worsening by the day.

Dr. Albert Levy still believed that an independent Texas would be key to a better future for him and his daughter. But this miserable army he was serving in was not good for him or his reoccurring and intense bouts of depression. Whether this siege eventually broke up and moved south for the winter or a battle for the city occurred, he planned to discharge the army as soon as possible.

From some of the officers in other volunteer groups, he'd heard stories of how a Texan navy was being formed. Maybe in the future months he'd make a better naval surgeon than this assignment he held here today. From his earliest days as a boy on the docks around Amsterdam and Vollendam, he'd always loved the sea and ships. On the sea voyage to America seventeen years earlier, he'd volunteered his services as an apprentice sailor and had loved every day of that rough and difficult voyage.

As his family had settled in Virginia, he'd continued sailing small boats whenever he could—an avocation he'd continued as a medical student later in Pennsylvania. Likewise, the short sea voyage from New Orleans to Velasco had been exhilarating to him while most of the other Greys had spent the three days in nausea. Yes, he thought to himself, when this mess here in Bexar was concluded, he'd try to obtain a commission in the new Texas navy.

His coffee cup was empty now, but before he could reach down to refill it, he heard his name being called. Turning on the stool, he saw a horseman approaching through the ramshackle tents of the camp. "Dr. Levy," the rider yelled, "better come quick. We've got an injured man over by the mill."

"Gunshot?" Levy called back as he reached for his medical kit.

"Nah," the rider answered as he rode up next to the doctor, "horse stumbled and pinned him. Think his leg's broken pretty bad."

Dr. Albert Levy hoisted his satchel behind the rider and lifted his foot into the empty stirrup being offered. With a grunt of his own, he swung up behind the rider and started off on another day of practicing camp medicine.

C3CS CS CS SO SO SO

San Antonio de Bexar had been the destination of both companies of New Orleans Greys from the very moment of their inception at Bank's Arcade. It was at San Antonio, or as the Mexicans called it, "Bexar," that the decisive battle of the Texas revolution was expected to occur. Even before the Greys left New Orleans in October of 1835, they were aware that a group of Texans was besieging the city.

During the first week in October a small group of Anglo settlers near the community of Gonzales had refused to return a small cannon to the Mexican army. A skirmish had resulted, and the Mexicans had withdrawn back to Bexar to await reinforcements while the colonists followed them— attracting additional volunteers along the way.

The New Orleans Greys were part of those additional volunteers they had attracted. But it wasn't until mid-November that they arrived at the Texan encampment about a mile outside Bexar.

A month earlier, as the Texans were just starting to grow in numbers, the Mexican garrison in the city was reinforced by the arrival of General Martin Perfecto de Cos, Santa Anna's brother-in-law, and his troops. By mid-October the Mexican force in Bexar totaled nearly 700 men. Mexican infantry backed by artillery held the two plazas west of the river, while the old Alamo mission compound was guarded by artillery and backed by over 400 cavalry in seven companies.[1]

By late October the Mexican forces had grown to over 750 men, and skirmishes were occurring almost daily between the two armies—particularly in the area along the San Antonio River near the century-old abandoned Franciscan missions outside the city.

On October 28 the skirmishes intensified and culminated in a major clash between Mexican forces and Texan soldiers led by James Bowie and James Fannin. The fighting that day, later referred to as the Battle of Concepcion, resulted in a substantial Texan victory that forced the Mexicans to retreat back into the safety of Bexar and the Alamo.

The Texan victory at Concepcion also established what would become the military posture of both armies: The Mexicans would maintain solely a defensive posture, and the Texans would be hesitant to mount an assault against the entrenched Mexican positions. Strategically, the conflict had become a siege situation.

The first week of November brought additional Texan reinforcements and supplies from the captured southern military outpost at Goliad. Accounts vary, probably because of confusion about two companies of Greys arriving at different times, but Morris' group is thought to have arrived at Bexar around November 9.

At this time both armies were roughly equal in numbers of men, however the Texans—for various reasons—were already becoming frustrated and leaving. By mid-November Texans were deserting in groups, and camp discipline had all but disappeared. Soldiers were refusing to follow orders, guards were sleeping on duty if they even reported, commissary stocks were being raided, and colonists were leaving to prepare for spring planting.

Shortly after the arrival of Morris' unit, word was received that Colonel Ugartechea had managed to slip from the Alamo and evade Texan patrols as he marched south to the Rio Grande to collect reinforcements for the Mexicans. The Texan "revolution" was clearly in trouble.

Less than two weeks after the first unit of Greys had established camp at Bexar, Captain Breece and the second unit rode in from Nacogdoches by way of Bastrop. Several sources report their arrival occurred on November 21. The addition of this second company of well-armed Greys in their distinctive uniforms boosted not only the Texans' dwindling numbers but also their morale.

Prior to Breece's arrival, the Texans had received several cannon from Goliad and had captured one Mexican cannon at Concepcion. Morris' unit had brought two more pieces, and the huge eighteen-pounder was en route from the coast.

During mid-November several of Morris' Greys worked their way out into a cornfield between the Texan camp and Bexar and had established a small redoubt where they positioned two of the Texan cannon. From this sheltered position, they were able to engage the Mexican ordnance in the Alamo in artillery duels that at times took on an almost burlesque atmosphere.

The Texan position was just close enough to the Alamo that the cannoneers, with good aim, could hit the crumbling north wall of the compound or even the old mission itself. While the bombardment was in itself basically ineffective it did achieve two goals: It weakened the north wall of the Mexican defenses while training the Texans—including the Greys—how to be artillerymen. Inevitably, the Mexicans would respond by returning fire with grapeshot and ball, and when the Greys ran out of cannonballs they would scamper around the desolate cornfield picking up spent Mexican rounds to fire back into the city.

The arrival of Breece's Greys failed to improve the conditions inside the Texan camp but seemed to inject some measure of activity and optimism into all of the volunteers encamped outside Bexar late in November.

For all the notoriety of the community of Bexar—the name was now famous throughout the United States—the community that both units of the Greys discovered at the end of their journeys was far from being a "city" in the American definition. San Antonio de Bexar lay in a gently rolling valley on the west side of the spring-fed San Antonio River. Stone buildings with thick walls surrounded two plazas that were intersected by broad streets. Between the main plaza nearer the river and the military plaza to the west stood a church whose tower overlooked the community of perhaps sixteen hundred people. West of the military plaza ran San Pedro Creek. Beyond the rock houses lay scattered log and mud huts. The river ran ninety feet wide but only a yard deep and formed a horseshoe bend east of the town toward an abandoned and crumbling Spanish mission called the Alamo. To the south along the river stood the ruins of four more missions that had been founded over a hundred years before, as was the town, but had been secularized in the 1790s with only their chapels used for services. Above and below the town lay fertile fields of corn.[2]

Immediately after arrival Breece's men located the other Greys and settled into the Texan camp quickly. While the New Orleans Greys may have brought uniformity and a military bearing to the Texan encampment, they did not add any measure of discipline to the troops. By Ehrenberg's own account, the Greys were as undisciplined as the other volunteers:

> If there were no necessary detentions, the troops appeared en masse. But with us here, we were more laid back. The roll was never called in the morning. After the signal to rise had been given and after the fire was made, we prepared breakfast. We then broke into small groups if there was nothing to fear from the Indians or large groups of the enemy and galloped away as we pleased.[3]

Stephen Austin was overjoyed at their arrival. He was so buoyed that he felt the time was right to take advantage of their presence in the Texan camp. He acquiesced to the demands of the volunteers and ordered an attack on the city and Alamo.

On November 22 Travis resigned the regular army and left camp. Austin planned an attack on the city for the early morning hours of the next day only to have several of his senior officers pass a petition urging the assault be delayed. In frustration Austin was forced to countermand his own order.

The decision was particularly harsh for Austin. He had previously been ordered to leave for the United States to do diplomatic work towards counteracting official U.S. neutrality, and this cancellation of the attack deprived him of any opportunity to take advantage of the Greys' arrival and lead an attack on the Mexican city.

With his departure, the volunteers elected Edward Burleson as their new commander. Temperatures dropped to near freezing, and sickness swept through the Texan camp.

Another brief flurry of action occurred on November 26 when James Bowie, in response to rumors that a Mexican column had been sighted escorting money to pay soldiers inside the Alamo, led a successful attack on the column only to discover the Mexicans had been out foraging grass for the starving animals inside the Alamo. Some of the New Orleans Greys participated in the "Grass Fight" according to Ehrenberg. "We liberated again (Mexican prisoners) during the night because they made us extra trouble and had to be fed from our provisions."[4]

But after the Grass Fight, Bowie also left camp. On November 29 New Orleans Grey Major Robert Morris wrote Sam Houston that "there are now here 225 men, nearly all from the U.S. who on no consideration will enter into any service connected with the Regular Army...."[5]

Morris also took the opportunity in his letter to suggest to Houston that the New Orleans Greys would not wait even another day to make a march to the "Interior"—meaning Matamoros. He also suggested to Houston that the Greys formed the elite nucleus of the Texan army and that they "without exageration form the best disciplind corps now in Texas."[6]

Morris' letter is one of the first suggestions that the Greys were considering abandoning the siege in favor of pursuing a Matamoros expedition—specifically at the urging of land speculator James Grant. In his correspondence, Morris declined a commission in the regular army and reported that he intended to lead the Greys to Matamoros on November 30.

Morris' letter to Houston threatening to take the Greys and depart for Matamoros is widely quoted in history books. What is often left out of the text, however, is the last sentence of the letter in which Morris states: "You will perceive

. . . that I am not a mere seeker of fortune, but one who has earnestly at heart the prosperity & liberty of your beautiful country."[7]

This reference to not being a "seeker of fortune" is significant—to Morris at least—in that it suggests he is sensitive to the charges of mercenary activity on the part of U.S. volunteers, including the Greys, inside Texas at that time. His attempt to assure Sam Houston of his interest in "prosperity & liberty of your beautiful country" may have been a reaction to Houston's stated opposition to the land speculators like Grant and Johnson.

The November 30 deadline passed without the Greys leaving for Matamoros; however, on December 1 Thomas Rusk also departed camp for east Texas.

If the Greys were free to pursue their own interests around the camp, they quickly found ways to involve themselves in the limited fighting. Immediately, they were drawn to the small cannon redoubt established earlier by Morris' Greys in the cornfield west of the Alamo. To reach the exposed position, any reinforcements were required to brave canister and grapeshot while running across a half-mile stretch of barren field.

Ehrenberg, who had arrived with Breece, later recalled how eight of the Greys decided one morning to join the cannon crew at the redoubt and started across the cornfield only to be pinned down behind the trunk of a leafless pecan tree while the Mexican artillerymen attempted to target them. When the Greys eventually made their way to the cannon, they found those already there wagering with regards to locations of their cannon shots. The usual bet, according to Ehrenberg, was the casting of musketballs by the loser or the loss of personal weapons.[8]

During one of these artillery duels, the Greys came under heavy rifle fire from snipers who had approached the bank of the San Antonio River between the Alamo and their position.

As the snipers succeeded in pinning down those in the redoubt, other Mexicans in the city began emerging to also open fire.

In response, a group of approximately thirty Greys grabbed their rifles and came to the aid of the stranded group in the cornfield. As they advanced, the Mexicans all retreated back into the city, and in a spur of the moment and unplanned move, the Greys rushed the city and found themselves occupying the outer houses without any resistance.

The "raid" then became one of breaking into houses and "appropriating" cookware—basically a "pots and pans" sortie. With the lack of any resistance, the Greys continued into the city on their raid, even capturing a Mexican cannon at one point. The raid ended when they came under fire from two artillery pieces in the San Fernando church tower, followed by a general sounding of alarm and a flood of Mexican soldiers rushing into the streets.

Forced to abandon the captured cannon unspiked, the Greys retreated only to find Mexican soldiers now occupied the cornfield. Nearly surrounded and pinned down, the foolhardy raid almost ended in tragedy until Deaf Smith led a force of Texans to their rescue.[9]

As stupid and risky as the Greys' raid into the city had been, it had achieved more than the procurement of cooking utensils. More importantly, it had proven what the Texan leaders advocating attack had been arguing for weeks: The Mexican defenses in the city itself could be breached by well-armed and aggressive Texas volunteers.

By December the Texan camp was becoming deserted. In desperation, Burleson agreed to a night assault, then, like Austin earlier, rescinded the orders to attack. The departures from the Texas camp now became a flood. The only volunteers remaining seemed to be the New Orleans Greys, a group of Mississippi volunteers, and a small unit of local Anglo settlers from Brazoria. Within the two combined units of angry, disillusioned, and frustrated Greys, one of the officers was silently weighing his options. . . .

William Gordon Cooke had been elected a New Orleans Grey captain immediately after arrival at Bexar when Robert Morris had been promoted to the rank of major.

By late November Robert Morris had become involved in the political intrigue swirling through the upper officer ranks of the Texan camp. His refusal to accept a Regular Army commission and his association with James Grant and the other land speculators indicates he had already decided by December to leave the New Orleans Greys and pursue his own interests in Texas.

Cooke, on the other hand, was now a commanding officer, and his company, formerly Morris', was now being referred to as "Cooke's Company" of the New Orleans Greys. And Cooke, unlike Morris, planned to cast his lot with the Texans here at Bexar.

After Burleson had cancelled the early December attack, he announced on December 4 that he was abandoning the siege and retreating to Goliad where Bowie had presumably arranged for winter quarters. Part of the rationale for canceling the orders to attack involved suspicion the Mexicans had been forewarned, but Burleson also had relied upon the advice of his senior officers—including Major Morris—who had advised against proceeding.

Burleson called a general assembly of the few remaining men. At this point Burleson was under a great deal of political pressure due to the demands of his leaders like Grant and Johnson, who were urging a Matamoros expedition to take the fighting to the Mexicans. To the few frustrated remaining volunteers—including the Greys—these arguments were falling on fertile ears. To many of the Greys, who had been vocally advocating an attack on the city, the thought of an expedition to the border to start a fight there sounded even better than an assault on Bexar under questionable odds.

It is obvious that James Grant was applying pressure on Burleson at this stage of the Bexar siege. Ehrenberg even suggests it was Grant, not Burleson, who called the general assembly of the men:

> Finally Colonel [James] Grant, who formerly was an officer in the Scottish Highlanders but now for a number of years a citizen of Mexico, succeeded in arranging for a general assembly of the troops, where General [he was elected brigadier general of the militia in 1837] E. [Edward] Burleson, the commander of the army [colonel of the infantry], would disclose his plans. If they should be approved, it was agreed to put them into action the next morning.[10]

There is some evidence to question if Grant, using Morris as a conspiratorial agent, may have sabotaged the attack plans in order to use the Greys for his Matamoros expedition, which, unlike the Bexar offensive, stood to help him restore his lost wealth and landholdings in northern Mexico. And Grant wasn't the only Texan leader attempting to sway Morris and the Greys to abandon Bexar for Matamoros.

Francis White Johnson also had ties in Coahuila and the northern regions of Mexico outside the area around Bexar. Earlier in the year, Johnson and two other speculators had visited the Mexican provincial legislature in Monclova as official "observers" and guests of the secretary of the legislature. The secretary happened to be none other than James Grant, who was heavily involved in internal Coahuilan politics, land speculation, and intrigue.

Through Grant, Johnson and the other "observers" obtained between 1,500 and 1,600 leagues of Mexican land in Texas to develop as entrepreneurs with rights to sell and part of the revenues being used to finance the Mexican Federalists in their opposition to Santa Anna and his Centralists.

The Coahuila Federalists, like the Texans, were wanting to secede from Mexico and start an independent republic.

Santa Anna quickly moved his army into Coahuila and occupied the legislature in Monclova, causing Grant and the American speculators to flee northward into Texas. Now, to retrieve their lost land and wealth, Grant and Johnson desperately needed to foment the Federalist revolution in Coahuila, and the New Orleans Greys were the perfect weapon with which to achieve a second revolution south of the Rio Grande.

Using Robert Morris, who had informed Sam Houston of the Greys' intent to leave Bexar for Matamoros on November 30, the two speculators stood to gain much by abandoning the planned assault on San Antonio. But Burleson had managed to foil their plans by keeping alive the hopes of attacking the city in the early morning hours of December 4.

Ostensibly, a "shadowy figure" was seen slipping into the Alamo that evening—assumed to be a spy disclosing the Texan assault plans. Later, Burleson was confronted by his senior officers, who unanimously advised the attack be cancelled.

Two New Orleans Greys later reported that their former captain, Robert C. Morris, was one of those who attempted to influence Burleson's decision. Captain William Cooke later wrote that just before the attack was to be launched:

> ... about this time Maj. Morris reported to
> Gen. Burleson that one of the centenils [sic]
> had observed a man pass from our camp to the
> Alamo and after a short conference with a cen-
> tenil on the walls had gained admittance—On
> this information Gen. Burleson thought proper
> to countermand the attack—This created great
> dissatisfaction among the men, in consequence
> of which a general parade was ordered and
> Gen. B. after giving Major Morris' statement as

his reason for withdrawing the order for attack, formally resigned his command....[11]

Ehrenberg, one of James Grant's staunchest supporters, also reported that Burleson had informed the assembled men:

> I have given the matter ripe consideration
> and have sought the advice of Major [Robert
> C.] Morris and Colonel [Francis W.] Johnson. It
> is my opinion as well as that of the colonel
> that, in view of the unfavorable season [December], we should withdraw behind the
> Guadalupe until spring, have some comfort in
> camp, await reinforcements from the States and
> undertake a sudden attack with renewed
> strength on San Antonio in February or March
> without setting up camp again as we are doing
> now.
>
> Cries of disapproval ran through the lines;
> and even Grant, the gallant Scot, shared our
> opinion.[12]

So, the actions of the two land speculators Grant and Johnson in conjunction with their new associate Robert Morris, appear to have been attempts to dissuade Burleson from attacking Bexar despite the general desire of the volunteers to proceed. This poses the question: Were Grant and Johnson attempting to stop the planned attack on Bexar and the Alamo so that they could utilize the New Orleans Greys as their personal mercenary force to recover lost possessions in Coahuila and Texas?

If so, they nearly succeeded as Burleson, or as Ehrenberg would have us believe—Grant, called the assembly of the remaining volunteers.

As Burleson announced that he planned to withdraw, the Texans began deserting the army in large groups. But it was also on this day that a Mexican officer approached the Texan camp and claimed to be a deserter. He reported that the morale and supplies of the Mexicans were in even worse condition than those of the Texans. Those hard-line Texans still campaigning for a fight took this as one last opportunity to win control of the city.

What happened next was an incident that became a mainstay reference to the Texas revolution: a statement nearly as recognizable as "Remember the Alamo! Remember Goliad!" According to most historical sources, it was after hearing the Mexican deserter's report that aging Ben Milam stepped forward and made his famous call: "Who will follow old Ben Milam into San Antonio?" or, by some reports, "Who will join old Ben Milam in storming the Alamo?"

The "Old Ben Milam" legend has, since 1835, been credited with rallying the Greys and other volunteers and saving the disintegrating Texas revolution. Without Milam's call, historians have contended, there would have been no victory at Bexar, no Alamo, no Goliad, and most importantly, no San Jacinto.

As early as 1841, just six years after the fact, Henry Stuart Foote wrote of Milam:

> One morning he steps out from the ranks;
> . . . and craves permission of the noble Burleson
> to beat up for volunteers to storm the town.
> Permission is granted. He exclaims aloud in a
> voice that will never be forgotten by those who
> heard it: "Who will join old Ben Milam in
> storming the Alamo".[13]

William Tennant Austin, who was present at the meeting and during the storming of the city, was later quoted as verifying Milam's role in rallying the troops that day:

> He (Burleson) accordingly authorized his
> adjutant and inspector general, F.W. Johnson
> and Col. Benjamin R. Milam, to raise a force of

volunteers from the army to attack the enemy the following morning. . . .[14]

Yet another account places Milam as the instigator at Burleson's headquarters that December 4:

> After hearing his report, Colonel Johnson suggested to Colonel Milam to call for volunteers, that "now is the time."
>
> Most of the army had gathered at the headquarters of General Burleson. Milam called in a clear, loud voice, "Who will go with old Ben Milam into San Antonio?" Many answered, "I will," whereupon they were requested to fall into line. After a respectable number had formed in the line, they were requested by Milam to assemble at the Old Mill, at dark, and there to organize.[15]

But in 1940 another version of the events leading to the storming of Bexar was published. Cooke's quote concerning Morris' reporting of the centenils (sentinels) sighting the "shadowy figure" going into the Alamo was contained in a letter to his brother James written on August 7, 1839.

That letter, discovered by Allen F. Adams and included in his graduate thesis, shed new light on the decision to storm the city and created considerable interest and some controversy when it was issued at San Marcos, Texas. The letter, which was at that time in the possession of Cooke's grandson in San Antonio, gave a considerably different version of the rallying call.

Cooke explains to his brother the confusion and frustration that the Greys and other remaining volunteers were experiencing as the meeting was being conducted by Burleson. Cooke wrote that around 4:00 P.M. that day he arrived to find the Texan leaders in conference with the Mexican deserter. His frustration at being denied the opportunity to storm the city finally boiled over and, in his words to his brother:

> I saw it was a favorable opportunity to prevent the retreat & called on my men to know if they were willing to follow where I would lead—Their answer was unanimous—yes—
> Immediately I faced them and marched them up and down the lines calling on the men to fall in & take the town rather than retreat—Breese's & Peacock's Companies immediately joined me & I succeeded in raising 300 men who were willing to undertake the attack—Many voices called on me to take command, but Col. B.R. Milam an old citizen and brave and good officer being present, I refused and proposed him—he was unanimously received. . . .[16]

Ehrenberg, who rarely passed up an opportunity to dramatize the events he was witnessing, was later surprisingly quiet about this development:

> A call was issued for volunteers to storm the town the next morning, "because only volunteers will fight for and win freedom." A list was passed from man to man, which everyone in favor signed. When the last had signed, the names of two hundred and thirty men could be seen on the paper. The names of only a few of our company were missing—the wounded.[17]

Ehrenberg's observation is particularly significant for several reasons. Most importantly, there is no mention of Ben Milam making the call for volunteers. Ehrenberg also verifies other reports that the Greys were almost unanimous in their eagerness to attack the city. And, in the last sentence, he discloses that several New Orleans Greys had, in fact, been wounded in the various skirmishes occurring around the city prior to December 4.

But, with regards to the call for arms, the disclosure of Cooke's letter in 1940 created considerable debate as to whether Ben Milam had actually issued his now legendary call to arms.

Adam's thesis was presented to the faculty of the graduate school of Southwest Texas State Teacher's College in May of 1940, but a review of his findings was reported in an April 21, 1940 issue of the *San Antonio Light* by columnist Sam Woolford.[18]

Woolford reviews the historical basis for Milam's credit in making the rallying call and previews the reports of those present at the headquarters when the call was issued. He states that of the later authors on the subject, only F.W. Johnson, William Tennant Austin, William Cooke, and Dr. Joseph E. Field were actually present at the time. While Johnson and Austin later wrote manuscripts supporting Milam's role in the matter, Dr. Field later wrote that:

> . . . Preparation for raising the siege and retreat to La Bahia. This order was received with great indignation by the soldiers, particularly the New Orleans Greys, who were very active in what follows. Two hundred and forty out of 600 immediately volunteered to storm the public square.[19]

Woolford then suggests that, given Field's statement that "the New Orleans Greys were very active in what follows," when placed in the context of Cooke's letter, suggests that "one cannot but assume that the famous Milam rallying call is still largely a matter of conjecture."[20]

But a rallying call was made that day outside Burleson's headquarters, and the United States volunteers, primarily New Orleans Greys, did respond to the request. So why would it be important who—Milam or Cooke—made the rallying appeal?

Adams suggested that a significant issue almost completely overlooked in this development of events was the fact that on December 4, 1835, the Texas revolution had been abandoned by the Texans and was being revived and carried on and principally officered by citizens of the United States.

If in fact the New Orleans Greys had followed Morris' threat to depart for Matamoros on November 30, there would have been little doubt that they had abandoned all pretense of fighting for individual liberties in Texas in favor of occupying Mexico for material gain. In other words, the New Orleans Greys would have come to Texas, as General Santa Anna claimed, in the role of pirates and mercenaries.

The attack on Bexar, however, was historically portrayed as a defense of the Anglo Texan settlers and their demands for constitutional freedoms under the Mexican Constitution of 1824. This, in future history books, made the New Orleans Greys at Bexar into fighters and defenders of personal freedoms.

Since the colonial Texans—soldiers and officers—were nearly all absent from Bexar on December 4, 1835, there is reason to doubt that the army remaining there was fighting for the constitutional freedoms of the Anglo settlers. There were no settlers at Bexar—or at least very few. The siege and eventual attack was launched almost entirely by United States volunteers led by American officers and wielding American-manufactured weapons and equipment. These facts would have been painfully obvious had New Orleans Grey captain William Cooke been credited at Bexar with issuing the final plea to attack the city.

Benjamin Milam, however, had been one of the first Americans to settle in Spanish Texas nearly two decades earlier. He had become a Mexican citizen and had even joined the Mexican army. He was a *bexarano*, and in history's eyes, his making the call to attack the city validated the viewpoint that the Texas revolution was a fight for personal freedoms.

But in 1940 Allen F. Adams asked the very poignant question: "Was it a war for independence, or a war of conquest? Was the 'Old Ben Milam' story invented to cover up the part played by the United States Citizens?"[21]

If Cooke's role had been historically portrayed at the headquarters, the Greys and other volunteers would have probably been seen in their mercenary role at Bexar. By portraying Milam as the rallying force for the attack, historians could comfortably refer to the Texas revolution in terms of "defending the local Anglo settlers like Ben Milam."

---

1   Alwyn Barr, *Texans in Revolt—The Battle for San Antonio, 1835* (Austin: University of Texas Press, 1990), pg. 13.

2   *Ibid.*, pg. 11.

3   Ornish, *Ehrenberg*, pg. 133.

4   *Ibid.*, pg. 140.

5   Jenkins, *The Papers of the Texas Revolution*, Vol. 3, pp. 31-32.

6   *Ibid.*

7   *Ibid.*

8   Ornish, *Ehrenberg*, pp. 134-6.

9   *Ibid.*, pp. 137-140.

10   *Ibid.*, pg. 140.

11   Letter from Cooke to his older brother, James, dated August 1839 and reported in Allen F. Adams, MA Dissertation, pg. 6.

12   Ornish, *Ehrenberg*, pg. 141.

13   Henry Stuart Foote, *Texas and the Texans in Two Volumes* (Philadelphia: Thomas, Cowpertwiat & Co., 1841)—Quoted in Sam Woolford, "Cooke Letter Coincides with Johnson's Report, *San Antonio Light*, April 21, 1940. Clipping from the archives of the Daughters of the Republic of Texas library.

14   Dudley G. Wooten, *A Comprehensive History of Texas, 1685 to 1897 in Two Volumes* (1898)—Quoted in Sam Woolford's *San Antonio Light* article, April 21, 1940.

15   Frank W. Johnson, *A History of Texas and Texans in Five Volumes* (Chicago: American Historical Association, 1914)—Quoted in Sam Woolford's *San Antonio Light* article, April 21, 1940.

16 Letter from Cooke to his older brother, James, dated August 1839 and reported in Allen F. Adams, MA Dissertation, pg. 7.

17 Ornish, *Ehrenberg*, pg. 144.

18 Sam Woolford, "Cooke Letter Coincides with Johnson's Report," *San Antonio Light*, April 21, 1940. Clipping from the archives of the Daughters of the Republic of Texas library.

19 Joseph E. Field, *Three Years in Texas, Including a View of the Texas Revolution, and an Account of the Principal Battles,....* (1836), reprint (Austin: Steck Co., 1935)—Quoted in Sam Woolford's *San Antonio Light* article, April 21, 1940.

20 Woolford, "Cooke Letter Coincides with Johnson's Report."

21 Adams, "The Leader of the Volunteer Grays: The Life of William G. Cooke, 1808-1847." pg. 10.

Chapter 5

Battle for San Antonio

San Antonio de Bexar, Texas, December 10, 1835: William Gordon Cooke leaned back against the adobe wall and stretched his legs out in front of him. Overhead on the log roof of the room he was occupying he heard the sounds of footsteps, but it was impossible to tell if they were those of his fellow Greys or Mexican soldiers.

Somewhere, very close by, a cannon thundered, and Cooke could tell by the direction and sound of the explosion that it was a large Mexican piece. Small arms fire never completely died out, and he could hear the sounds of the ineffective Mexican Brown Bess rifles somewhere to his right and the responding fire of the Greys.

The fighting was entering into the fifth day, and Cooke, like the rest of the Greys, was surviving on a combination of adrenaline and fear. He knew that if he surrendered his body to fatigue, he would sleep indefinitely. So, leaning against the wall, he vowed to himself to rest but not close his eyes.

The past four days had been pure hell. The fighting had started out as street fighting, but the deadly canister from the Mexican artillery had forced the Greys to take refuge inside the rows of houses along the street.

Since the Mexican adobe houses were all adjoined, the Greys had begun tearing holes through walls to form a protective covered tunnel adjacent to the street. But this, in turn, had become room-to-room and, ultimately, hand-to-hand combat, and the advance had been terribly slow and difficult and had continued up to this moment. Cooke knew that when the Greys resumed their advance, it would again be hand-to-hand fighting.

William Cooke was an introspective man, and instead of dwelling on the danger and discomfort of the moment, he used this period of rest to examine his impressions of Texas this past two months.

Velasco had been a terrible first impression. No place on the face of this earth, he reasoned, could be as dirty, disease-ridden, and pathetic as that tiny hamlet where he, Morris, and the Greys had arrived in Texas. The stench and insects had seemed to follow them up the Brazos River to the frontier settlement in Columbia. From there, however, they had marched overland across a kind of saltgrass prairie, and Cooke had come to appreciate this new land.

While the old Spanish fort at Goliad had fascinated him, it had been radically different from what the Greys had found here in Bexar. La Bahia had been Old Spanish Mexico while San Antonio de Bexar was Tejano Mexico, and the two were very different. Interspersed between the two was Anglo Texas, and Cooke liked the mixture. He planned to stay in Texas after the fighting was over.

He and the other Greys had anticipated—even campaigned for—this fighting here in Bexar, but the Mexicans had proven to be more tenacious than expected. Still, as dangerous and arduous as his life was right now, it still beat dispensing pills in the family pharmacy at Fredericksburg, Virginia.

He had maintained contact with his brother James and through their letters knew that he had made a good decision to leave Virginia and move to New Orleans to start his own life and career as a druggist. Still, as exciting as New Orleans had been, he had no regrets for having signed up as a soldier with the Greys at Bank's Arcade less than two months earlier.

Despite his lack of military background, he had proven to be a good leader. The Greys had elected him a first lieutenant after their arrival at Velasco, and now, in the midst of fighting in central Bexar, he was a company captain and seemingly held the respect and obedience of his men. This part of soldiering came easy for him.

Part of his success as captain was due to the support he had received from Robert Morris, his captain at Velasco and now a major and second in command of the assault forces in Bexar. Morris had confided in him and nurtured his leadership position within the Greys.

Cooke respected but didn't completely trust Morris, and he wasn't sure if he really liked the man or not. Morris was without question a very ambitious man and made it clear that his goals in Texas were not revolutionary, but financial. Cooke suspected that Morris' relationship with the Greys was based upon his using the conflict as a stepping-stone to greater things after the war.

Still, Cooke thought to himself, his own personal goals were not all that different from Morris' except that he planned to stay in Texas and become involved in the political structure of post-war independent Texas whereas Morris seemingly was only interested in making money—whether it be here, Coahuila, or New Orleans.

Like Morris, Cooke planned to leave the Greys and join the regular Texas army after Bexar was captured. He wanted to meet and cast his lot with Sam Houston. True, Houston was often cursed and maligned by the men around Bexar these days, but Cooke had no reservations that Houston would be the key to post-revolutionary Texas. He planned to be a close political contact when that happened.

If he could first make a name for himself here at Bexar, he knew that Houston, who was desperate for military men he could trust and depend on, would welcome him into his confidence.

And he knew that so far he had distinguished himself. The men respected his leadership and appreciated his quartermaster duties. He had led his men in some of the heaviest fighting, and he had kept his personal politics in order while doing so.

He somewhat resented the fact that Ben Milam, and not he, was getting all the credit for mobilizing the disintegrating army and rallying them to the cause of attacking the city. Especially since his death, Milam was rapidly achieving martyr status among the men here at Bexar.

"Who'll follow old Been Milam?" was the quote most often heard in memorial of the crusty old warrior. If Cooke had held mixed feelings about Morris, he had no reservations about Milam. He'd liked the man and respected him as a person and a soldier.

But in fact, it was William Cooke who had been instrumental in traveling through the ranks and mobilizing the deserting soldiers. True enough, the Greys were among the few still remaining and spoiling for a fight, but that fact had made the job easier when campaigning for additional soldiers.

Cooke, like most of the other Greys, resented the fact that the resident Texans had all but disappeared when the fighting had begun. Except for a few volunteers from Brazoria, the entire fighting force—including the Greys—were from the United States. But still, he reasoned it would be from these men that most of the leaders of an independent Texas would be chosen in the future. And he intended to be one of them.

Reflecting back, he felt he had kept his political cards in order during that period. It had been Cooke, not Milam, who the Greys had wanted to be commander-in-chief, but it had also been Cooke who had nominated and promoted Milam. In return, he had gained Milam's confidence and been given a company command—something he was sure Sam Houston already was aware of.

So his immediate goals were to stay alive, play an important role in the capture of Bexar, and then become involved in

Texas politics. There would be no more drugstores in his future.

At this point, his brief respite from the fighting was interrupted as a young New Orleans Grey private stepped into the small room. Cooke recognized him as William Davis Durham, a twenty-year-old Englishman who had arrived in Texas with the Greys at Velasco.

"Mexicans, sir," he told the captain, "not more than twelve inches behind your head on the other side of that wall. They entered the building under cannon fire with axes and crowbars. They'll be coming through the wall any moment now."

Cooke forced himself to his feet and motioned the young private back out of the room. "Fetch me five longriflemen," he told the young soldier, "and we'll be waiting when they break through."

For now, the fighting had begun again. All thoughts of military and political ambition would have to be put on hold for the time being.

ଔଔଔଔ

*E*hrenberg's diary suggests that Breece's unit of the Greys was obsessed with arriving in Bexar before the fighting had begun. On that late November day when their escort reunited them with Morris' company, they must have been elated that the assault on the city had not started.

That elation, however, would have been short-lived as the Greys realized they had traveled from New Orleans to Bexar in time to find a disintegrating Texan army.

With the attack plan—at least a modified version—established, the Texan forces spent the night of December 4 cleaning weapons and discussing among themselves the anticipated combat facing them in the early morning hours.

During the night one of Texas' infamous "blue northers" arrived. In the relatively short period of Anglo settlement in Texas, these climactic aberrations had already become well known, and although the recently arrived members of the New Orleans Greys had never experienced one, there were plenty of Texans at Bexar who had.

One of those early settlers present that night was Dr. John Washington Lockhart who, some years after the Battle of Bexar, wrote:

> . . . a "Blue Norther" would come up, and for three days it would almost freeze the life out of every living thing. But on the fourth day the atmosphere would be as genial as the quietist spring day. We always had warning of the approach of a Norther. The weather for a few days preceding one of these would be oppressively hot and remain so for two or three days. At this juncture a very black cloud could be seen approaching from the north, and often its pace would be very swift. As it arose above the horizon its appearance would be very angry in the extreme, well calculated to strike terror to the newcomer, especially if he had come from a country where storms were prevalent. It had an inky blackness, its outer edges sometimes taking on a greenish cast.
>
> As it came bounding and leaping along it looked as if it might be carrying death and destruction to everything in its path. At its approach, loose horses, cattle, deer, and every living animal would flee as fast as their legs could carry them to the timber, or if not convenient to timber, to the south side of hills, deep valleys and ravines, or anywhere to escape its cold blast.[1]

And so the young Greys, already occupied with precombat stress that evening, were also faced with one of these infamous Texas blue northers. Probably to the advantage of these New Orleans volunteers, the unsuspecting Mexican sentries in Bexar were also preoccupied with finding warmth and comfort that night.

James Neill's instructions were to maneuver a twelve-pounder under the cover of darkness across the San Antonio River to the Mexican-occupied side and advance to within effective shelling distance of the Alamo—a considerable military maneuver in itself.

If successfully deployed, Neill and his crew would have the responsibility of launching a diversionary attack just before dawn. If he succeeded in decoying the Mexicans, the Texans would launch an attack into Bexar with the objective of driving the Mexican garrison stationed there out of the city.

Just before daybreak—and Neill's attack—a heavy fog developed, providing additional cover for the combined companies of Greys huddled with the other men of Johnson's division poised to enter the city along Soledad Street.

At the signaling sound of the cannon, the Greys and other Texans hesitated in the foggy darkness to gauge the Mexican response. Almost immediately there was shouting and small arms fire followed by an artillery response. Neill's diversion had succeeded. The Greys started moving into San Antonio de Bexar.

Just before reaching Soledad Street and Calle de Acequia, the two divisions split. The Greys, mostly assigned to Johnson's division, entered the city along Soledad Street that ran directly parallel to the San Antonio River. Milam's division entered the city simultaneously one street over on the Calle de Acequia.

Although Bexar was considered a hostile zone during the Texan siege, the city was not an unknown factor. Many of the Texans had lived and conducted business in the city, and there were several Tejano guides to lead them. Preliminary scouting reports indicated the Greys would be advancing between two rows of adobe buildings interspersed with small gardens and patios. Much of the bank of the San Antonio River would be obstructed by heavy underbrush that might provide cover for Mexican snipers.

Still, in the darkness and heavy fog, landmarks were blurred and the progress was slow in order to maintain quietness and the element of surprise.

Milam's division was entering the city with two cannon—a twelve-pounder and a six-pounder—and fifteen artillerymen, while Johnson's division and the majority of Greys would enter the city on foot and move steadily toward their objective of the Veramendi House near the central quadrangle. Very quickly they advanced down Soledad Street toward the city's central plaza. Single-story square adobe buildings with their parapets, massive oak doors, and barred open windows lined both sides of the street.

The streets of Bexar were mostly dirt with some areas around plazas paved with adobe brick. But for the most part, the streets were bare, narrow passageways without sidewalks or curbs and offered no cover to those moving along them.

On at least one occasion, Mexican sentries were observed, but to maintain the element of surprise, the Greys bypassed them in the dark and continued toward the Veramendi House. Their initial entry into the city had succeeded as planned.

New Orleans Grey Thomas R. Stiff, who would in the coming days participate in some of the heaviest fighting in the campaign, recorded that "when we came within about 200 yards the Houses we Droptd all our Blks (blankets) and our Coates in order that we might not be seen so plain."[2]

The uncontested entry down Soledad Street ended when, approximately two hundred yards from the Veramendi House, their advance was discovered and challenged by Mexican small arms fire from posted sentries.

Immediately the Mexican garrison was alerted and quickly opened volleys of grapeshot and canister—some of it being fired from only eighty feet away—and the Greys found themselves completely exposed in the street.

To escape the devastating cannon fire, they beat and kicked in doors of the buildings and charged inside for refuge. Some of the buildings were businesses and warehouses, but many were private residences whose occupants had just been awakened by the cannon fire. In some of the homes, Mexican soldiers were being quartered, and some of the Greys found themselves in hand-to-hand combat at the very beginning of the battle.

Mexican buildings in the 1830s were generally of standard construction. Designed to protect against Indian raids, they were built of adobe brick with walls up to three feet thick. Each room was built like a small fortress with usually one door leading to the street and no interior doors for passage from room to room. Each building also usually had at least one large window with heavy bars and wooden shutters.

The roofs were mostly flat and constructed of a layer of logs often covered with adobe brick. Most of the buildings had low parapets extending two to three feet above the roof and containing drainage spouts of tile or hollowed logs. Some of the more complex buildings featured a patio on the roof with a staircase located either on the outside of the building or inside the room below.

While designed for security purposes, the buildings also were constructed to take advantage of the Texas climate. With the adobe brick fashioned from mud and straw and sun-dried, the walls and roofs were also good insulators against the hot sun. But since the bricks were not fire-baked, they were not particularly strong, and for that reason many of the buildings had very thick walls.

For the next several days this building construction would be significant, since the Greys and other Texans would find themselves fighting from room to room and forced to literally tunnel their way between rooms through the bricks. The bricks could be torn out fairly easily, but the thickness of the construction would prove to be a formidable obstacle.

In the darkness and fog of that first morning on December 5, the Greys had no idea what to expect as they kicked in doors and occupied buildings. One of the buildings occupied in those early hours was their strategic objective: the Veramendi House. They found, however, that even after taking refuge in these small fortresses, they were still highly vulnerable to the devastating cannon fire, especially from one piece located about eighty feet away.

Using the limited cover from inside the buildings, the Greys immediately focused on that cannon, and Ehrenberg reported that the Greys sharpshooters quickly drove the Mexicans back away from the piece, effectively silencing it.[3]

Small arms fire and other cannon fire from the Mexicans stationed in the Alamo and near the central plaza in the city continued to pin the Greys down, effectively eliminating any communications between their positions and Milam's division.

Although safe inside their positions, the Greys also realized that this security was temporary at best and that they would have to launch a counterattack soon.

Since the Greys at this point were basically an infantry unit, they had to rely upon rifle firepower, and the decision was made to occupy the roofs of some of the buildings to elevate their position and take advantage of the low-lying parapets on the buildings they were occupying.

On one building Greys Second Lieutenant John H. Hall climbed to the roof with Deaf Smith only to discover the Mexicans had already established rooftop positions, and both men were immediately wounded and retreated back to safety below.

Hall, an Irishman who had enlisted with Morris' group and been elected fourth corporal, had just been promoted to second lieutenant and was probably the first New Orleans Grey to become a casualty in the battle for Bexar. His injuries that day would later result in his being listed as "severely wounded."[4]

Other Texans made the same mistake of ascending the rooftops that first morning, and nearly all of them suffered the same fate as Smith and Hall. As the Mexicans intensified the small arms fire onto the rooftops, they also began firing canister and grapeshot from artillery positions. Ehrenberg reported that incoming fire from the bell tower of the San Fernando church was particularly devastating.

As they continued to be pinned down under the heavy fire, the Texans began scrambling from rooftop to rooftop to gain the best possible cover. In the process, many were wounded—some so seriously that they were unable to climb back down without assistance.

In desperation, their comrades began tearing holes in the roofs in order to lower the wounded to safety inside. While many of the roofs were so thin as to be dangerous to walk on, others were constructed of heavy logs and adobe bricks and required hard chiseling with knives and hatchets.

Once a hole was created, another danger existed: Were there Mexican soldiers stationed in the room below? While the seriously wounded were being lowered into the rooms, the uninjured Texans often dropped through the hole first not knowing if they would be greeted by gunfire.

As the sun rose that cold morning, the Greys found themselves firmly entrenched in the city as far forward as the Veramendi House, but they also found themselves isolated under heavy fire from the Mexicans. Part of that isolation was the result of the lack of any communication with Milam's division just one street over.

Around eight o'clock in the morning, they also came under small arms fire from their right flank and prepared to launch a counterattack in that direction to stop the assault. Before they could move out, however, it was determined that they were actually receiving incoming "friendly fire" from Milam's soldiers. Word was quickly sent back to Burleson in reserve, who notified Milam, and the sniping was stopped—but not before at least three of Johnson's division were wounded including one killed.

To prevent a similar occurrence in the future, both divisions began digging trenches toward each other in order to establish a reasonably secure and safe line of communication. The lack of proper tools made this a slow, difficult, and dangerous job.

The Greys and other Texans had entered Bexar that morning with each soldier carrying two days' rations and a limited supply of canteen water. The unexpected heavy fighting, trenching, and securing of positions had resulted in most of the food supplies and virtually all of the water being consumed during the first day.

Water, in particular, posed a critical problem for the Greys, and with Mexican snipers hiding in the brushy area along the banks of the San Antonio River, any attempt to approach the river for water was extremely dangerous.

Ehrenberg reported that at one point the Greys were preparing to rush the river for water when a Mexican woman in one of the buildings they were occupying offered to go for them—insisting that the Mexican soldiers would not open fire on one of their own citizens, especially a woman.

Against their protests, the woman left the safety of the building to approach the river, and to the Grey's dismay and horror, she was quickly cut down by sniper fire. As several of the Greys attempted to rescue her and return her to the building, others took advantage of the situation to charge the riverbank and fill containers with water.

As the afternoon progressed, the continuous exchange of firepower resulted in the brush along the river igniting, and the fires burned well into darkness that evening. As a result, in future days the Mexican snipers would be deprived of cover, and access to the river was made a little easier and safer for the Greys.

As the evening approached, those Greys assigned to Cooke's company occupied yet another house. Plans were drawn up to assault another building between them and the river the next morning with the objective of establishing a secure water source for the remainder of the battle.

In these last hours of fighting on that first day, the Greys began taking Mexican prisoners. But having no extra manpower to serve as guards, they were forced to parole them out with a questionable promise not to take up arms against the Texans again.

From this point on, it was obvious that much of the fighting would be house to house. As darkness settled over Bexar that night, both Texan divisions took inventory of the day's fighting. The results had been mixed: Resistance had been much stronger than anticipated, and the fighting had become mired down; however, the initial assault on the city had developed almost exactly as planned, and the execution of the battle plan had been nearly perfect. Although under heavy Mexican fire, the Greys were well established in their positions that first night.

A head count indicated that Johnson's division, to which the Greys were assigned, had suffered one dead and six wounded that first day—most of those due to "friendly fire"—while Milam's division reported four wounded. With communication between the two columns now established, a popular consensus between the two groups indicated a desire to renew the attack the following morning.

Milam's group reported one serious blow—the loss of the twelve-pounder cannon to Mexican fire. The six-pounder had been of only limited military advantage due to the inability to establish secure cover from which to set up and fire it.

Although Mexican fire continued intermittently throughout the night, the Greys and other Texans were secure and spent the night fortifying their defenses: filling sandbags, cleaning weapons, and strengthening the lines of communication with Milam's group.

For the young Greys in Bexar that night, the day's fighting had been truly a baptism of fire. No longer were they simply enthusiastic, inexperienced young men filled with bravado and dressed in distinctive military uniforms with new rifles.

On the night of December 5, 1835, some of them were wounded, all of them were now combat veterans, and their distinctive military uniforms were now dirty, torn—and in several cases—bloodied. The boasts of "we had in our imagination conquered all Mexico" made earlier at Brazoria and Courtman's pledge to spill the last drop of his blood for the new republic made at Nacogdoches had been challenged by the fierce Mexican resistance that cold December day.

December 6 dawned cold and crisp. In the early morning hours the Greys discovered that the Mexicans had also been busy overnight fortifying their positions and occupying even more elevated rooftops.

As the firing began in the early light that morning, one of the most serious problems facing the Greys was the lack of rations. The solution would come from one of their own: Captain Cooke.

Upon the conclusion of the battle at Bexar, Cooke would emerge as one of the most acclaimed veterans of the battle. His duties were many, his leadership inspirational, and his courage established beyond any question. On this second day of fighting, however, it was his quartermaster duties that endeared him to the Greys and other Texans in both divisions.

Burleson had not been simply an observer in his reserve role outside Bexar that first day. He had sent scouting parties out around the countryside attempting to intercept Colonel Ugartecha's anticipated arrival with Mexican reinforcements.

While Ugartecha had not been found that first day, the scouts did kill and butcher beef and hogs and returned them to the reserve base camp. Overnight, other reserves had cooked the meat over fires, and around nine o'clock that morning, Cooke managed to have some of that food delivered to the soldiers in Bexar. The food arrived none too soon, as the situation was becoming serious. James T. DeShields later wrote:

> . . . thanks to Quartermaster Wm. G. Cooke, about 9 o'clock that morning and while the air seemed filled with flying missiles, and the smoke from the enemy's guns hung in dense clouds over the old town, he sent forward an abundant supply of nicely barbecued beef. This was issued to the men while they stood or crouched under cover of fences, walls of houses, etc., and was devoured with a relish. . . . It was thus during the entire siege, and no man went hungry as long as he was within reach of the Quartermaster. The Captain became a favorite with the men who fought at Bexar, and he later won great distinction in camp and forum.[5]

Replenished and ready to resume the attack, the Greys pressed forward, occupying more buildings and slowly driving closer to the final objective of the central quadrangle. On this, the second day, the fighting intensified and the room-to-room fighting expanded into heavy hand-to-hand combat.

The fighting this day was particularly dangerous. The closer the Greys moved to the central plaza, the stronger the resistance became. Now, literally fighting from one room to the next, the Greys would use crowbars, axes, knives, hatchets, and any other heavy tools to punch holes in the thick walls. Once a hole was established, another Grey would thrust his rifle through the opening and fire into the adjacent room, not knowing if it were empty or filled with Mexican soldiers. When the rifle barrel was removed to allow reloading, they had to watch that a Mexican weapon was not thrust through from the other side to return the fire.

Another problem was that as the Greys slowly moved forward inside the buildings, they also moved under the roofs of structures occupied by Mexican sharpshooters. Then they were faced not only with the room-to-room fighting but also from hostile fire from above as the Mexicans turned their weapons down through the ceilings.

Slowly the holes would be expanded, and finally the Greys would charge into the next room, often finding that Mexican soldiers were waiting there. Then close-quarter hand-to-hand combat occurred, but often the Mexicans would simply surrender, creating another unanticipated problem: what to do with the captured enemy.

With no extra men to assign for guard duty, the Greys were forced to resort to what other Texans were doing that morning: parole the prisoners with unreliable pledges to leave Bexar.

Since the Mexican Brown Bess rifles were old surplus issue weapons and considerably inferior to the Kentucky long rifles, most of the captured weapons were simply made inoperable and cast aside. Sometimes their barrels were used as crowbars to assault the next wall or door.

The promises of the Mexican soldiers were generally not trusted, and as the day progressed and the number of prisoners increased, a practice developed in Milam's division to make the parole oath more binding:

To administer an oath after the American usage had no effect on a Mexican. He regarded it as a form of no value and, if a prisoner, he was liable to be found the next day in battle, ready to shoot at you again. The Mexicans were Catholic, and no oath was binding upon them unless the Roman cross figured in the proceedings. So with a charcoal snatched from an abandoned "brasero" it took Captain York but a few minutes to make a cross for each captive on the white lime-plastered wall. The men were marched up, the right hand of each on an outlined cross, their left hands on their breasts, and the oath was administered—and they observed it.[6]

Throughout that second day of intense combat, the Greys fought room to room: chiseling holes, firing inside, enlarging holes, and finally, charging inside to fight the occupants. As the day ended, the fighting had progressed but at a much slower pace than the Texans had hoped for.

Another twelve-pounder was brought forward from the reserve position, and several of the Greys attempted to position it and cut portal holes. Although not utilized very effectively the second day, the piece expanded the military role of the Greys from footsoldiers to that of artillery-backed infantry.

As darkness fell on Bexar December 6, the Greys found themselves again entrenched under intermittent fire and once more spent the night fortifying their defenses, strengthening positions, and continuing to expand and connect communications trenches with Milam's division. As these lines were developed, the two divisions began to support and reinforce each other, resulting in details of Texans being reassigned and transferred back and forth and probably moving some of the Greys to Milam's division.

Again, on the dawn of the third day, the Greys would quickly discover in the early morning light that the Mexicans had also continued to fortify their defenses. Of particular concern was a redoubt that had been constructed overnight on the Alamo side of the San Antonio River. In the early daylight, the Mexicans opened cannon fire on the Greys and were silenced only after several Texan sharpshooters succeeded in driving the cannoneers back from the pieces.

The fighting resumed immediately upon daylight and again quickly intensified. Johnson requested and received the six-pounder from Milam's division, giving the Greys temporary possession of both Texan artillery pieces.

On this third day, the artillery began to play a pivotal role for the Texans and Greys. It was also on this day that many of the Greys became true artillerymen. And it was at this stage of the fighting that all Texan artillerymen sustained heavy casualties.

Ehrenberg reports the twelve-pounder, manned by a Brunswickian named Langenheim (not a Grey), destroyed part of the San Fernando church dome and forced the Mexican sharpshooters perched there to retreat, eliminating a considerable volume of firepower against the Greys. He also reports that all of the artillerymen except Langenheim were wounded in his group including at least one New Orleans Grey—Private John Cook—who was killed in action.

Cook, an Englishman, was one of the few Greys enlisting in New Orleans who had military experience. As Ehrenberg later wrote: "We, also, had a serious loss today; a good artillery man, an Englishman name Cook, was killed. Formerly he had been a gunner in the English fleet, and in Texas he had immediately taken his place with the artillery. He was the first one to be killed in operating the twelve pounder."[7]

Around noon the fighting reached a stalemate, although the incoming fire from Mexican cannon continued. Frustrated with the lack of progress, a young Tennessean in

Milam's division named Henry Karnes single-handedly charged a Mexican stronghold and successfully battered in the door. His actions prompted a charge by his company, and this seemed to motivate all of the Texans in both divisions to renew the attack.

Room by room the fighting continued toward the central quadrangle. Crowbars and axes chopped holes, battering rams were fashioned from scrap wood, and much of the actual combat was hand to hand. Progress that afternoon was literally measured in feet and inches.

In the afternoon Ben Milam called for a meeting of the company commanders near the Veramendi House. The two New Orleans Grey leaders—Morris and Breece—were summoned with the others, and around three o'clock that afternoon the group assembled outside the massive wooden doors of the Veramendi House. At this meeting, a Mexican sniper's bullet dropped Ben Milam—killing him instantly.

Milam's loss represented more than a military casualty. Whether he—or Cooke—had been the motivating force for the assault on Bexar, it was Milam whom the Texans including the Greys saw as the hero of Bexar. His death that afternoon profoundly affected all of Texas fighting forces in the city.

Still the fighting continued, and around seven o'clock that evening another meeting was held. Johnson was elected commander-in-chief to replace Milam and a New Orleans Grey—Major Morris—was chosen as second-in-command.

By ten o'clock that night, an exhausted group of Greys reached and occupied the Navarro House where they established night quarters. As in the previous two nights, there was little chance for rest as the enemy was literally next door. The weather remained cold and wet, and the night was spent again filling sandbags and preparing weapons for the coming day.

December 8, the fourth continuous day of fighting, dawned cold and wet with intermittent rain. The full moon had been largely blocked by the cloud cover. Cooke later wrote that "after four days fighting with but partial success, and our men becoming wearied out with fatigue, a council of war was called, and an attack on the public square determined on—."[8]

In assessing their position that morning, the Greys realized that they were within fifteen yards of the central plaza. They were entering the most dangerous phase of the fighting. Cos had positioned the majority of his garrison in the central plaza, and the location was open to artillery fire from the Alamo across the river.

Around nine o'clock that morning the soldiers occupying the Navarro House were reinforced by another detachment of New Orleans Greys, and the combined force then advanced and occupied Zambrano's Row, which led to the square.[9]

At this point all fighting had become room to room, and that morning the Greys were again thrust into intense combat.

> A heavy fire of artillery and small-arms was opened on this position by the enemy, who disputed every inch of ground, and after suffering a severe loss of officers and men, were obliged to retire from room to room until at last they evacuated the whole house.[10]

Dr. Lockhart later recalled that one Grey in particular, Private William Graham, merited mention for brave conduct. Graham, a Grey volunteer from Nova Scotia, would again be cited for bravery under fire later that day. Lockhart also reports that at this time the Greys received reinforcements from York's company under the command of a Lieutenant Gill.

The Mexicans continued heavy fire by cannon attack during the day but caused little damage. Around five o'clock that afternoon Ehrenberg's group of Greys launched yet another assault against a building near the central plaza.

In attacking this building the familiar room-to-room scenario quickly developed. Ehrenberg reported that the Texans chiseled holes in the wall only to be met by Mexican muskets being fired into their faces. When the Mexicans withdrew their rifle barrels, the Greys would thrust theirs through and return the fire. While the Greys reloaded, the Mexicans would again fire into them. While all of this fire and counterfire was going on, the Greys with the axes and crowbars continued to chip away and enlarge the holes.

Finally the wall gave way, and the Mexican soldiers retreated into an adjoining room—this time barricading themselves with a heavy wooden door. This fire and counterfire continued again as the Greys chopped holes in the door and battered it in. At least two Greys sustained minor injuries before the door gave way.

By now it was early evening, the sun had set, and the second room, as the Greys cautiously rushed in, was completely dark. Again the Mexicans had retreated to another adjoining room, and the Greys could hear them through the wall.

Groping the walls in darkness, they found another door and began battering it down. As they succeeded, they charged into the third room only to find the Mexicans had retreated from the house.

This one single incident of room-to-room fighting was typical of the hourly physical and emotional stress that the Greys were being subjected to. Cooke understood this and also understood that even these brave men could not sustain this level of fighting indefinitely.

At this point only one more house stood between Johnson's company and the military plaza one block over from the central plaza. That house was a solidly built stone, not adobe, house called the Priest's House.

Occupation of the Priest's House would give the Texans an excellent point of assault on the central plaza and the church depot there, which was serving as the Mexican ordnance supply point.

After Ehrenberg's group of Greys had successfully assaulted the third room and occupied the house they were attacking, reinforcements were moved up to Zambrano's Row immediately behind them.

Cooke now plotted his battle plan for the attack on the Priest's House. He later wrote that battle casualties had reduced the Greys under his command to only thirty-seven men, so Brazoria volunteers from Captain W.H. Patton's company were brought up to combine with the Greys, giving the company a combined force of approximately forty-nine men.[11]

Thomas Stiff would later recall:

> ...that night Capt W. G Cook determined to enter the public square and asked if there was any person who would go with him, the Grays all with exception of 3 said they would follow him to the devil, there was also Capt W H Patton and 10 or 12 of his company who were willing to follow also, at 11 ock, at night we were waiting for the word "March" under the comd. Of Capt Cook, Piloted by J.W. Smith, the company did not know where they were going—Smith said that he would carry them to a house on the square; when they reach the house they found the door barricaded and Smith the (P) became confused and told Capt. Cook he did not [know] where to go....[12]

The attack on the Priest's House was launched before midnight in the light of the full moon and, as anticipated, was contested fiercely by the Mexicans.

This was Cooke's moment of decisive leadership and personal heroism during the battle for Bexar. Later in August of 1839 he would recount the assault on the Priest's House in a letter to his older brother, James, and in February of 1844 he would again chronicle this assault in a report to Mirabeau Buonaparte Lamar. From these correspondence we have the best record of this furious and deadly assault that became the decisive victory in the battle of Bexar.

The Priest's House was constructed with a material used by the early Franciscan priests and was known as *tufa*. A mixture of crushed limestone, sand, water, and clay, tufa typically formed stone walls two to three feet thick. Examples of this construction material are evident in San Antonio today in the original unrestored areas of the Alamo and other Spanish missions.

It was not a material that would give way to crowbars and axes. More ominously, the house was constructed, because of threats of Indian raids, as a small fortress with rifle portholes along the walls. In 1835 it was one of the most secure houses in Bexar.

Cooke knew this assignment was risky. The full moon provided direction for the Greys but also denied them cover in the open street. As Cooke would later recall:

> About 12 oclock at night we left our
> position in the Beremendi's (Veramendi)
> House, passed through that of Garza and one
> in advance which had been taken from the
> enemy a day or two before and was then occu-
> pied by Capt York—Guided by Jno W Smith we
> proceeded to attack the rear of Yturri's House
> which is on the square—Immediately on issuing
> from Yorks house (the moon shining almost as
> bright as day) a tremendous fire was opened
> on us from every position occupied by the
> enemy—Finding it impracticable to gain

> entrance in Yturri's, in consequence of the
> strength of the barricade and the severe firing
> kept up from it, we determined to attempt an
> entrance into the priest's house at the other
> extremity of the square—In accomplishing this,
> we had to pass within a few feet of a line of
> loop holes for seventy or seventy five yards
> from which a constant firing of musketry was
> kept up—[13]

When their advance stalled, Cooke again assumed leadership. According to Thomas Stiff:

> Capt: C. then said follow me boys, which
> was done immediately by all, he mounted the
> walls after passing the fire of five or six hun-
> dred guns through the port holes of the houses,
> we passed in hunting a safe retreat, we finally
> succeeded in getting into Square by climing
> over the wall one by one, after getting in the
> square we found ourselves exposed to the
> Enemys cannon and musketry, we were then
> Led by Cook to the right....[14]

For the second time that day, Private William Graham is cited for his role in the conflict. Cooke continues:

> Graham, of my company led off, followed
> by myself, Patton, Smith & the others—On
> arriving in rear of the Priest's house we found
> the doorway barricaded up to the arch which
> was higher than our heads and left a space
> hardly sufficient to admit one man at a
> time—we climbed up one at a time and fired
> off a few guns as we dropped down on the
> inside. The house was filled with Mexican sol-
> diers who fled upon our firing and left us in
> possession—[15]

Stiff was more specific: "where we entered the doors of the Priest's House, we found the priest, 1 son and 3 Daughters the son attempted to make his escape through a window but was shot by one of the Grays."[16]

The Greys had succeeded in occupying the Priest's House, but the success had been costly. At this point the Greys were at the foremost position of all the Texas forces and were virtually face to face with the heaviest concentration of Cos' soldiers in the central plaza.

Immediately the Mexicans swarmed to the area of the plaza nearest the Priest's House, and two six-pounders—one only about six feet from the hole by which the Greys had entered the house—were concentrated on their position.

Not only were the Greys under devastating fire, they were also effectively cut off from the other Texan forces and isolated with no hope for reinforcements. Knowing they could not sustain the artillery bombardment long, Cooke ordered a charge against the plaza. He later recorded:

> Immediately on gaining entrance we rushed upon the Square where [document blank] large number of Soldiers collecting, but evidently in great confusion—One piece of Artillery was placed immediately in front of the door through which we entered the Square at the distance of two or three yards, this we took possession of and attempted to pull in the house, but by that time the fire from the enemy became so severe, we were compelled to retire to the house after spiking the piece, in performing which, one of my men (John Belden) lost his eye from a musket ball—On regaining the house we barricaded the doors, Windows, passages &c as well as we could—which (having lost our sand bags)—we accomplished. But very imperfectly—using our

blankets, shirts, the library of the priest &c for
that purpose—[17]

Spiking a cannon involved wedging a slender metal
"spike" into the vent at the rear of the barrel and snapping it
off. This prevented any subsequent use of the cannon since
the primer could no longer be used to set off the powder
inside the piece.

Belden had rushed out of the Priest's House and spiked
the cannon "in defiance of their shot from every corner, and
returned unhurt, until the moment of closing the door after
him, when a shot through the door cut away part of his nose
and one of his eyes."[18]

Driven back into the Priest's House for cover, the Greys
discovered about twenty terrified women and children whom
they hid in the most secure part of the building.

Among those prisoners, the Greys also discovered the
priest. Stiff reported:

> We kept the old priest and 3 daughters until
> the surrender, the Priest informed us as soon as
> we got into the house, that Ugartechau had just
> arrived in Town with 1000 men and that he
> had no doubt but we would be all killed but we
> all proceded to dig up the dirt from the floor
> with our Bowie Knifes to help to barricade the
> doors and windows we also took the beds and
> trunks that were in the house to aid but as fast
> as we wold put them up against the doors and
> windows they were Shot out by the Canon of
> the Enemy, several Balls came through and fell
> in the floor by us, Capt Cook found our Situa-
> tion such that we were in great danger, the
> Cannon balls passing through the house con-
> stantly, he then turned to the Company and
> asked them any which they would choose,
> retreat, Surrender, or die, they all answered

they would die or do,—destitute of Provisions—we then recommenced our labours,
barriccading the doors and windows and making port holes—at the dawn we commenced
firing through the holes that we had made with
our Knives We fires some Eight or ten times
Killed 3 or 4 Mexicans. . . .[19]

The priest's announcement that Ugartechea had arrived
with Mexican reinforcements was particularly disturbing to
the Greys in his house. The news outside their position, however, was even more ominous.

During the hectic fighting, all lines of communication
between Cooke's Greys and the other Texans had been severed. The Greys were now completely isolated only yards
away from the Mexican infantry garrison and protected only
by the stone walls of the Priest's House.

Captain York, in this absence of communication, also lost
touch with the Greys and reported the unit probably had
been killed in the furious fighting. This communiqué led Burleson to recommend a withdrawal from the town.[20] Had his
recommendation been followed, Cooke and the Greys would
have been left stranded in the heart of Bexar and at the
mercy of the Mexican army. As it developed, York did pull
back, but the Texans did not abandon their hard-won positions in the city.

Inside the Priest's House, the Greys—having voted to fight
rather than surrender—attempted to fortify their position as
best they could. They used Bowie knives to loosen the earth
underfoot and piled it against the walls. They stacked chests
and furniture against doors and windows, yet the Mexican
artillery, only yards away, blew holes in these defenses. Their
situation seemed hopeless as they were nearly out of powder
themselves. The close-proximity artillery blasts were shower-
ing them with debris and spent ammunition.

Then at three o'clock in the morning, the firing stopped.

To Cooke and the Greys inside the Priest's House, the silence must have been both welcome and foreboding. What they could not have known was that it was the result of what had become almost total disarray within the Mexican forces.

The priest had been correct: Ugartechea had arrived at the Alamo with additional troops, but those soldiers were conscripts who had no military training and were not in a disposition to fight a war.

After initially attempting to use some of the new conscripts to assault the Greys inside the Priest's House, General Cos had realized their ineffectiveness and withdrawn them, leaving only the two cannon outside the house and a small detachment of men. In their place, cavalrymen were ordered into the plaza, but four of the Mexican cavalry officers instead led their companies out of the Alamo and towards the Rio Grande.

Their departure created pandemonium in the Alamo, and in the frenzy General Cos himself was nearly caught in the stampede of horses. Rumors quickly circulated among the Mexicans that he had been killed. This in turn created confusion among the remaining soldiers in the plaza, who had been assaulting the stone walls of the Greys' fortress.

With the Mexican cavalry deserting, the conscripts refusing to fight, and chaos in the only remaining combat-tested troops, the military position of the Mexican army was as critical as that of Cooke and his Greys.

Cos realized that with the arrival of daylight the Texans would begin reinforcing the defenders near the plaza, and so he reluctantly ordered his senior officers to negotiate a surrender.

For nearly four hours inside the Priest's House, the Greys continued to use the respite from the fighting to reinforce their seemingly hopeless position. Then, to their complete surprise, they heard Mexican bugle calls outside their position sometime around seven o'clock that morning. Unsure what the buglers were signaling, the Greys maintained their position without responding until Lieutenant Colonel Jose Juan Sanchez Navarro ordered a white flag hoisted in the plaza.

Cautiously, Cooke emerged from the Priest's House and met the surrendering Mexican officers and personally led them to Burleson. There, negotiations took place in which another Grey, Robert Morris, was instrumental in designing the final agreement, which ended the fighting and surrendered Bexar and the Alamo to the Texans.

After considerable negotiating, the Mexicans were allowed six days to prepare for their withdrawal south of the Rio Grande. For their journey south they were allowed a limited amount of arms and ammunition and one cannon to protect against Indian attacks. The rest of their supplies and equipment—including a considerable number of artillery pieces—were to remain behind as property of the Texans. Since the Texans had neither the resources nor the food to maintain a large number of prisoners, all captured soldiers were to be freed to join the retreat.

The small "city" of Bexar was left in shambles, but almost immediately upon cessation of the fighting the local population began moving back into their homes. By arrangement, the Texans remained in Bexar during the six-day period while the Mexicans were allowed to remain in the Alamo until ready to depart.

The New Orleans Greys had been badly bloodied in the battle for Bexar, but Texan casualty numbers were amazingly low given the ferocity and duration of the fighting.

As a unit, the Greys had led the decision to mount the assault and had then taken a lead in virtually every aspect of the five-day battle. William Cooke and his company of Greys were unquestionably responsible for the Mexican decision to surrender with their daring and successful assault on the Priest's House at the very perimeter of the elite Mexican garrison in the plaza. It was a Grey—Captain William G. Cooke—who accepted the Mexican surrender and another Grey—Major Robert Morris—who helped negotiate the final terms of surrender.

The battle for Bexar was recorded in history as a Texan victory over a Mexican army superior in numbers, ordnance, and supplies. In many ways, however, it was a validation of the New Orleans Greys as the most effective—and combat-experienced—military unit operating inside northern Mexico in the waning days of 1835.

---

1 Dr. John Washington Lockhart, *Sixty Years on the Brazos* (Los Angeles, CA: Privately Printed, 1930), pg. 335.
2 Jenkins, *Papers of the Texas Revolution*, Vol. 3, pg. 390.
3 Ornish, *Ehrenberg*, pg. 151.
4 Jenkins, Vol. 3, pg. 240.
5 James T. Deshields, *Tall Men with Long Rifles* (San Antonio: Naylor Co., 1935), pp. 68-69.
6 *Ibid.*, pg. 71.
7 *Ibid.*, pg. 156.
8 Lamar Papers, Mirabeau B., Texas State Library, Vol. IV, Part 1, pg. 45.
9 D.W.C. Baker, *A Texas Scrap-Book* (Texas Historical Association: Austin, 1991), pg. 222.
10 Lockhart, pp. 322-3.
11 Letter from Cooke to his older brother, James, dated August 1839 and reported in Allen F. Adams, MA dissertation, pg. 7.
12 Jenkins, Vol. 3, pg. 391.
13 Lamar Papers, Vol. IV, Part 1, pg. 45.
14 Jenkins, Vol. 3, pg. 391.
15 Lamar Papers, Vol. IV, Part 1, pg. 45.
16 Jenkins, Vol. 3, pg. 391.
17 Lamar Papers, Vol. IV, Part 1, pg. 45.
18 Jenkins, Vol. 10, pg. 185.
19 Jenkins, Vol. 3, pg. 392.
20 Alwyn Barr, *Texans in Revolt—The Battle for San Antonio, 1835*, pg. 54.

Chapter 6

Winter Quarters

*A*lamo *Compound at San Antonio de Bexar, Texas, February 20, 1836:* The squeaking axles of the oxcarts could be heard clearly from inside the Alamo compound. From several positions inside the fortified walls, New Orleans Greys watched the activity below in Bexar.

Today was February 20 and the Mexican civilians were once again evacuating the city. Rumor had it that tomorrow the Tejanos serving in the Texas army would be discharging and that soon Travis would be withdrawing the rest of the military from the city into the old mission compound.

Santa Anna had crossed the Rio Grande four days earlier and was headed toward San Antonio, while General Urrea had also crossed into Texas and was headed toward Goliad. A week earlier there had been no Mexican military presence in Texas; today two massive divisions were moving north, and the Mexican civilians in Bexar were evacuating their property and livestock before Santa Anna's anticipated arrival.

Surprisingly, this abandonment of the city didn't seem to have a sobering effect on those Greys and other Texans watching from the walls of the compound. Instead, there was light banter and cheering as each fully loaded oxcart worked its way down the road out of the city.

But one Grey watching from the southwest corner was not smiling or cheering. That soldier, a captain, was studying the scene below with regards to logistics. He was standing beside the massive eighteen-pounder cannon.

Positioned atop an earthen ramp, it was pointed directly into Bexar and the tallest building in the city—the San Fernando church. One of the Greys, Private Francis Johnson, had helped wrestle it across the plains from Copano Bay to San Antonio.

True, the cannon had arrived three days after the fighting had ended, but it added to the significant artillery ordnance that General Cos had left behind, and the Texans now had considerable—and formidable—firepower.

Captain William Blazeby ran his hand over the breech of the giant gun and looked back into the Alamo compound. "Not much of a fort," the thought to himself, "but I guess it was never designed for warfare—just Indian attacks."

The adobe and log walls were crumbling all around the perimeter, and the north wall, in particular, had required heavy makeshift patchwork repairs. The north wall had been the object of target practice by the Greys during the siege of Bexar, and now they were trying to rebuild it as a defense.

The building known as the Long Barracks along the western wall was made of secure stone, but the roof had required extensive work, and the horse and cattle pens directly behind it were of no defensive use at all. Still, Green Jameson had positioned a captured six-pounder at the corner of the pen and a swivel gun atop the two-story part of the barracks serving as a hospital.

South of the hospital and extending out on the west wall was the old church with its spiral columns. The Alamo, they called it, and the chapel had long ago lost its bell tower and roof. Cos and the Mexicans had formed the rubble into a long ramp on the back wall. Perched atop the ramp were three twelve-pounders that could be maneuvered in all directions. A few of the Greys had earlier taken up residence inside the old church.

Jameson and Neill had done a commendable job with the cannon, Blazeby thought to himself. With nearly thirty tubes, the Greys and others remaining behind had managed to mount twenty in various other positions around the perimeter.

Blazeby took a certain pride in the extent to which the compound defenses had been developed. He was, after all, a veteran of the battle for Bexar and afterwards had been promoted to captain. Neill, whom he genuinely admired, had made him captain of the remaining Greys and designated his unit as an infantry company.

But Blazeby also knew that the Greys were sorely hurting in other supplies such as food, clothing, and medical supplies. And all because of that bastard Grant. So anxious to pursue his dream of riches to the south, he had talked many of the Greys into leaving San Antonio for Matamoros and, in doing so, had stripped Bexar and the Alamo clean of food and supplies.

Neill and Jameson had written letters to Sam Houston to no avail. Even Bowie had tried to get help for them. Looking down at his own filthy uniform, he thought to himself that if he were back in Virginia or New York—or especially back in his native England—he would be considered a scoundrel in these rags.

He thought back to the time they had crossed Gaine's Ferry and been met by the settlers—especially the pretty girls who had presented them with their unit flag. That seemed like another era but had been less than four months earlier. The Greys had been sharply dressed that morning.

While their uniforms had not been completely alike, they were all grey and of the same basic cut. Still fresh from the boat trip and short march across Louisiana, they had been crisp and clean as the unit had stood at attention before the settlers.

But by the time they had reached Bexar, Breece's company had marched through rain, prairie fire ashes, and bright sun, and the formerly grey uniforms had taken on a sooty, charcoal look. Now, after the terrible fighting in Bexar, most of the uniforms were torn or completely replaced with non-uniform accessories.

As an officer, Blazeby had made a point to try and maintain his uniform and his status as a Grey. With satisfaction, he felt most of the other Greys had done so also. True enough, some of his men had joined Bowie in his infamous fandangos and all-night drinking sprees, but for the most part those Greys remaining behind in Bexar had conducted themselves well.

The same couldn't be said for that alcoholic James Bowie. The slave trader had been drunk for as long as Blazeby and the other Greys had known him since his arrival in San Antonio after the battle for the city. Ironically, Blazeby had voted with the other Greys to elect Bowie as leader of the volunteer Texans—a co-commander with that pompous, posturing, egomaniac Travis.

Bowie might be a drunk and bully, but he was also a fighter—no one ever questioned that in Bexar. He also seemed to respect the Greys, and several of the volunteers had established careful relationships with the knife fighter and brawler.

Personally, Blazeby didn't like the man although he'd voted for him as commander. And frankly, he didn't trust Bowie or Travis, but under the circumstances he felt safer casting his lot with a proven fighting man.

Bowie had celebrated that election by throwing a fandango and getting riotously drunk. His behavior that night had been particularly bad—even by his standards. He had organized a drunken mob—including several of Blazeby's Greys—and marched on the Bexar jail where he released all the prisoners.

In the aftermath another of the Greys, John Baugh, had to write a report to the Council concerning Bowie. Personally, Blazeby was glad it had been Baugh and not he who had been requested to write the report. Bowie, drunk or sober, would not be a good man to have as an enemy.

And yet the morning after, Bowie had shown genuine remorse and had initiated a meeting with Travis to establish a joint command. But now Blazeby wondered if it even mattered. Bowie, it seemed, spent most of his time confined in the Low Barracks on the south wall. . . .

And below him in Bexar, the oxcarts continued their noisy exodus.

CRCRCRRØRØRØ

*T*he Greys emerged from the battle for Bexar as combat veterans—some of the best Texas had to offer in 1835. As such, they became the targets of political intrigue that would require future fighting against the Mexicans. One such conspiratorial scheme involved Dr. James Grant's dream of recouping his lost empire in Coahuila.

Even as General Cos was preparing to leave Bexar and return to Mexico, Grant began campaigning among the Greys and other Bexar veterans to organize a "Matamoros Expedition" to take the fighting into Mexico itself and encourage other secessionist movements against Santa Anna.

Under the terms of surrender, which many of the Greys felt were far too lenient, Cos was allowed to remain in the Alamo compound for six days to prepare for his return to Mexico. During this period, the Texans generally remained in Bexar and the Mexicans in the Alamo—ostensibly to prevent further hostilities.

But as the gunfire died out, the Mexican civilians began returning to their homes in Bexar to inspect the damage to their houses and businesses. Almost immediately, Texan and Mexican civilians and even soldiers began intermingling again.

When Cos left in mid-December, the Greys and other Texans entered the Alamo compound and began inventorying the supplies and ordnance left behind.

Several days after the fighting had ended, the massive eighteen-pounder arrived from the coast. Some speculated that its anticipated arrival had been a factor in Cos' decision to surrender when he did. Despite the fact the cannon had played no part in the fighting for the city, the Greys were nevertheless encouraged to see the huge weapon that Morris' group had transported from New Orleans on the *Columbus*. Few if any of the Greys believed that Cos and his soldiers would honor the terms of their parole and remain south of the Rio Grande long.

For New Orleans Grey Private Francis Johnson from Maine, the arrival of the eighteen-pounder was especially eventful. He had remained behind at Copano and helped transport the weapon across the south Texas plains—a remarkable engineering feat not diminished by its late arrival.

One problem, however, involved ammunition for the huge cannon. Initially left behind at Velasco and transported to Copano because no ammunition had been shipped from New Orleans, the gun now arrived at Bexar still with no ammunition. Even so, the gun inspired confidence in those who manhandled it into the Alamo compound.

With the departure of the Mexicans, some of the Texans remained in Bexar while others assumed control of the Alamo compound. Several of the Greys, including Ehrenberg, moved into the old roofless Alamo chapel and established living quarters among the rubble.

The Mexicans had taken the rubble from the collapsed roof and crumbling walls and built an earthen ramp, extending from the front door up to an embankment at the rear of the church, that was designed for artillery placement.

Ehrenberg reported that "each one, according to his own pleasure, searched out a favorite retreat for protection against the cold and storm of winter.[1] He continued to record how the Greys spent the days hunting, gambling, and lounging around at leisure and the nights drinking and dancing at fandangos. After the hard fighting, the rest and recreation were initially a welcome diversion for the young Greys so far away from their American and European homes.

In the period just before departure on December 30, two of the Greys in Bexar were scouting around the area and made a discovery that would prove to be significant to those Greys and other Texans who chose to remain in Bexar and guard the Alamo compound there.

Joseph Spohn, Herman Ehrenberg, and another non-Grey volunteer mounted horses and followed the San Antonio River south to where the other abandoned Franciscan mission ruins—Conception, San José, San Juan, and Espada—were located.

About a mile from the Alamo they found the Mission Conception where, just before the two companies of Greys had arrived at Bexar, James Bowie and James Fannin had successfully engaged a Mexican force five times their size and had succeeded in driving them back and capturing the twelve-pounder cannon that had been so valuable during the subsequent siege of Bexar and the attack on the city.

The next mission along the river was the Mission San José, which they explored and found inside several Mexican families living in hovels. As opposed to the open friendliness of the Mexicans in Bexar, Ehrenberg reported these families to be suspicious, even hostile.

While the Alamo is the oldest of the San Antonio de Bexar missions, the most successful during the period of the Franciscans was the *Mission San José y San Miguel de Aguayo* which grew to become known as the "Queen" of the San Antonio missions. In its grandeur and beauty, Mission San José had had one other feature not found in the other missions: a gristmill.

Behind the massive church and stone presidio wall, the old gristmill was built under the supervision of a Franciscan friar named Father Pedrajo. Ingeniously, the padre had tapped the San Antonio River by means of an *acequia madre* ("mother ditch") in which the water was trapped at a dam on the river and channeled to the mill. Being a scarce commodity during the long, hot summers, the water was directed through the mill to the two-and-one-half square miles of field crops nearby.

Built between 1789 and 1794, the mill used its great wooden wheel placed nearly fifteen feet underground to drive two millstones and grind wheat into flour for bread. Water was diverted to the lower chamber through use of a stone waterway constructed six to twelve feet below ground level and extending over thirty feet.

The 1794 Franciscan inventory listed "one operating grain mill." There are no records available with regards to production, but the mill must have been very efficient and successful because nearby, inside the presidio walls, a mammoth granary was built in 1749 and is thought to be the oldest stone building in Texas.

In 1835 the ruins of Mission San José were serving as crude living quarters for several Mexican families and, unknown to the Greys, the location of a considerable amount of feed and grain hidden inside the ruins of the granary.

Prowling around, Spohn and Ehrenberg found what they estimated to be twelve to fifteen wagonloads of corn. Returning to the Alamo, they reported their find to the quartermaster, who dispatched six wagons the next morning. After bartering, the Americans ended up purchasing three wagons of feed from the Mexicans.

Following his third trip to Mission San José, Ehrenberg returned to the Alamo to discover the arrival of another volunteer group from Mobile, Alabama, also calling themselves the Greys. More importantly, his arrival back in Bexar this day also signaled the decision to move toward Matamoros on December 30.

But while this period was one of jubilation and pride for the combat-hardened Greys fresh from their victory over the Mexicans, it was also a period of turmoil for the unit.

Not only were the Greys being divided along lines of loyalty by Grant advocating the Matamoros expedition and Neill counseling consolidation of the Alamo, but they were also considering other options being offered to them during this period.

Several of the Greys left the unit for various reasons. Captain Breece had so impressed Texan leaders with his leadership in capturing the Veramendi place during the battle for Bexar that he received orders on December 21 from Sam Houston in Washington-on-the-Brazos. His orders, Houston wrote, were to leave Bexar to "whatever point you may deem best for the interest of the service & there recruit as many men as you possibly can." Breece was then to report to Copano or Matagorda by March 1, 1836.

Given the undisciplined reputation of Texan regulars and many of the volunteers during the revolution, the New Orleans Greys experienced—on the available records, at least—relatively few desertions and expulsions.

Walter Lord, in his book *A Time to Stand*, states that during a period of low morale, one man "actually mutinied and was finally drummed out of camp."[2] Texas General Land Office archive records indicate that only three Greys were formally expelled from their ranks[3]. Two Irish privates from Breece's company—John Casey and John Coffee—were listed as expelled but no dates, locations, or reasons were given. Another private with Breece, Louisianian William Ross, was also expelled without notation.

Only two Greys were listed officially as deserters—again without notation on the General Land Office rosters. James Fitzgerald of Louisiana and Englishman John Shaw, both privates with Breece, are the lone deserters listed.[4]

Several Greys were furloughed—usually back to New Orleans—for health-related reasons. Private Michael Cronican, a printer and newspaperman from Boston, was one Grey who left Bexar for medical treatment as did Captain Thomas William Ward, who had lost a leg in the fighting.

John L. Hall, the Irishman who had climbed with Deaf Smith onto the rooftops and been wounded early in the fighting at Bexar, was granted an unlimited furlough on December 29. John Belden, who had lost an eye spiking the cannon during Cooke's desperate assault outside the Priest's House, was discharged on January 20, 1836, and received $40 mustering out pay.[5]

One post-battle medical report listed eight New Orleans Greys as wounded in action. In a December 17 letter to the governor and General Council, surgeons Samuel Stivers and Amos Pollard reported Greys volunteers James McGehee, Thos W. Ward, George Alexander, Lieut. George W. Main, Alexander Abrams, James Noland, James M. Cass, John Hall, and John Beldon as wounded in action. Their report listed a total of twenty wounded, which indicated the Greys comprised forty percent of the casualties at Bexar. Revised reports would raise the total number of wounded to between thirty and thirty-five including five or six killed,[6] but the fact remains that the Greys were active among the most aggressive fighting and suffered proportionately heavy casualties. John Cook, the English naval artilleryman, was the only Grey reported killed in action.

Marshall R. McIvor, from Kentucky, was not listed as wounded in action but also received a five-month furlough on the eleventh of January 1836 (listed as "McKeever" from Jefferson City, Kentucky). Private William Davis Durham, one of Morris' men, also received an unlimited furlough on the eleventh of January.

After the fierce fighting around the Zambrano Row during the battle for Bexar, Private William Graham of Nova

Scotia was cited later by several leaders for his heroism and bravery in that particular stage of the battle. He, too, received a four-week furlough from the Greys on the fifteenth of December 1835—less than a week after the fighting had ended.

While these furloughs do not specifically list injuries or wounds as the basis for mustering out of the Greys, in all probability recuperation was the reason for the leaves of absence. Hall and Graham, in particular, had been in the midst of the heaviest fighting.

During the divisive and tumultuous weeks following the victory at Bexar, the Greys—who had been so cohesive as a military unit during the fighting—were also caught up in the turmoil of Texas politics.

While several Greys left, furloughed, or were discharged, one member rejoined the group after the battle. Johann George Andreas Voss, the twenty-six-year-old German who had been captured the day before he and Morris' unit had arrived in Bexar, had been released from jail by the Mexicans and was now reunited with the Greys.

Joseph Spohn, who was captured with Breece's group entering Bexar also reappears in post-combat records, but it is unclear if he escaped prior to the surrender or was released after the fighting.

In the midst of all this, Grant decided to make his move towards advancing on Matamoros. On December 30 he set out with two hundred men including most of the New Orleans Greys. To make matters worse, he also requisitioned most of the Texan supplies—clothing, food, medical supplies, small arms, and ammunition. Even the valuable horses were taken—leaving Neill and the remaining Texans without the resources to scout the countryside for food or approaching Mexican troops.

Nevertheless, Neill—who was receiving conflicting orders from the Council at San Felipe and from Sam Houston—

decided to reinforce the compound with what resources he could muster. On January 6, 1836, he wrote a letter to San Felipe complaining of the shortages of materials due to Grant's departure. He reported in that letter that he had only 104 men with which to shore up and defend the Alamo should the Mexicans return to Bexar.

Of those 104 men, approximately one quarter were New Orleans Greys who had opted to remain in Bexar. On January 15 Neill was down to eighty men including "a handful of shivering New Orleans Greys."[7]

Once Neill had decided to remain at the Alamo and fortify the compound, he had to reorganize his existing soldiers while at the same time appeal for reinforcements. For his adjutant, he chose a New Orleans Grey officer, First Lieutenant John Baugh, whom he promoted to captain and stationed in Bexar. Baugh's critical role as executive officer is often overlooked in Alamo literature. In the event of the death of the commanding officer, it would be John Baugh who would be responsible for the command of the Alamo forces.

By early January 1836 the remaining Greys at the Alamo had lost their leaders. With Breece being furloughed to recruit volunteers and Morris and Cooke departing for Matamoros, those Greys remaining in Bexar and the Alamo were without a commanding officer. One of Breece's second lieutenants, Englishman William Blazeby, was promoted to captain and placed in charge of the remaining Greys, who were officially then listed as an infantry company.

With Albert Levy discharging the Greys to join the Texas navy, William D. Howell was the only remaining Grey with professional medical training, and Neill assigned him to Blazeby's unit as surgeon. Grey Sergeant John Jones was promoted to lieutenant and also assigned to Blazeby's infantry.

Those seriously wounded from the fighting in Bexar were moved into the Alamo compound and housed in the two-story building at the end of the Long Barracks near the chapel. In a

December 17, 1835 report, Dr. Amos Pollard listed New Orleans Grey George Washington Main, one of Breece's lieutenants, as "severely wounded," so he was probably initially interned in the hospital unit. He was later assigned to Captain Robert White's Bexar Guards, suggesting that he had at least partially recovered from his wounds by March.

George Nelson, another of the Greys wounded at Bexar, was not listed on Dr. Pollard's December 17 report and was subsequently assigned to Blazeby's infantry, so he probably was not seriously wounded.

Bill Groneman, in his book *Alamo Defenders*, lists James Nowlan, an Englishman who "probably came to Texas as a member of Captain Cooke's company of New Orleans Greys. The name 'James Nolind' is listed on the roster of Cooke's company." Groneman also states that he took part in the siege and battle of Bexar and was severely wounded in the battle and that it is unlikely that he was able to play an active part in the Alamo battle.[8]

The Muster Roll, "New Orleans Greys, Capt. Wm. G. Cooke, in the Army before Bexar 1835" does, in fact, list an Irishman named "James Noland" on the roster. A later muster roll of "Capt Pettus Compy. 'New Orleans Greys' massacred at Goliad on Mar 27, 1836" also lists a "( ) Noland Wounded & afterwards massacred."[9]

This roster and the fact he is listed as Irish—not English—would place him not in the Alamo hospital, but at Goliad in the early months of 1836. His name is engraved on the Fannin Monument outside La Bahia, and Harbert Davenport, in his 1939 treatise "The Men of Goliad" also lists a "James Noland" as having been wounded at Coleto and massacred at Goliad.[10]

Several other Greys remaining at the Alamo were also listed as "wounded" but evidently not seriously enough to prevent their being assigned to Blazeby's infantry company. Among those wounded Greys veterans were Robert

Crossman, a twenty-six-year-old Pennsylvanian, and James Magee from Ireland.

Henry David Hersey, a thirty-one-year-old Englishman, was also wounded at Bexar but later assigned to Captain William Carey's artillery company inside the Alamo. Joining Hersey as an artilleryman was fellow Grey Thomas Waters from England.

Hersey and Waters were the only two Greys officially listed as artillerymen at the Alamo. These two, and George Washington Main who was assigned to Captain White's infantry company, were the only Greys not assigned to Blazeby's infantry unit.

Henry Courtman, a twenty-eight-year-old German remained at the Alamo with Blazeby. Groneman records that "His brother George F. Courtman, was killed in the Goliad Massacre."[11]

Of those Greys leaving for Matamoros with Grant, the muster roll for Pettus (called the San Antonio Greys) does not list a "Courtman," however the muster roll for Burke's Company of Mobile Greys does include a "George F. Courtman [Curtman]" and identifies him as a former member of Breece's New Orleans Greys.

So while there appears to be no records of a George F. Courtman—or Curtman—on either Breece's or Morris' rosters from Bank's Arcade, a New Orleans Grey named George F. Courtman is listed as traveling from Bexar to Goliad with the Mobile Greys during the Matamoros expedition.

Ehrenberg further documents this in his diary when recalling the moment the Mexicans opened fire on the Greys during the Palm Sunday massacre at La Bahia: "Close to me Mattern and Curtman were fighting death."[12] Davenport likewise records a "George F. Courtman" as dying in the massacre.[13]

Given this documentation of two different "Courtmans" from Germany, with one serving at the Alamo and the other at Goliad, it appears that there were two brothers serving in the Greys—making them the only known siblings to serve with the unit.

Another Alamo defender, Charles Despallier, was not a Grey but was the brother of furloughed New Orleans Grey Bexar veteran Blaz Phillipe.

Robert B. Moore, from Martinsburg, Virginia, was also assigned to Blazeby's company. Moore had the distinction of being the oldest New Orleans Grey and Alamo defender at age fifty-five. His twenty-eight-year-old cousin, Willis, was also serving inside the Alamo but was not a New Orleans Grey.

Robert Mussleman, now a veteran of the Seminole Wars and Bexar, was promoted to sergeant with Blazeby's unit. Englishmen Stephen Dennison and James Dickens (also occasionally listed as Dimkins), Louisiana native James Girard Garrett, and Tennessean James Halloway were also placed under Blazeby's command.

Virginian William Linn, who had been captured briefly during the Bexar fighting, joined William Marshall of Tennessee, Englishman Richard (sometimes listed as Robert) Starr, and Henry Thomas of Germany in completing the list of New Orleans Greys assigned to Blazeby.

Groneman lists a Charles Henry Clark as remaining in the Alamo but lists no assigned unit other than the fact he had been a New Orleans Grey.[14]

The *New Handbook of Texas*, however, states that the Charles Clark who died in the defense of the Alamo was not a Grey but one of at least four "Charles Clarks" who served in the Texas revolution. The *NHT* also reports that Charles Clark, a native of Louisiana, was a private in Captain Breece's company that served in the siege of Bexar and was reportedly killed in the Goliad massacre.[15]

Muster rolls for Breece's volunteers list a Charles Clark from Louisiana who died with Fannin at Goliad, therefore the

Charles Henry Clark who perished in the Alamo almost certainly could not have been a Grey.

And so, when Neill complained again on January 14, 1836, about the lack of provisions, these Greys were assigned and manning the Alamo garrison, which at this point totaled only about eighty men counting themselves.

January 14 was also the date that Sam Houston arrived in Goliad to try and dissuade the volunteers there—including the Greys—from continuing with Grant's Matamoros folly. One of Houston's first acts at Goliad was to dispatch James Bowie to the Alamo to assess the situation and, if he deemed wise, to destroy the Alamo compound and retreat to Gonzales.

Bowie arrived at the Alamo five days later, on the nineteenth, and like Neill he became obsessed with fortifying and defending the old mission compound. Bowie, despite his violent reputation, had an uncanny ability to forge useful working relationships, and it appears that he and Neill were able to cofunction during this period despite the fact they both shared the rank of colonel.

By February 2 Bowie was joining Neill in writing the Council in support of maintaining the Alamo, and by this date much of the considerable artillery ordnance left behind by Cos was being remounted and positioned along the reinforced perimeters of the old mission grounds. Equipment and supplies were located in the city and transported to the Alamo compound. Even ammunition for the eighteen-pounder was located. There seemed to be genuine consensus among those Greys and other defenders remaining in Bexar that the Mexicans would return to Bexar and that the Alamo compound could—and would—hold.

This spirit of consensus was shattered the next day when William Barret Travis arrived at the Alamo with thirty regular army cavalry and yet another Alamo commission as colonel. Travis, with his pompous personal bearing and elitist approach to military leadership, was a direct contrast to

Bowie's hard-drinking, knife-fighting, cantina-brawling "one of the boys" leadership style. The Greys, who had been effective—but undisciplined—fighters in Bexar, would be naturally attracted to Bowie.

All pleas for reinforcements were still going unanswered. Five days after Travis' arrival, David Crockett arrived at the Alamo with twelve Tennessee volunteers. The already legendary frontier luminary was more than welcome despite the small number of men he brought with him. With his famous name and almost mythical reputation, he lent credibility to the defenders at the Alamo, and surely his presence would encourage a flood of additional volunteers to their cause.

Crockett wisely realized that there were already too many colonels serving the garrison and requested to be assigned as a "high private" with his own men.

Three days later, on February 11, Neill mysteriously furloughed and left Bexar. Various reasons have been given, but Neill must have realized that leadership of the garrison, in what was surely going to be a dangerous future, could not continue indefinitely with three men vying for loyalty of the Greys and other defenders.

With his departure, he appointed Travis—the regular army commissioned officer—officially in charge. Within twenty-four hours this arrangement had fallen, and most of the volunteers were clamoring for a popular election of leaders. The vote was predictable: The regular army defenders elected Travis while the volunteers—including the Greys—overwhelmingly voted for Bowie. One exception to this vote may have been New Orleans Grey Adjutant John Baugh whom Travis chose to retain as the executive officer for the garrison.

The night of the election, February 12, Bowie celebrated his victory among the volunteers by getting roaring drunk. This was not Bowie's first drunken rampage at Bexar, but it was, even by his standards, an extraordinary binge. He started by hosting a fandango that evening, and before the

night was over he had led a group of drunken volunteers—almost certainly including some of the Greys—to the
city jail and began releasing prisoners under the threat of
storming the building if necessary.

John Baugh, the adjutant, was requested the next morning to file a report of the episode with the Council, which he
did in the form of a letter to Governor Smith on the thirteenth. In that letter, Baugh recorded:

> Lt. Col. J.C. Neill being suddenly called
> home, in consequence of the illness of some of
> his family, requested Col. Travis, as the Senior
> officer, to assume command of the Post during
> his absence,—Col Travis informed the volun-
> teers in the Garrison, that they could, if not
> satisfied with him as a commandant Pro Tem,
> elect one out of their own body—The volun-
> teers being under a wrong impression, and ever
> ready to catch at any popular excitement,
> objected to Col Travis upon the grounds of his
> being a Regular Officer, and immediately
> named Col Bowie as their choice.
>
> An election was consequently ordered by
> Col. Travis and Bowie was elected.—without
> opposition none but the volunteers voted & in
> fact not all of them—The consequence was a
> split in the Garrison. Col Travis, as a matter of
> course, would not submit to the control of
> Bowie and he (Bowie) availing himself of his
> popularity among the volunteers seemed anx-
> ious to arrogate to himself the entire control.—
>
> Things passed on this way yesterday &
> to-day until at length they have become intoler-
> able—Bowie as Commandant of the volunteers,
> has gone so far as to stop carts Laden with the
> Goods of private families removing into the
> Country. He has ordered the Prison door to be

opened for the release of a Mexican convicted
of Theft who had been tried by a Jury of 12
men, among which was Col. Travis and Col.
Bowie himself—

He was also ordered, and effected, the
release of D.H. Barre a private in the Regular
army attached to the Legion of Cavalry, who
had been tried by a court martial and found
Guilty of mutiny, and actually liberated him
from prison with a Corporal Guard with Loud
Huzzas.—

But the most extraordinary step of all, &
that which sets aside all Law, civil & military, is
that which follows—

"Commandancy of Bejar Feby 13th 1836
Capts of co'ys.
You are hereby required to release such
Prisoners as may be under your direction, for
labour, or otherwise—
James Bowie
Commandant of the volunteer forces of Bejar'

Under this order, the Mexicans who had
been convicted by the civil authorities, and the
soldiers convicted by Court martials, & some of
whom had been placed in the Alamo, on the
public works, were released—

Antonio Fuentes who had been released as
above presented himself to the Judge under the
protection of Capt. Baker of Bowies volunteers
& demanded his Clothes which were in the
Calaboose, Stating that Col. Bowie had set him
at Liberty, whereupon the Judge (Seguin)
ordered him to be remanded to prison, which
was accordingly done,—As soon as this fact was
reported to Bowie, he went, in a furious

manner, and demanded of the Judge, a release of the Prisoner, which the Judge refused, saying that "he would give up his office & let the military appoint a Judge"—Bowie immediately sent to the Alamo for troops and they immediately paraded in the Square, under arms, in a tumultuously and disorderly manner, Bowie, himself, and many of his men, being drunk which has been the case ever since he has been in command.—

Col Travis protested against the proceedings to the Judge, and others, and as a friend to good order, and anxious to escape the stigma which must inevitably follow, has, as a last resort, drawn off his Troops to the Medina, where he believes he may be as useful as in the Garrison, at all events, save himself from implication in this disgraceful business—

I have ventured to give you a hasty sketch of passing events in justice to myself and others who have had no hand in this transaction.

John J. Baugh
an Antonio de Bexar, Texas
2/13/1836[16]

Bowie, on the morning after, tried in his own way to make amends with Travis. Requesting a meeting, Bowie agreed to a joint command in which both men would sign all correspondence and military decisions. Travis would retain his command of the regular army and Bowie would lead the volunteers—including the New Orleans Greys.

Some kind of agreement was crucial at this point. Two days later, on the sixteenth, Santa Anna crossed the Rio Grande at Paso de Francia and started up the Camino Real to approach Bexar from the west. The next day General Urrea crossed the Rio Grande at Matamoros with 550 men and started his march toward Goliad.

When Cos had withdrawn from Bexar and retreated south of the Rio Grande in December, Texas had been completely free of Mexican military presence. Now, less that two months later, Texas had two giant Mexican armies returning and advancing in two directions—Bexar and Goliad. At both locations, their objectives included New Orleans Greys defenders.

On February 20 Mexican civilians in Bexar began loading their possessions and evacuating the city. The following day the Tejano volunteers in the Alamo garrison began discharging the army and leaving the city as well.

Both Travis and Bowie felt these moves were far too premature—that Santa Anna couldn't possibly reach Bexar that soon. Nevertheless, on February 23 the bell began clanging in the San Fernando church tower. The Texan sentry posted there had spotted Santa Anna's army outside Bexar, and the Greys and other Texans were now face to face with the president of Mexico and his considerable Mexican military force.

The siege of the Alamo had begun.

---

1   Ornish, *Ehrenberg*, pg. 165
2   Walter Lord, *A Time to Stand* (Lincoln: University of Nebraska Press, 1961), pg. 76.
3   Texas General Land Office Archives, [A2, Section C][list].
4   *Ibid.*
5   Jenkins, *The Papers of the Texas Revolution,* Vol. 4, pg. 136.
6   Barr, *Texans in Revolt—The Battle for San Antonio, 1835,* pg. 57.
7   Lord, pg. 59.
8   Groneman, *Alamo Defenders,* pg. 87.
9   Texas General Land Office Archives, [A2, Section C][list][tran][note][A3; T1 p37].
10 Harbert Davenport, "The Men of Goliad," pg. 35.
11 Groneman, *Alamo Defenders,* pg. 26.
12 Ornish, *Ehrenberg,* pg. 251.
13 Davenport, pg. 34.

14 Groneman, *Alamo Defenders,* pg. 23.
15 Thomas W. Cutrer, "Clark, Charles A." *New Handbook of Texas.*
16 Groneman, *Alamo Defenders*, pp. 151-2.

Chapter 7

South with Grant

Colony of San Patricio, Texas, February 14, 1836: Samuel Overton Pettus was a soldier, not a politician, and it was getting more and more difficult to tell the two apart in Texas these days. But he was a soldier and now, in some forlorn Irish colony far south of San Antonio, he was captain and commander of the New Orleans Greys or, as the politicians liked to refer to them, the San Antonio Greys.

Captain Pettus liked being a unit commander, but he was leery of being stationed in this abandoned hamlet called San Patricio—Mexican for Saint Patrick—so far from supplies and reinforcements.

His fellow Greys were clamoring to return to Goliad and resupply—by use of force if necessary—before continuing back so San Antonio to relieve the other Greys, who were about to be abandoned by the politicians in San Felipe and Washington-on-the-Brazos. Samuel Pettus intended to lead them on that quest.

The gaunt Virginian glanced around the one-room hut that he and three other Greys were billeting in. The building was completely empty of furnishings—the Irish Papists had packed everything before running toward the Rio Grande. Only a crude wooden cross remained above the single door. Pettus recognized it as a Gaelic, not Mexican, cross.

He was uncomfortable here. This house... this village... this beautiful but isolated part of Texas gave him an unexplainable nervousness, and he was not by nature a nervous man.

He could feel it. People were going to die here and soon. And he didn't want the dead to include his Greys. The Texans, including his men, hadn't learned the most important lesson in storming Bexar. In their youthful naivete they still saw themselves as bulletproof and invincible and the Mexicans as cowardly and unable—or unwilling—to fight.

But Pettus knew better, and the other Greys should too. They, of all Texans, should have recognized the fierce resistance the Mexicans had put up during the tunneling through Bexar. There had been no cowardice, and if the Mexicans had had any type of effective weapons, the casualty list of the Greys would have been devastating.

If Pettus agreed with the politicians on one thing, it was that the Mexicans would be coming back to Texas. San Antonio for sure and almost certainly through this place on the way to Goliad.

He missed Cooke being gone from the Greys but figured the former Grey captain had the right idea—aligning himself with Sam Houston. Morris, on the other hand, was headed for disaster with that unreliable Scotsman.

Cooke had been a good man and a valuable leader for the Greys. Pettus figured the former Greys captain would go far in post-revolution Texas—maybe even one day be a governor of the state of Texas when this war was finally won. And Pettus harbored no illusions that it would not be won. But not here, not in this isolated area. And not by Texans.

Samuel Overton Pettus was a soldier, not a politician, but he had learned to listen to those officers who were politicians. Sam Houston had left Goliad for east Texas last month, supposedly to negotiate a treaty with the Indian tribes in that area to prevent Santa Anna from using the Cherokees and others to open a second front against the Texans from the north. But Pettus suspected the old soldier had another, bigger plan.

He figured that what Houston really had planned was for his Greys, the Greys in San Antonio, and all the other Texan volunteers to withdraw to Gonzales and abandon La Bahia and the Alamo once Santa Anna and the Mexican army arrived. Then from Gonzales old Sam would lead the Mexicans right up El Camino Real to the Sabine and General Edmund Pendleton Gaines with his U.S. Army regulars at Fort Jesup and Camp Sabine, just waiting for an excuse to flood over the boundary and help the Texans.

Sure, General Gaines, President Andrew Jackson, and the U.S. Army were officially "neutral" in this rebellion against Mexico, but with the right reason, the United States would jump into the fray. And that reason was why Sam Houston was in east Texas right now.

Sam Houston, the stories had it, was half-Cherokee himself, if not by blood at least by his past. Sure The Raven, or Big Drunk, or whichever name the Cherokees called him, would negotiate a treaty with his former allies so they would be left out of the war. But the other tribes in east Texas—the Comanche and Apache—were anther story. Should they mount an attack on white American settlers in Texas, both Jackson and Gaines would have a free rein to enter Texas and protect U.S. citizens.

With American soldiers occupying east Texas, Santa Anna would have to choose between retreating and granting Texan independence or fighting the U.S. Army. Either way, the Mexicans—and the Indians—would lose and the Texans would win, and the United States would march uncontested to California and the Pacific Ocean.

"Yeah," Captain Samuel Overton Pettus thought to himself, "I've got to get these Greys out of here before we get trapped. There's going to be a great battle before this is all over, but it's not going to be at San Patricio, it's going to be at Nacogdoches.

೮೮೮೮೮

Dr. Grant's expeditionary force—including the majority of New Orleans Greys remaining in Bexar—left that city on December 30, 1835, with a planned layover at the La Bahia presidio 100 miles to the south. Under Grant's leadership they were to proceed to the Rio Grande and Matamoros where they would join the Mexican Federalists.

Captain Robert C. Morris, who had distinguished himself in Bexar and been promoted to major, appears at this time to have withdrawn from the New Orleans Greys but traveled with them in the army leaving Bexar. He seems to have had a dark foreboding of the future of the expedition, for he wrote his will leaving the lands he would earn as his military bounty to his sisters back in New Orleans. He sent the document to his brother-in-law, Doctor Vail, who was then at Nacogdoches, with a letter in which he wrote:

> I am in a dangerous land and may be
> knocked off at any time. If so, I leave my lands
> to my sisters and will leave an immortal name.
> I will have accomplished what I came for in
> having aided to win the freedom of Texas.[1]

With Captain Breece furloughed for recruiting duties and Captain Morris joining Johnson and Grant as their third in command, the remaining Greys were reorganized.

The majority of those Greys leaving on the Matamoros expedition were now under the command of Captain William Cooke, one of the heroes in the storming of Bexar. Cooke's company was comprised of former members of Morris' original roster from Bank's Arcade. They still often referred to themselves as "New Orleans" Greys, but their official unit title was now "San Antonio" Greys since their ranks also included volunteers from several other units.

A smaller number of Greys from Breece's original New Orleans roster also joined the Matamoros expedition in a reorganized unit known as Captain David Burke's Mobile Greys.

Together, the two units left Bexar that December 30 morning and camped the first night just six miles south of the Alamo on the Salado River. The following day they arrived at Juan Seguin's plantation on the San Antonio River where they spent New Year's Eve.

Since the Greys were now part of a much larger force—estimated at around 400 men—movement was slower, and it was not until January 4, 1836, that they finally reached Goliad and camped one mile outside the old Spanish fort called La Bahia.

George Collinsworth and a small group of men had captured the old presidio from the Mexicans the previous October. The attack had been successful beyond all expectations: possession of the most fortified military installation in northern Mexico with only one man injured in the assault. And there were other prizes of war as well—supplies, small arms, and artillery.

Soon after assuming control of the fort, Collinsworth left Philip Dimmitt in charge. Under Dimmitt and his men, who were neither Texan regular army nor part of the revolution army volunteers, they had issued a unilateral declaration of independence from Mexico and raised a defiant flag over the compound—a flag depicting a severed bloody arm holding a sword.

Dimmitt, who had considered himself the originator of the plan to attack Matamoros, now had second thoughts and opposed the scheme. When Grant arrived on January 4 with a large force intent on carrying out the plan anyway, conflict was inevitable between the two leaders.

Grant, who desired union with Mexican Federalists and a coalition with Coahuila so he could regain his land and holdings, was in direct opposition to Dimmitt, who had declared complete independence from Mexico, which, if successful, would assure Grant's Coahuillan property would remain in Santa Anna's Mexico.

Increasingly, the Greys were finding themselves pressured to choose between fighting for Texas independence or creation of a new Mexican state. To further complicate their dilemma, the General Council in San Felipe had not endorsed either scheme.

But the January 5 conflict between the two groups, with the Greys allied with Grant, centered on Dimmitt's refusal to share supplies. Grant, who had virtually strong-armed all the Alamo supplies and provisions before leaving Bexar, now intended to do the same with the well-stocked fort that Collinsworth and Dimmitt had so successfully attacked and captured three months earlier.

After arriving at Goliad on January 4, the Greys camped across the river from the presidio near the grounds of the abandoned Mission Espritu Santo. Cooke would later recall the turmoil immediately after their arrival:

> Some difficulty occurred between the commandant of that place (Capt. P. Dimitt who had hoisted the flag of independence) and Col Grant, and we all expected to have a fight with his forces—Dimitt refused to furnish us with provisions, of which he had a large store, upon the grounds that we were acting contrary to the wishes of the people of Texas, in uniting with the Mexicans west of the Rio Grande—The next day however, he consented to furnish us with Coffee, Sugar &c &c for a three months campaign—During the time of the altercation both parties were kept in readiness for a fight—after the supplies were furnished we were permitted to exchange civilities. . . .[2]

For five days the Greys remained encamped across the river, capturing and attempting to break wild mustangs and, on one excursion, unsuccessfully chasing after some local marauding Indians.[3]

For the Greys assigned to Cooke's unit—almost all of whom had formerly been in Morris' company—this was their second visit to Goliad. After departing Velasco the previous October, they had marched here through Victoria and stopped long enough to take control of some wild mustangs with dubious success.

On January 9, with an agreement between Grant and Dimmitt in effect, the Greys moved from their campsite into Goliad. As they rode into the town, all appeared deserted except for a few remaining Mexicans, who peered out at them from behind shuttered windows. For the most part the Mexican locals, who were almost unanimously hostile to the Texans, had left the town for safer areas south of the Rio Grande or on local nearby ranches.

Since the Texas revolution, the town of Goliad has relocated across the San Antonio River behind the old Mission Espritu Santo, some three miles from the reconstructed Spanish presidio. But in 1835 the town of Goliad was literally built around the old fort.

The fort itself was built atop the highest hill in the area overlooking the southwest bank of the San Antonio River across from the old mission for which it was designed to protect by quartering Spanish soldiers for defense against hostile Indian raids.

Heavy stone walls three feet thick and ten feet high surrounded the three-and-one-half acre quadrangle parade ground that included barracks, offices, a jail, and a small chapel. Unlike the Alamo mission compound in Bexar, this presidio was designed as a fortress, and the sally port, or main gate, was located on the south side. The only other entrance was a small gate on the north wall called a "water gate" which allowed access to the San Antonio River.

Bastions were located on each corner and were of sufficient size to accommodate artillery pieces. The inner barracks were located along the south wall for the enlisted men, and the officer's quarters and offices were located along the west wall. A small jail, or calaboose, was located inside the fort on the west side of the sally port.

As the Greys entered the town that January 9 morning, the prominent feature they would have first noticed would probably have been the Our Lady of Loreto chapel with its distinctive bell towers and octagonal window. Designed for use by soldiers and their families, the chapel was tiny by mission standards, eighty-five feet long and about thirty feet wide with a small alcove on one side.

The Greys riding into town that morning probably paid little attention to the small chapel located inside the northeast corner of the fort, but the church would soon become an integral part of the unit's history.

Despite the agreement to share provisions, all was not cordial between the two groups. The political bickering taking place at Goliad that day was just a microcosm of the greater political turmoil taking place in Texas.

The next day, January 10, in San Felipe, Governor Smith attempted to dissolve the council, which in turn impeached him. Smith refused to resign, and Texas was left in a political vacuum for the next six weeks.

Now, with the Council and governor's office divided, the military situation was also deteriorating. Sam Houston, angered over Grant's stripping of the Alamo, now decided to head the Scottish land speculator off at Goliad. He arrived the evening of January 14, five days after the Greys had entered Goliad and the presidio.

Houston arrived at La Bahia with a disputed command and unclear orders. Acting on behalf of an impeached governor and dissolved council, his command was disputed by both Dimmitt and Grant. By this time Houston, like Dimmitt, had changed his opinion about the Matamoros expedition and was now opposing it.

Grant, however, was determined to proceed at all costs, and Houston's immediate objective after reaching Goliad was to dissuade the troops—including the Greys—against continuing to the Rio Grande.

He was, according to Cooke's account, at least successful in diffusing the hostilities but unable to stop Grant's excursion south. In Cooke' words:

> Genl Houston who had been recently
> appointed Comdr. In Chief, arrived at Goliad a
> few days after this occurrence—He ordered a
> general parade, for the purpose (as was stated)
> to reorganise the troops and explain to them
> the desire of the Provisional Govt—He did so,
> and his address completely defeated the object
> of Col Grant—Houston was accompanied by
> Cols. James Bowie, Hockley Nibbs and several
> staff officers—A company under the command
> of P S Wyatt from Alabama was at Goliad on
> our arrival there—King's compy of about 30
> men were stationed at Refugio—It occupied
> several days to arrange matters between Houston & Grant. . . .[4]

On the seventeenth Houston received by messenger Neill's urgent request from the Alamo. Houston, the Greys, and other Texan volunteers at Goliad now learned that Santa Anna had invaded Texas.

Cooke does not mention this in his later correspondence, however he does touch upon the relationship between Bowie and Houston at this difficult time:

Bowie's object appeared to be to induce
our men to return to San Antonio—He used
every means in his power to effect this object—
They however at length determined to recognize the order of Genl Houston, and marched
to Refugio. . . .[5]

This would appear to suggest that Houston and Bowie were at odds concerning the role of the Alamo and its defenders while at Goliad.

It was Houston's plan to regroup outside Bexar in the community of Gonzales, and before his retreat from Goliad, he wanted first to go to Refugio to meet Colonel James Fannin and his men and supplies as they arrived by ship at nearby Copano Bay. Then, united with Fannin's forces, Houston planned to return to Gonzales.

But now, with Neill's urgent request, Houston needed someone he could trust—in this quagmire of political intrigue—to go to Bexar and, if necessary, destroy the Alamo compound and retreat to Gonzales with Neill's considerable artillery and firepower. The man he felt he could trust—possibly the only man he felt he could trust in this situation—to make the determination concerning the ability to defend or destroy the Alamo was James Bowie. It appears Bowie left Goliad for Bexar on the seventeenth in complete agreement with Houston's directive.

Thus it was on the seventeenth of January 1836 that the Greys in Goliad first learned of the serious situation their fellow unit members in the Alamo were facing. From that date, those Greys outside the Alamo appear to have had only one objective: to rejoin their fellow Greys in Bexar. Every record, every correspondence, and every reference to their objectives indicate they wanted to return to Bexar to help the Greys there.

It was also on this date that Houston formally re-enlisted Captain Cooke and the rest of the Greys into the provisional army for a term of three months. In a brief communiqué he penned:

> To William G. Cooke
> Headquarters, Goliad, January 17, 1836
> To Capt. William G. Cooke,
> Sir, I have the pleasure to acknowledge the tender of your services, and those of your company, to Texas, for the term of three months.
> The same are accepted, in behalf of Texas with pleasure, for the term of three months.
>
> Sam Houston[6]

After enlistment, the Greys continued on to Refugio to meet Fannin but then attempted to return to Bexar and the besieged Alamo. Only Fannin's refusal to outfit them prevented the New Orleans Greys from reuniting at the scene of their previous victory. Their decision not to return to Bexar with Bowie on January 17 quite possibly sealed the fate of those Greys in the Alamo. And their own fate.

As Bowie left for Bexar, Houston joined the Greys in Grant's estimated 200-man force as they left for Refugio some thirty miles south of Goliad. In addition to Fannin's forces, Houston expected to meet Colonel William Ward and his Georgia Battalion whom he believed had already arrived at Refugio. Riding along beside the volunteers on the two-day march, Houston spent the time singling out small groups of men and attempting to dissuade them from following Grant south of Refugio.

The main body of the army arrived in the Irish colony on the night of January 20 and was met by several other volunteer forces; however, neither Fannin nor any of his supply ships had arrived. Nor had Ward or his Georgia volunteers.

Almost immediately upon arrival at Refugio, Houston received a request from one of Grant's couriers for a meeting with Major Morris. Houston responded:

> To Robert C. Morris
> Headquarters, Refugio, January 20, 1836
>
> General Houston will be happy to see Major
> R.C. Morris, at Captain Westover's, whenever it
> will suit his convenience, as he wishes to make
> some communications through him to the vol-
> unteers at this post.[7]

In a January 30 letter to Governor Smith, Houston would
reveal that Morris had requested food supplies and informed
him that he wished to move troops further west, which Houston advised against.

The next morning more bad news arrived for Houston.
Francis W. Johnson, Grant's co-conspirator in the Matamoros
expedition and Mexican land grab, arrived in Refugio from
San Felipe with an explanation for Fannin's lateness. After
impeaching Governor Smith, the General Council had
replaced Sam Houston as commander-in-chief, making Fannin the new head of the army. Fannin was en route and
already in possession of Ward's army and supplies.

Houston's reaction was to spend the day lobbying the soldiers against continuing to Matamoros. In an inspired speech
under incredible pressure, Houston's words had to have had
an impact on the already disillusioned Greys. An artillery
captain named Pearson entered into a rebuttal, and the
words of the two men exemplify the dilemma that the Greys
and other volunteers had to ponder that day:

> Comrades! began General Houston, it is
> with pleasure that I find myself in your midst
> again after such a long separation, and I notice
> with astonishment that the keenest anticipa-
> tions that I had of the patriotic spirit of the
> army, in reality, have been even surpassed.
> Comrades, we must seek to maintain such patri-
> otic fire and not use it up where it will be of no
> benefit. Soon, friends, I believe, soon will the

enemy under Santa Anna raid our peaceful
savannahs, soon will their bugles urge their soldiers to our destruction; but that mighty
word—freedom—will inspire us, the thought of
right, and of religion, of wife and child, will
make us heroes. And, disregarding the superior
number of the enemy, I hope that our army will
defeat his purpose on the foaming Guadalupe;
and before the next summer, the flag of Texas,
the true symbol of freedom, will wave in all the
ports of the land. But to be victorious, citizens,
it is necessary that we stand united, and that
we extend our hands to one another in firm
union. Our weapons will be victorious—separated we shall lose.

You intend to take Matamoras. I praise your
courage. But I must candidly tell my friends
that this plan does not please me; I see no
advantage that can emanate from it; I see only
an unnecessary sacrifice of the blood of Texans
for a town that can have no value for us and
that lies beyond the border of our territory. If
the enemy is to be harmed, let us await him
and let his forces, fatigued by long marches and
privations, feel the work of our guns. Let us
prove to him what a nation can do which is
united. Though weak in numbers, it will rise up
en masse and boldly speak out: "We want to be
free." Let us show them that when nations rise
up for the cause of justice, the Almighty will
carry the banner. But I see, comrades, by the
expressions on your faces, the disapproval of
my opinion; it is, however, my judgement I
want to act only in the interest of the new
fatherland; but my voice is only one, that of
yours is—to Matamoras. Well, then to

Matamoras be it. But at least wait a short time
until the troops from Georgia and Alabama
land, and united with them, what power of the
enemy can withstand us?[8]

Upon the conclusion of this speech, Captain Pearson then
stood before the soldiers and addressed them:

Comrades! As much as I respect General
Houston, I cannot approve his suggestion. We
already have lain idle here too long and the
consequence is that the larger part of the army
has left us in disgust. Too long we have waited
in vain for munitions; in vain we have looked
for reinforcements from day to day that the
government had promised. It would be for
nothing that we would stay here longer, hesitat-
ing, idle, enduring the hardships of a campaign.
If we shall endure, let us be acting and I here-
with call on all who are in favor of an
immediate departure for Matamoras. Colonels
Johnson and Grant and Major Morris are in
favor of the expedition and will participate in it.
Once more, let us not hesitate longer, and, all
who endorse my position, be ready at noon—to
leave for Matamoras![9]

After these two speeches, Ehrenberg reported that the
Greys were overwhelmingly in favor of continuing the
Matamoros expedition. But Houston was not finished:

Comrades, Citizens of Texas!
Once more I come before you, and it is with
the most fervent desire that this time my words
will find general approval.
Our proclamations to the other states of the
Mexican confederation, asking them to support
us in our struggle for the restoration of our
former rights and for the protection of the

Constitution of 1824, have, as you all know, been without results. Even many of the Mexicans who live between the Sabine and the Rio Grande have disdainfully forsaken the cause of freedom, and have not only denied us their support but also united themselves with the troops of Santa Anna and, as enemies, waged war against the land. Others have gone beyond the Rio Grande in order to smother us by combining themselves with the next best power. Still others have remained on their plantations on the banks of the forested rivers apparently to idly observe the war. These, comrades, are for us the most dangerous, because he who is not with us is against us. Also, from the otherwise liberal inhabitants of Zacatecas we have observed no movement in our favor. No other help remains for us now than our own strength and the knowledge that we have seized our arms for a just cause. (Hear!) Since it is impossible to call forth any sympathy from our fellow Mexican citizens and no support is to be expected from this side and as they let us, the smallest of all the provinces, struggle without any aid, let us then, comrades, sever that link that binds us to that rusty chain of the Mexican confederation. . . .

My friends, I must ask for a few moments more of your attention. There is general complaint about the negligence of the government in supplying the troops with war materials. But to eliminate the causes for this complaint lies beyond the power of the governor. Ship loads are on the sea, and only unfavorable northwest winds have prevented their running into our harbors. Possibly even now they may lie safe in

> Matagorda Bay, and the citizens will rush to
> deliver the cargoes to the army.[10]

In this brief follow-up speech, Houston managed to hit
upon the fears and resentments of the Greys and satisfacto-
rily answer them. Like many of the volunteer groups at Bexar
and now in Refugio, the Greys were vocally wondering
where the Texas settlers were when the fighting was going
on. More unsettling to them, they saw the governor and
council as insensitive to their needs in providing desperately
needed supplies and food.

One of Fannin's stated policies had been that, under his
command, the troops would be paid out of the "spoils taken
from the enemy" during the attack on Matamoros—effectively making the Greys and other volunteers pirates.

But now, in Houston's final address to them, the Greys
were reassured that the governor and council had not given
up on them and that the local Texans did support their
efforts. They were soldiers—not pirates—and Houston had
also given them a clear objective: separation and independence from Mexico. And he had given them a promise of
supplies. Once again they were fighting men with military
objectives. Grant's promises of the pleasures of dark-eyed
senoritas and untold riches to be plundered south of the Rio
Grande no longer seemed that enticing.

Ehrenberg described cheers of joy as the general finished
his speech. The Greys surrounded him and grasped to shake
his hand as if he were a politician announcing election victory. More importantly, the Greys also decided to remain at
Refugio and wait for Fannin and Ward to arrive.

Houston, feeling he could do no more in the south, left
that night for east Texas to negotiate a treaty with the Indian
nations there.

Grant, absolutely refusing to be detoured from his
Matamoros dream, left the next morning with Johnson, Morris, and about seventy men. Robert C. Morris, at this point,

seems to have severed all ties with the Greys and cast his lot with the land speculators. One of Morris' New Orleans Grey volunteers, James M. Cass of Connecticut, also joined Grant's group as did William Jones Gatlin, a Tennessean formerly of Breece's company. Their immediate objective was another Irish colony to the south named San Patricio.

With Houston, Grant, Morris, and Johnson gone, the Greys chose to remain at Refugio to await Fannin and Ward. They moved two miles outside the town and camped on the plantation of a local ranchero named Lopez, who proclaimed to be loyal to the Texan cause. Later, Ehrenberg would report, Lopez would turn out to be another of the local spies reporting on the Texan movements in the area.

While most of the remaining army at Refugio billeted in the local houses, nearly all of which were abandoned, the Greys remained outside of town hunting game and capturing wild horses.

On January 24 five Greys including Herman Ehrenberg were dispatched to Copano to meet the ships carrying Fannin and Ward. The Greys reached the coast to find an angry sea of raging waves whipped by what Ehrenberg described as "hurricane-like" winds. Taking residence in an abandoned house on the coastline, the Greys spent eight days, hunting and fishing and watching the horizon for Fannin's ships.

Finally, on February 2, 1836, two frigates appeared and soon docked. Aboard were Fannin with his men along with Ward and his Georgia Battalion. Altogether, their combined force numbered 200 men. Between the rough seas and the amount of supplies, it took the Greys and the newcomers nearly two days to unload the ships.

On February 4 and 5 Fannin marched his army to Refugio where he, under his new orders from the divided council, attempted to assume overall command. They arrived to find the Refugio army had dwindled even more due to desertions and furloughs.

On February 7 Fannin received from San Patricio a letter from Major Morris stating that a force of 1,500 Mexicans was within a few hours' march of him. Fannin immediately dispatched the two companies of Greys, under the leadership of Cooke, to assist Morris.

Morris may have effectively discharged the New Orleans Greys after Bexar but the two companies of current Greys who left Refugio that day were intent on racing to the aid of their former leader. In an incredible forced march that totaled forty-eight miles in one day, the Greys reached the tiny Irish hamlet of San Patricio Hibernia.

The feared Mexican invasion, it turned out, was a false alarm. Again the Greys declined housing in the abandoned huts of San Patricio and set up camp just outside of town. Grant received word from Matamoros that the Federalists were awaiting him and would join his forces in overthrowing and occupying that city once he arrived.

Knowing that Grant would never return to Goliad and submit to Fannin's command, the Greys attempted to convince him to, instead, return to Bexar and help reinforce their fellow Greys threatened there by Santa Anna's impending arrival.

Grant, however, absolutely refused to abandon his assault on Matamoros, and on February 9 he, Johnson, and Morris led their small army south once more while leaving Cooke in charge of the two artillery pieces and the post at San Patricio.

Within a few hours after their departure, Cooke later wrote:

> . . . a Mexican officer in full uniform came into town, and with a passport and letters from Grant & Morris to me—The amt of Grants letter to me was that he had recd through this officer information from Vital [sic] Fernandez, comdg Genl. Of Tamaulipas who offered to unite with him (the moment he reached the Rio Grande),

with 1800 men—Morris letter stated that he no
longer intended to serve the Govt. of Texas—
that he had received the appointment to the
command of a Regiment in the Federal service
of Mexico—I forwarded copies of these letters
to Col Fannin, who ordered me to fall back to
Goliad, then his Hd quarters, bringing with me
all the artillery, ammunition &c which I accordingly did, arriving there about the 12th of
Feby—[11]

Immediately after leaving San Patricio on the ninth, it
appears Morris obtained a commission with the Federalists in
the Mexican army. Now he was no longer affiliated with the
Greys or the Texans—he was a Mexican soldier in the midst of
a civil war and, for better or worse, his future and fortunes lay
with the Scottish land speculator. Only two months earlier, on
November 29, 1835, he had declined Houston's offer of a
commission in the Texan regular army and carefully empha-
sized that he was not a "mere seeker of fortune." By early
February, on the south Texas plains, he accepted a commission
in the Federalist Mexican army. All pretenses of "prosperity &
liberty" for Houston's beautiful country were gone.

Cooke returned to Goliad on the twelfth and was dispatched with two prisoners to Washington-on-the-Brazos on
February 14—thus ending his career as a New Orleans Grey.

Back in San Patricio, Samuel Overton Pettus was placed
in command of Cooke's company. With Cooke's departure, all
three of the original Greys leaders were now gone. Pettus, a
Virginian who had enlisted with Morris in New Orleans, had
been promoted during the Bexar fighting and was now commissioned a major. He was, like Cooke, one of the original
Greys and a highly respected combat veteran.

On February 18 Pettus and the Greys returned to Goliad
from San Patricio with the objective of restocking supplies
and continuing on to Bexar. Dragging the two artillery pieces

Grant had left behind, they arrived in Goliad only to learn that Fannin would not supply them for a Bexar trip. Two supply ships, he assured them, were being loaded in New Orleans and would shortly be en route to Lavaca Bay.

When Sam Houston departed Refugio, he took with him Captains Lawrence and Wigginton. Davenport reports that "many men of both their companies, and a number from Captain Cooke's, dissatisfied, and some of them ill, were released from the service at the same time."[12]

On February 23 Fannin's diary indicates he furloughed or discharged fifteen volunteers with partial payment including New Orleans Grey Francis Leonard, a Louisiana native who had enlisted with Morris and traveled to Texas through Velasco. Fannin's entry was recorded:

> Recd 23d Feby 1836—Fort Defiance from
> J W Fannin Jr Agt Provl. Govt of Texas the sum
> of Twenty Dollars in part payment for services
> rendered as a Volunteer in the N.O. Greys, Capt
> Cook's Company—and regularly credited in my
> discharge—
> $20   F.G. Leonard[13]

Two days later Fannin mentioned Leonard once more in a letter to the General Council. In that letter, Fannin outlined expenses he was incurring at Goliad in which he enclosed drafts for, among other charges, "two hundred and ten Dollars . . . (being the articles furnished them for private purposes, to wit seventy gallons of Brandy) and will be deducted from their pay—private G.F. Leonard is in the same situation and will be deducted from their pay by the proper officer . . ."[14]

No reason is listed for Leonard's discharge, and his name is not found in any subsequent documents. It is not known if he was wounded, sick, or had a family emergency back home in Louisiana.

For the next week the Greys assisted the other Texan volunteers in fortifying the presidio. Much of the work involved the destruction of huts and outbuildings adjacent to the fort's walls. Underbrush and trees were burned away from the perimeter of the fort to allow artillery clear access around the stone walls.

These were clearly difficult times for the Greys, and the situation began to deteriorate quickly after the twenty-third. Two days later they received—through Travis' urgent message to Fannin—news that the Greys in the Alamo were now trapped by Santa Anna's forces, who were threatening to kill all defenders if they refused to surrender.

In response, Fannin left Captain Westover and his men in charge of the presidio and headed north to Bexar and the Alamo. While still within sight of the fort, Fannin attempted to cross the San Antonio River only to have one—some reports claim as many as three—wagon break down. The Greys and other volunteers camped out overnight on the other side of the river, separated from their supplies and ammunition, and awoke the next morning to learn that the inexperienced wagoners had allowed the oxen to graze unfettered overnight. The animals had wandered off, leaving the army with no way to transport any supplies or food on the trip to San Antonio.

Fannin hastily consulted with his officers and decided to abort the disastrous relief mission and return to La Bahia. The New Orleans Greys were not included in the decision, and that may have been by design given the animosity and opposition the Greys had shown toward Fannin since his refusal to supply their return to Bexar from Refugio.

Now, in near rebellion but with no means to break away on their own, the Greys were forced to return once more to the fortress at Goliad and abandon their comrades in the Alamo. What had been initial elation at leaving the presidio became dejection and hostility.

The Greys had barely resettled inside the fort again when Colonel Johnson arrived with four men from San Patricio.

Grant's Matamoros expedition was beginning to unravel with disastrous results. Grant and Morris were still in the field south of San Patricio, but Johnson and his men had been ambushed in the early morning hours of the twenty-seventh and all captured or killed except for the five returning to Goliad.

After making a successful trip to the Rio Grande to capture wild horses, Johnson, Morris, and Grant had returned to San Patricio where Johnson stabled the horses on a nearby ranch. He then bivouacked in the abandoned colony with a small force while Grant and Morris left to obtain more horses.

During the night of the twenty-sixth, in the midst of a brutal "blue norther," General Jose de Urrea surrounded the ranch and captured the horses and eight Texans while killing four men. In San Patricio, Captain Pearson and eight Texans were camping in the public square while Johnson and the rest were billeting in abandoned houses. At 3:00 A.M. on the morning of the twenty-seventh the Texans were awakened by gunfire followed by a cease-fire in which the Mexicans offered Johnson's men a free pardon if they would surrender. They ignored the offer and continued to fight throughout the night until daylight when they surrendered in order to obtain aid for their wounded.

Legend tells the story that Urrea sent word ahead to loyalists to leave a light burning in their homes and they would not be molested. It so happened that Johnson was working late—with a light.[15] In the midst of the initial firefight, Johnson and four others did escape to return to Goliad. In San Patricio, eight Texans were killed, including two Mexicans loyal to the rebel's cause, thirteen were taken prisoner, and six, including Johnson, escaped. Morris and Grant, on another horse-gathering trip during the attack, maintained their position twenty-six miles to the south near Agua Dulce Creek.

Back in Goliad, Johnson's arrival and his story of the defeat of Texan forces at San Patricio confirmed reports that General Urrea was in their immediate vicinity. Still Fannin refused to abandon the fort and march to join Sam Houston at Gonzales. Within days more bad news arrived at the presidio.

William James Gatlin, the New Orleans Grey who had cast his lot with Morris and Grant earlier, now appeared at the gate of the fort with four other of Grant's men to announce that Urrea's soldiers had surprised them at Agua Dulce Creek and destroyed their force. Major Robert C. Morris and Private James M. Cass—two New Orleans Greys— were among the dead. Morris was killed early in the encounter; the details of Cass' death are unknown. A total of twelve Texans were killed at Agua Dulce; four were captured and six—including Gatlin and the four others who returned to Goliad—escaped.

Dr. James Grant, the Scotsman who refused to abandon his dream of reclaiming riches in northern Mexico, was captured in the ambush and, while a prisoner, murdered. There are several accounts of his death: He was trampled under the hoofs of the wild horses he was herding; he was viciously set upon with swords; or he was tied to the hoofs of a wild mustang and dashed to death on the prairie. But it is certain that his Mexican captors were aware of his political treachery and land grabbing prior to the revolution, and his death was particularly vengeful.

The captured at Agua Dulce and those prisoners from San Patricio were imprisoned at Matamoros, making them, ironically, the only men in Grant's expedition to actually reach their destination.

The Greys, although heavily involved in the military theaters of Texas during this period, had been astonishingly fortunate in that they had sustained very few casualties despite their involvement. The first known Greys casualty to the Mexicans had been Charles W. Connor, murdered while separated from Morris' unit en route to Bexar. John Cook, the English naval artilleryman, had been killed in the storming of Bexar, and several other Greys had been wounded. But, considering the fact that the New Orleans Greys were the most combat-experienced unit in Texas at this time, they had sustained few casualties.

Now, with the deaths of Morris and Cass at Agua Dulce, the realities of this complex revolution in which they were participating were beginning to take an ominous toll.

On March 5 the Greys and other volunteers at La Bahia—now renamed Fort Defiance—received word that a new Texan government had been established in Washington-on-the-Brazos with David G. Burnet as president and Sam Houston once again appointed commander-in-chief of all the various armed forces serving in Texas. It was also official now: Texas had declared independence from Mexico.

This development was welcome news for the Greys. It now meant that Sam Houston, whom the Greys had grudgingly respected and acquiesced to at Refugio with regards to abandoning the Matamoros folly, was now in a position to dictate direct orders to Fannin, toward whom they were openly hostile. Given the disasters to Johnson at San Patricio and Morris and Grant at Agua Dulce, their alliance with Houston had been a wise decision. Now they needed to advance on Bexar to relieve the Greys surrounded by Santa Anna's troops outside the Alamo.

In fact, one of Houston's first correspondences to Fannin after being re-elected commander-in-chief was to order him once again to abandon and destroy the fort and depart Goliad to join forces with him north of the Guadalupe River. The Greys stationed at Goliad had no way of knowing that March 5 was the last day in the unit history of the Greys surrounded inside the Alamo. Within twenty-four hours they would all be dead.

A subsequent order, according to Ehrenberg, included the offer by Houston to meet the Greys and other Goliad volunteers at Seguin's ranch forty miles from the Alamo.[16]

Fannin refused, however, to abandon the fort with some justification due to other events surrounding his position at that time. Still, the Greys fumed and hovered near open rebellion. Ehrenberg's diary entries during this period detail the opinion of the Greys toward the commander they saw as indecisive and insensitive to their comrades in Bexar:

> But Fannin was inclined neither for the retreat nor for the march to San Antonio. On the contrary, he would rather face the enemy in the fort of Goliad as fortified by him. In Goliad he held undisputedly the first position, which rank, however, he would have had to resign if he combined with the main Army. Our efforts to induce him to march to San Antonio were fruitless. . . .
>
> From where Fannin derived his conclusion that the Volunteers were not inclined to rescue the lives of their brothers in the Alamo was not explained to us, and without taking the vote of the army, everybody went back to Goliad.
>
> The Greys moaned and complained about the fate of the besieged ones for whose reinforcement they had been on the march but were then detained by Fannin. . . .
>
> As said before, Fannin could not be moved to evacuate Goliad, and he still believed that the besieged forces (in the Alamo), if they wanted to, could surely withdraw. . . .[17]

Fortification continued on the fort, and a covered trench was constructed from the "water gate" to the San Antonio River to assure access to water in the event Urrea's men surrounded them.

Not only was morale down among the volunteers, but discipline was also becoming a problem. The Greys, who as young men had enjoyed the interaction with the Mexicans in

Bexar by gambling, drinking in cantinas, and dancing at fandangos, found the deserted and dirty streets of Goliad depressing and boring.

The few Mexicans who remained in Goliad were suspiciously considered to all be spies; however, they did, at considerable profit, supply some needed foodstuffs and supplies. Some of the garrison did go into town to patronize a cantina, and there are stories of one lieutenant who occasionally got drunk and kicked in doors, a performance not designed to gain much friendship from the local population.[18]

Inside the presidio, the loyal Mexican artillery company, which had joined to support a return to the civil liberties under the Constitution of 1824, now withdrew their services since the new declaration of independence forced them to fight against Mexico rather than campaign for constitutional reforms. Fannin now had to train artillerymen to man his cannon.

There is a popular conception of the New Orleans Greys suggesting they were artillerymen, or at least an artillery unit, while in fact they never were. The image of them as artillerymen probably stems from Ehrenberg's description of the Greys—prior to the storming of Bexar—using cannon to target practice on the Alamo chapel.

During the storming of Bexar, the Greys served purely as an infantry assault unit, while the other division under Milam manned the two cannon and Neill maintained his reserve position firing a cannon as diversion and protecting the rear flank. During the heat of battle inside Bexar, the Greys requested and received the artillery from Milam's division and fired it effectively—due, no doubt, in large part to their prior target practice. But their primary functions were footsoldiers and riflemen.

Now, inside Fort Defiance at Goliad, the Greys no doubt also trained again on the artillery in possession there. Given their reduced numbers, the Texans almost certainly were required to man the guns with far less than the recommended gunnery practices for the pieces they possessed. This would require that virtually every man be at least familiar with the firing procedures to replace fallen gunners in the course of battle. To the north, their fellow Greys inside the Alamo compound had also trained in firing drill but remained officially an infantry unit: Blazeby's Infantry Company.

Meanwhile, the ever-tightening ring of military disasters continued to plague the Goliad garrison. On the night of March 10, carts arrived at the fort from Lavaca containing supplies that had been delivered to that port. Fannin had earlier received a request for evacuation aid from Lewis Ayres for himself and several other Anglo settlers who had remained behind at Refugio. At the time of the request Fannin had no carts with which to dispatch, but these returning carts from Lavaca would allow him to respond to the settler's request.

On the twelfth he dispatched Captain Amon King with twenty-eight men to Refugio with the objective of evacuating the Anglo settlers to Goliad. In doing so, Fannin also depleted the fort of almost all the wagons that would be necessary if he did decide to evacuate. Had King concentrated on his mission, all would have gone well, but his men, no doubt suffering from "barracks boredom," chose instead to use this excursion as an opportunity to harass and punish local Mexicans whom they perceived to have been disloyal to the Texan cause.

Urrea's soldiers quickly engaged King and his men and cornered them in the abandoned Mission Nuestra Senora del Rosario, but one of the Texans escaped to return to Goliad and inform Fannin.

The next day, the thirteenth, Fannin dispatched Colonel William Ward and the Georgia Battalion to rescue King. Joining Ward's force was New Orleans Grey John Bright, a North Carolinian who had joined with Breece.

Ward arrived at the old mission that afternoon and quickly drove off the Mexicans, but instead of joining King and returning to Goliad, both commanders chose to continue the harassment of the local Mexicans and split their command that evening. Ward remained at the old mission while King traveled to the nearby Lopez ranch where the Greys had camped during their stay at Refugio—an area that Ehrenberg had identified as a haven for spies.

Ehrenberg had evidently been correct in his assessment since King's men were obviously entering a trap as they approached the plantation. After a fierce firefight they were driven back to the mission for cover. Meanwhile Ward's men were already pinned down inside the old structure, and both he and King effectively used their men to hold off the Mexicans until, later in the day, they ran short of ammunition and powder. Holding off the Mexicans until after dark, the Texans managed to escape but again split forces.

King's men were quickly captured and returned to Refugio. Ward's men, including New Orleans Grey John Bright, successfully eluded the Mexicans by traveling to the southeast along Copano Road. In the midst of the fighting and escapes, Fannin's wagons—so critical for an evacuation from Goliad—were lost to the Mexicans.

The day after dispatching Ward to King's rescue, the thirteenth, Fannin received a direct order from Houston to retreat from Goliad. With King and Ward missing, however, Fannin spent March 14 and 15 awaiting word from them. Without their wagons, he was also dependant upon Captain A.C. Horton and his Matagorda volunteers to arrive from Victoria with wagons and teams.

On the sixteenth he received word that King's men had been captured and summarily executed in Refugio. Ward and his soldiers had escaped and their fates were unknown. To the Greys this meant that one of their ranks, John Bright, was missing in action.

They could not have known that Ward's men were slowly being encircled near Victoria and that Bright, serving on a water detail when they were attacked, was able to escape (one record indicates he was "lost") and was one of the very few to avoid capture and execution.

On March 17 Fannin received word that King himself was dead. Now, finally, he made the decision to destroy Fort Defiance and follow orders to retreat to the north.

---

1   Wharton, *Remember Goliad*, pg. 39.

2   *Lamar Papers*, Vol. IV, Part I, pg. 42.

3   Ornish, *Ehrenberg*, pg. 176.

4   *Lamar Papers*, Vol. IV, Part I, pg. 42.

5   *Ibid.*

6   Amelia W. Williams, and Eugene C. Barker, *The Writings of Sam Houston 1813-1863, Vol. I* (Austin: Pemberton Press, 1970), pg. 342.

7   *Ibid.*, pg. 343.

8   Ornish, *Ehrenberg*, pp. 181-2.

9   *Ibid.*, pg. 182.

10   *Ibid.*, pp. 183-4.

11   *Lamar Papers*, pg. 43.

12   Davenport, "The Men of Goliad," pp. 16-7.

13   *Lamar Papers*, Vol. 5, pg. 92.

14   Jenkins, *The Papers of the Texas Revolution*, Vol. 4, pg. 429.

15   Keith Guthrie, "San Patricio, Battle of" *New Handbook of Texas*.

16   Ornish, *Ehrenberg*, pg. 205.

17   *Ibid.*, pp. 205-7.

18   Pruett, *Goliad Massacre*, pp. 43-4.

Chapter 8

Alamo Defenders

***Roof of the Long Barracks, Alamo Compound, March 6,
1836:*** John Baugh was a natural leader of men. That had been
evident in Alexandria, when Breece's men had elected him first
lieutenant. He had served well on the trip to Bexar, and his
leadership during the siege and battle for the city had gained
him the respect of the Texan leaders.

When Baugh had spurned Grant's offer of an officership in
the Matamoros expedition, Neill had been quick to assign him
as the adjutant for the remaining Alamo compound force.

The thirty-three-year-old Baugh prided himself on working
well with proficient, effective men no matter how difficult they
might be to deal with. His role as adjutant under the quiet,
unassuming Neill had been easy, almost effortless. The Alamo's
apprentice engineer, Green Jameson, had likewise been a
pleasure to work with, and they had teamed well together to
procure equipment and supplies.

The adjutant stopped walking and peered out into the
darkness over the rooftop along the eastern wall. Unable to
see any movement in the partial moonlight, he concentrated
instead on listening. Just a few scraping sounds and the shuf-
fling sounds of the cattle penned up there. He turned and
started walking back toward the north wall.

"Bowie," he thought to himself, "now there's a difficult
man to work with." Actually, Baugh enjoyed working with the

famous knife-fighter as much as any other Texan in the compound—at least he had while Bowie was still healthy.

Most of the Greys and other volunteers liked Bowie simply as an alternative to Travis. Sure, they respected and even feared Bowie's fighting skills, and many of them had enjoyed joining the Louisiana slave-trader on his drinking binges, but their acquiescing to Bowie's leadership was based on the "survival of the fittest" principle.

Baugh, on the other hand, saw in Bowie not a belligerent, dangerous bully good to have on his side in a fight, but instead he saw Bowie as a cunning, although crude military tactician and calculating leader of soldiers. "Crazy like a fox," Baugh had thought to himself on more than one occasion. He genuinely liked James Bowie and deeply regretted seeing the man incapacitated on a cot in the Low Barracks.

That Travis would keep Baugh as his adjutant after Neill's departure also spoke well for the Grey officer's ability to work with leaders of different temperaments. Baugh didn't like Travis—didn't like him at all. None of the Greys did. But Baugh respected him—just as he had respected Bowie—only for different reasons.

Travis was shrewd and clever but in a pompous, self-promoting, pretentious way. He was also effective, and Baugh placed a high priority on effectiveness—especially in this difficult situation they were in here at the Alamo compound tonight.

Reaching the northeast corner, Baugh stepped over the sleeping body of another New Orleans Grey, George Washington Main. Main had been severely injured in the battle for Bexar and had been recuperating in the hospital when Blazeby's company of former Greys had been formed. Baugh had kept an eye on Main, a fellow Virginian, during his recuperation, and the poor soldier was still in serious condition.

Dr. Amos Pollard had listed Main, one of Breece's lieutenants, as "severely wounded," and although Blazeby and the

Greys had wanted him assigned to their company, Main had realized his inability to fight and requested to serve as a lookout with Captain Robert White's Bexar Guards.

Baugh took one last look to the northeast before climbing down from the Long Barracks roof. Walking over to the earthen ramp in the center of the north wall, he climbed the ramp, and, leaning on one of the three eight-pounders there, he resumed his watch. The *Fortin de Teran*, they called this position. At least Travis did. It was his command post on the wall and typical of the man that he'd give it some kind of foreign name.

The adjutant wanted to look at his watch, but without a light he couldn't read the time, and it didn't matter anyway. He could feel that daylight was less than two hours away.

All of a sudden he also had another feeling—one he couldn't readily identify, but he did recognize it as an uneasy feeling. Then he knew what it was. It was the same eerie silence they had all felt just after the shelling had stopped the previous afternoon. All of a sudden everything was too quiet, but it was as if he could feel, rather than hear, a thumping.

He peered out over the north wall into the darkness. A half-mile to his left was Bexar, and he suddenly realized it was abnormally dark. Every night shift he'd walked before, there'd been scattered small fires and candlelight in at least some windows. But now it was so black he couldn't even see the town.

He fought back a sinking feeling in his stomach. It was too quiet and too dark. Was something wrong or was he falling victim to fatigue and frayed nerves? Was his mind playing games with him? All of a sudden he felt dizzy, as if the dark night in front of him was dancing up and down.

Keeping absolutely quiet, he leaned forward over the wall and stared again in front of him. He wasn't dizzy: The up and down movement was the movement of hundreds of Mexican soldiers running toward him. Then he heard the yell.

ᘓᘓᘓᘔᘔᘔ

*F*or the Greys in Bexar, the morning of February 23, 1836, began as just another routine day. There would be more fortification of the defenses around the perimeter of the mission grounds necessary, and probably Green Jameson would have at least some of them performing mock drills on the artillery pieces. Nearly all of the Texan volunteers left behind were being familiarized with the artillery drill since they were so short-handed.

Despite the constant repairs and fortifications taking place, there wasn't a real sense of urgency. Most Texans believed Santa Anna would lead a force into Bexar but not before spring. The general feeling was that he would wait until the severe winter had passed and he could take advantage of the spring grasses to feed his horses and teams as he moved from Mexico City into central Texas.

Just the same, there had been persistent rumors that he was already in Texas, and at the fandango last night a messenger had appeared with a report that Mexican soldiers were just outside San Antonio.

Because of the late-night party, most of the Greys probably slept late in the Mexican houses they were leasing or simply occupying. Travis, however, had given the report enough credence to post a lookout in the bell tower of the San Fernando church.

The sounds of what had become almost a mass exodus of Mexican citizens from the city may have been the noise that awoke most of the Greys that particular morning. After their morning routines, they would have begun the half-mile trek over to the old Alamo compound. All in all, February 23, 1836, promised to be just another routine day of "barracks boredom" for the Greys of Blazeby's Infantry Company and the other Texan volunteers in Bexar.

At least until the bell started clanging in the tower of the church.

While most of the volunteers probably just stopped what they were doing and stared at the tower, several began walking to the plaza in front of the church. As they watched, Travis and Dr. John Sutherland climbed into the bell tower to question the lookout and survey the surrounding countryside.

As those Greys in the plaza looked up into the tower, there appeared to be no particular panic or distress from the highest vantage point in San Antonio. But upon returning to ground level, Travis ordered a formation and requested volunteers to scout the countryside.

The problem was that all the horses were being stabled at Salado Creek, nearly five miles away. Dr. Sutherland and another volunteer named John W. Smith had horses at hand, so Travis dispatched them with orders to the bell tower lookout to sound the alarm immediately if he were to see Sutherland and Smith racing back into town.

The Greys, sharing the overall Texan view that this whole episode was just another false alarm, probably relaxed and returned to their chores as the two mounted volunteers left to scout the countryside.

Smith and Sutherland, however, had traveled less than two miles from town when they confirmed their worst fears and the tower watchman's adamant claims. Sutherland recognized that the Mexican forces were huge—he couldn't have had time to estimate that 1,500 soldiers were assembled—and he and Smith wasted no time barreling back into San Antonio. Almost immediately the bell in the church tower began clanging frantically again.

By the time the two scouts had reached the plaza, the city was empty of Texans. The Greys and other volunteers had already evacuated into the confines of the old Alamo mission compound. For better or worse, the Greys had made their stand.

The siege of the Alamo had just begun.

As the Greys withdrew into the Alamo compound, they carried their small arms and personal gear with them. Cattle that had been penned in side streets of the city were herded into the stock areas behind the Long Barracks and hospital building.

New Orleans Greys Henry David Hersey and Thomas Waters took up quarters in the Long Barracks with the rest of Captain William Carey's artillery company. George Washington Main, who was assigned to Captain White's infantry company, would have been assigned to barracks along the east wall near the center of the compound as would have been the majority of Greys assigned to Blazeby's company.

The blue silk flag presented to the Breece's company of the Greys at Gaine's Ferry was hoisted onto the roof of the infantry barracks—perhaps during that first day of the siege.

Also during that first day, as the Greys and other volunteers peered over the Alamo compound walls at the growing Mexican military force assembling in Bexar, Travis retired to his quarters and penned a dispatch for help, which he sent by courier to Gonzales. He had, he wrote, one hundred fifty men inside the Alamo that morning.

For the Greys, the seriousness of the situation was evident, but there was also the sense that reinforcements would soon be coming and their predicament wasn't as bad as it appeared. After all, Fannin had a huge force at Goliad, including the combat-experienced Greys and they, for certain, would return to help their fellow soldiers.

Later in the afternoon, however, they watched two ominous developments in the city below them. The first was a series of signals from Santa Anna. He ordered a red flag signifying no quarter placed in the San Fernando tower and then commanded a savage burst of cannon fire. Next, he ordered the white pennant raised to signal for a parley.[1] Travis responded with a thunderous round from the eighteen-pounder on the southwest corner of the compound.

The second and perhaps more disconcerting signal came from one of their commanders—James Bowie. The smoke had not cleared from the cannon exchange when Green Jameson emerged from the Alamo with a white flag and a hand-written note in Spanish from James Bowie.

While Travis had responded to Santa Anna with a unilateral blast from the giant cannon, Bowie had independently responded to the white flag that Santa Anna had raised requesting a parley. After a brief discussion, Jameson returned to the compound with the Mexican terms: unconditional surrender at Santa Anna's discretion.

Travis was furious with Bowie, and the incident demonstrated all too clearly the danger of defending the Alamo compound with a dual command. Surrender for Travis or Bowie, however, was out of the question at this point, and the Mexicans now began bombardment of the compound walls.

The bombardment was continuous, and had the Mexicans had heavy siege guns, the ancient walls and earthen barricades of the compound would have crumbled immediately. But Santa Anna didn't have heavy siege guns—only light field pieces and probably no more than ten of them. Lacking heavy ordnance, the gunners had to place their smaller cannon closer to the walls. But venturing within two hundred yards of the fort in daylight was an invitation to the deadly Texian riflemen.[2]

Most of the Greys remaining in the Alamo after Grant's departure had been former members of Breece's Company. At least fifty New Orleans Greys—the first fifty to sign up at Bank's Arcade, had received new rifles compliments of Adolphus Sterne. Breece's Company, traveling through Nacogdoches, was supplied with additional equipment from Sterne, probably including at least some additional weapons. The remaining Greys now aimed some of those long rifles over the compound walls at the Mexicans as this siege began.

To avoid the Texan sharpshooters, the Mexicans began a nighttime construction of trenches that would allow the light artillery to slowly move closer to the walls of the Alamo fortress as the siege progressed.

The first day, however, the Mexican bombardment was probably more of a psychological ploy than a legitimate military assault on the Alamo defenses.

On the second day, February 24, Travis wrote his famous plea for help in which he reported he had sustained a continual bombardment for 24 hours without sustaining a casualty. This was due, in large part, to the fact that Santa Anna was bombarding from a long range with light field artillery pieces.

Travis, whose personal life has been vilified—with a degree of just cause—perhaps cemented his place in Texas history with the words he penned in that letter. And, as the correspondence left the compound in the possession of a courier, it also cemented the place of the New Orleans Greys in Texas and Alamo history: There would be no surrender to the Mexicans. Or, in Travis' words, "Victory or death."

It was also on the twenty-fourth that the dual-command problem was unexpectedly resolved. Bowie, who had been sick and drunk for weeks, now collapsed and was completely incapacitated. Various reasons have been offered for his ailment, but it is thought he probably was suffering from some type of respiratory problem. Neither Dr. Sutherland nor any of the other doctors, including Greys physician Dr. William Howell, could properly diagnose it, and Bowie was removed to a stretcher located in officer's quarters along the south wall in the Low Barracks.

In his last act as joint-commander of the defenders, Bowie relinquished his authority and instructed the Greys and other volunteers to follow the command of Travis. With this act, all the remaining Greys in Texas were now under the command of leaders they had neither elected nor wanted: Fannin at Goliad and Travis at the Alamo.

Outside the Alamo walls, the Greys watched as the Mexican artillery began to creep forward. The warm, cloudy morning found them busy digging a new earthwork on the riverbank about 400 yards away. Still out of rifle range . . . but they were closer than the night before.[3]

That evening, in addition to the cannon bombardment, the Mexicans began intermittent bugling—keeping the Greys on edge since they never knew if the trumpets were signaling an attack. The evening of the twenty-fourth would be the second of what would become many sleepless nights for the Greys.

With only 150 defenders attempting to patrol the perimeter of a three-acre compound, manpower was stretched pitifully thin. Jameson had constructed earthworks for much of the artillery, and some footpaths existed along the walls, but much of the perimeter defense was located atop buildings, and the Greys, with the other Texan volunteers, were stationed around these vulnerable positions.

Even where sentries could be relieved, those who attempted to rest could not sleep due to the cannon bombardment and bugle calls. Eventually, the defenders would have to resort to one of the most dangerous military practices in time of war: sleeping at their posts while maintaining a solitary watch.

The morning of the twenty-fifth dawned with overcast skies and light drizzle. Again, the Mexicans had spent the night trenching ever closer to the walls of the compound—this time from the south just across the river toward an area known as "La Villita."

La Villita had long been a disreputable area near the Alamo where the soldiers previously garrisoned there—Spanish, Mexican, and Texan—had visited for various vices. Located close to the Alamo compound wall, the shacks of La Villita were now the objects of a Mexican advance. Occupation of the huts would give Santa Anna's army a close and protected position from which to attack the Texans.

Travis responded with intense cannon fire from the Alamo chapel ramp, the lunette outside the main entrance of the compound, and the two-gun dirt redoubt in the yard. Under fire, the Texans sent out three volunteers to burn the huts and eliminate the cover outside the walls. One of those dispatched on this extremely dangerous mission was Charles Despallier, brother of furloughed New Orleans Grey Blaz Philipe Despallier. The Mexicans had claimed La Villita, but the Texans succeeded in destroying the cover. Santa Anna's soldiers ended up retreating and abandoning their hard-won position.

The rainy morning weather cleared up, and the temperature warmed in the afternoon. That evening a "blue norther" blew in, and temperatures plummeted to near freezing. Under the cover of darkness, Santa Anna spent the night strengthening the circle around the compound. The defenders were not completely trapped inside now, but it was becoming more and more difficult for couriers to enter and leave the compound.

February 26 was another cold and overcast day. Work continued fortifying the defenses in what had become a round-the-clock assignment now, but the Texan artillery fell silent. To conserve powder, Travis depended upon the riflemen—including the Greys—to hold the Mexicans at bay. Artillery, especially the huge eighteen-pounder, was quickly exhausting the Texan stock of powder.

Cold, damp weather was not the only misery the Greys and others were suffering now. Food consisted of corn and unsalted beef. There was no coffee available so no stimulant with which to fight fatigue. And for the Greys, being riflemen, the days were filled with constant sharpshooting and the nights with restless attempts at sleep knowing that in the darkness outside, the Mexicans were always creeping closer.

Saturday the twenty-seventh found no respite from the near-freezing weather. Mexican soldiers were observed attempting to dam off the Alamo compound supply of irrigation water, so Jameson detailed a squad to dig in the courtyard well. The men hit water, but they also undermined an earth and timber parapet by the low barracks. The mound collapsed, leaving no way to fire safely over the wall.[4] That night, Travis sent one last appeal to Fannin at Goliad. The messenger, James Butler Bonham, successfully slipped through the Mexican sentries. With this message, it was felt that the Greys to the south would be arriving soon to help out.

The twenty-eighth brought continued rain, but the extreme cold temperatures seemed to be breaking. February 29 (1836 being a leap year) did result in warmer temperatures. Unknown to the Greys and other defenders, relief was finally on its way to the Alamo. Only it wasn't from Fannin.

Around 3:00 A.M. one of the sentries detected movement outside the perimeter and opened fire. The other volunteers, rushing to the wall, heard voices speaking English, and the gates were swung open. Thirty-two men rode in. In the dim lights of the torches, the Greys peered in the darkness at the new volunteers. There were no New Orleans Greys among the newcomers.

The Gonzales Ranging Company of Mounted Volunteers must have brought hope into the compound that March 1 morning; however, for the Greys inside the Alamo, it must have also been a shallow and disappointing development. It was a disappointment that would carry over into the next day. Where were their fellow Greys?

Nevertheless, the success of the Gonzales volunteers in "breaking" into the Alamo demonstrated that relief was, at least, possible.

From the time Bonham left for Goliad on February 27, the men in the Alamo began counting the days. He should get there early on the twenty-ninth . . . Fannin's force would start that morning . . . they were bound to arrive before dawn on March 2 . . . at the very latest March 3.[5]

But March 2 arrived and passed with no word from Bohnam or Fannin. Unknown to the Greys inside the Alamo, the politicians at Washington-on-the-Brazos declared independence from Mexico that day. It would probably have been an empty declaration to those New Orleans Greys as they maintained constant vigil over the walls against nearly 2,000 Mexican soldiers.

The Mexican breastworks grew ever closer on the third, and the Greys watched as General Antonio Gaona arrived with his forces and artillery. The Mexican army in Bexar now numbered about 2,400 men and supported heavier field artillery pieces—at least two nine-pounders.

Then the Greys noticed something else: A second blood-red flag had been hoisted—this time at Power House Hill. They would not know until early afternoon that it was raised to symbolize the Mexican victory at San Patricio. They would only learn that when James Bonham arrived with news from Goliad.

The Greys from Goliad were not coming.

The news must have been devastating to Blazeby, Baugh, and the others inside the Alamo compound. Bonham must certainly have given them the reasons Fannin had aborted his mission: the wagon problems crossing the river, concern for the settlers in the outlying colonies, troops and supplies supposedly coming in at Lavaca. . . .

Maybe Bohnam even told them about Fannin's refusal to supply the Greys who wanted to relieve the Alamo defenders. But the reasons rang hollow. They were now surrounded and abandoned.

March 4 dawned to reveal Mexican artillery approaching what had previously been no-man's land—a range of about 200 yards where the Texan rifles could accurately pick off the Mexican artillerymen.

The men were becoming more completely trapped. With the new battery to the north, the Mexican ring seemed tighter than ever. The two long nine-pounders just across the river continued to pound the west wall, while howitzers made life especially miserable by lobbing bombs into the innermost areas. Enemy entrenchments were now on all sides. To use Travis' own estimates: "in Bexar, four hundred yards west; in La Villita, three hundred yards south; on the ditch, eight hundred yards northeast, and at the old mill, eight hundred yards north."[6]

The closer the artillery moved, the more devastating the impact of the rounds smashing into the walls. The north wall, in particular, was requiring 24-hour maintenance and reshoring. And the bombardment continued throughout the night.

Sunrise on March 5 revealed a clear, warm morning. But the Mexican artillery attacking the north wall had moved within 200 yards, and each round was landing with terrible impact.

This continued throughout the day and mysteriously began to slack off as the afternoon progressed. Around 5:00 P.M.—with a little more than an hour of daylight left—the shelling stopped. The immediate silence was eerie, and for a while the Greys simply froze in their defensive positions waiting for the attack to resume.

The Greys and other volunteers slowly began to emerge and wandered around the pockmarked courtyard surveying the condition of their fort. It was during this period, according to legend, that Travis called them together in front of the chapel. Whether or not he drew a line in the dirt with his sword will probably always remain subject to conjecture, but almost certainly he used the break in the fighting to question if any man wanted to leave. At least one did, but no New Orleans Grey chose to abandon his post that afternoon.

The silence continued into the night. No doubt Travis suspected that the Mexicans were trying to lull the defenders into a sound, deep sleep after nearly two weeks of constant cannonading. But nothing he could have said or done would have prevented sleep from coming to the men posted along the walls. Physically exhausted himself, he retired to his quarters but only after assigning his adjutant, New Orleans Grey John Baugh, as commander of the watch that evening. In turn, Baugh posted several sentries outside the walls to serve as an early warning system should any activity take place during the night.

Shortly after midnight and the beginning of March 6, the Mexican camps began preparing their weapons and issuing tools—ladders, crowbars, ropes. Between 5:00 and 5:30 A.M. the soldiers silently moved out toward the compound walls from all four directions.

John Baugh continued to walk the catwalks along the perimeter and listen to the darkness. He, like the others, had grown accustomed to the false alarms sounded by the buglers, but this morning all was quiet. Earlier in the evening he had picked up sounds from Bexar—metallic clanging, scraping noises—but such sounds were typical of an encamped army.

Meanwhile the approaching armies overtook the napping Texan sentries and silently killed them. John Baugh heard nothing until, from nowhere, the cry of "Viva Santa Anna" rang out followed by hundreds of shouts and then a cadre of bugle calls. Peering into the very earliest of the morning light, he couldn't believe what he thought he was seeing.

Sounding the alarm, Bough brought many of the defenders out of their sleep immediately, but others, in their fatigue-induced slumber, awoke slowly and were confused. One of the first to his post was Travis, and the colonel was also one of the first—perhaps the very first—Texan to die in defense of the Alamo. With his death at the onset, the adjutant—New Orleans Grey John Bough—became the acting commandant. Little matter, events were beyond the ability of any one man to control by now.

The Texan artillery fire was initially devastating to the Mexicans. Round after round of shrapnel was fired almost point-blank into the attackers. After that, grapeshot and then ball ammunition followed. Somewhere along the perimeter, New Orleans Greys Henry David Hersey and Thomas Waters performed the drill on the cannon that they had practiced so many times before. Other Greys, unknown and unnamed, almost certainly were helping man the understaffed cannon.

Around the perimeter, except for the Alamo chapel palisade manned by Crockett and his men, the New Orleans Greys were firing at the oncoming Mexicans.

The Mexican attack stalled, and three of the armies fell back while the other battalion attempted to take refuge in the burned out *jacales* of La Villita. After a brief hesitation the attack resumed with the majority of the soldiers now concentrating on the weakened north wall, and the southwest force charged the position of the giant eighteen-pounder.

The first breech of the perimeter probably occurred on the west wall through barricaded openings, followed by a massive surge of soldiers over several points on the vulnerable north wall. Those soldiers, in turn, opened the postern, and the army of Santa Anna then had almost unrestricted access to the Alamo compound.

That access, however, was not without cost. Once the courtyard began filling up with Mexicans, the Texan cannoneers, through rote drill, turned their guns inward and continued loading and firing shrapnel, metal hinges, rocks, chopped-up horseshoes—anything that could kill.

But, as they finally did fall back and abandon their pieces, they failed to perform the universal artilleryman's retreat tactic: They did not spike their guns. Assuming control of the unspiked cannon, the Mexicans pushed them into the center of the courtyard and began blasting the barracks where many of the Texans were taking refuge. Particularly deadly was the eighteen-pounder—the massive piece so carefully shipped from New Orleans, salvaged from Matagorda Bay, and manhandled from Copano to Bexar.

While some of the defenders on the rooftops continued to fight until overwhelmed, most of the carnage took place along the Long Barracks. On the south wall, in the Low Barracks, the defenders there—including Bowie—were systematically killed. The last defenders to fall were probably the cannoneers positioned on the dirt ramp at the rear of the Alamo chapel.

Halfway down the eastern wall of the compound, atop the Long Barracks, the blue flag of the New Orleans Greys fluttered in the early morning light. The Jiminez Battalion, which had entered the compound from the south, attempted first to reach the flag. Three times battalion sergeants scaled the building only to be dropped by Texan rifle fire. Finally, Lieutenant José Maria Torres of the Zapadores Battalion succeeded in reaching the rooftop and pulling the flag down. Then he, too, was killed by Texan bullets.[7] But the azure, silken flag of "The First Company of TEXAN Volunteers from New-Orleans" had fallen.

After a thirteen-day siege, the Battle of the Alamo had concluded in approximately one hour. There were no Texan military survivors. All of the New Orleans Greys inside the compound died that morning. Less than five months had passed since they had—full of youth, bravado, and probably more than a little liquor—stepped up in Bank's Arcade and signed their names. Now only their names belonged to Texas.

---

1   Lon Tinkle, *The Alamo: 13 Days to Glory* (McGraw-Hill: New York, 1958), pg. 39.

2   Hardin, *Texian Illiad*, pg. 129.

3   Walter Lord, *A Time to Stand*, pg. 106.

4   *Ibid.*, pg. 116.

5   *Ibid.*, pg. 133.

6   *Ibid.*, pg. 144.

7   *Ibid.*, pg. 163.

Chapter 9

Battle of Coleto

Plains of Coleto, March 20, 1835: George Voss had moved from the cluster of New Orleans Greys along the right front perimeter and was slowly working his way through the Alabama Red Rovers toward the wagon Fannin was using as a command post. Fannin himself was now outside the battle formation, assisted because of his own wounds, trying to negotiate a surrender. Voss secretly hoped the fickle Fannin would drive that Prussian imposter Holzinger crazy with his pompous manners and indecisive nature.

This was Fannin's second trip out to negotiate this morning. Voss and the rest of the Greys knew what was developing: Fannin would negotiate a surrender and the Texans would, against their wills, become prisoners of the Mexicans. All night, during the lull in the fighting, they had talked among themselves and had almost unanimously chosen to fight their way out during the darkness.

He'd concede one thing to Fannin: the Georgia dandy could talk like a politician. It was probably the only thing about the Texan colonel that Voss could admire. And that was because it was a trait they both shared.

Despite his thick German accent, Voss spoke English fluently and, since being assigned to Goliad, had picked up enough Spanish to make himself understood around the local Mexicans living near the fort. He figured that after Fannin was finished this morning, speaking Spanish might be a real asset in his own future.

By now he had worked his way back to the command wagon, and he gently stepped among the wounded lying around the cart and climbed up onto the wagon so he could watch the parley. Around him, the Texans formed a square—actually it had now disintegrated into a rough circle—and most were standing or kneeling with their weapons primed and staring toward the negotiators.

The Greys had been nearly unanimous in choosing to fight on rather than surrender. Even Fannin's eloquent speech had failed to persuade them until he hit upon the one thing they were not prepared to do: leave their wounded behind at the mercy of the Mexicans. In the end the Greys, in concert with the Red Rovers, had to choose between fighting their way out in the darkness while leaving their fallen comrades or remaining in their miserable defensive position and sharing the fate of the wounded—whether it be a fight to the finish or surrender.

From atop the wagon, Voss could see the negotiators, and he concentrated on watching Holzinger. "Juan José" he called himself. Voss smiled as he mentally repeated the name. The fool seemed to forget he was a German, not a Mexican. Voss, being a northerner from Hamburg, wondered if he would have trouble understanding Holzinger's southern Mainz dialect. Probably not, he was good at languages. And in a few minutes he was going to be good at medicine, too.

Voss had been on a raiding party earlier at one of the Mexican ranches when they were looking for horses. In the early morning hours, they'd caught a Mexican local on the trail, and Duval's men had beaten him until he admitted being a spy. He had also talked a great deal about the German who was traveling with Urrea as an engineer and artillery colonel.

Rumor among the Mexicans had it that Holzinger was really chosen by Santa Anna, not Urrea, to be the artillery commander. Supposedly, Holzinger had been a mining engineer when Santa Anna had contracted him to build one of his mansions and then commissioned him into the Mexican army as an engineer. From engineering, he moved to artillery and had risen to the upper ranks that included several other European officers.

Voss, who had manned a few cannon himself, wondered what kind of artilleryman the German was. So far this morning he had only ordered two rounds fired over the breastworks into the Texan camp, and that had been enough for Fannin. In truth, it had been enough for Voss, too. And, although he'd never admit it to the Greys, surrender sounded much better than continuing to fight this obviously lost cause on the prairie.

He knew that a lot of the Greys didn't trust him personally. It all went back to that period when he had been with Morris' group and had been captured outside Bexar. The Mexicans were going to kill him that night, but Cos had given him reprieve. He'd learned during that captivity that the Mexican army was short of virtually every type craftsman and that they protected prisoners who had skills they needed. And he learned something else about being a Mexican prisoner: It wasn't all that bad.

Pulling his eyes from the cluster of negotiators, he looked back over his shoulder at the Texans wounded on the ground behind him. Many were feverish and begging for water. Others had lost a great deal of blood. Voss estimated that over seventy men were lying there, although many of them were not mortally wounded. He saw the kindly doctor from Alabama, Jack Shackleford, doing what little he could without water to clean and dress the worst of the wounds. Nearby, Dr. Barnard was similarly attending the worst injuries. Below him, next to the wagon, Dr. Fields was attempting to sterilize something over a small smoldering fire.

From the wounded, he looked up at the perimeter and at the Greys standing there in small groups talking among themselves as they speculated on the negotiations. Voss didn't share their intense dislike—almost hatred—of Fannin. He saw

Fannin as a fool, while they saw him as a traitor. He was more than a little concerned that if Fannin surrendered unconditionally, the Greys might revolt and involve everybody in a massacre. He watched the other Germans closely. Eigenauer was dead, but Mattern, Courtman, and Ehrenberg were huddled together whispering among themselves. They, too, had been distant towards him since his captivity at Bexar earlier.

"To hell with them," he thought to himself, "especially that *wunderkind* Ehrenberg, who had gone to sleep on guard duty and let Urrea surround all of them." Not a lot had been said yesterday about it, only Dr. Barnard had been vocal, but everybody knew that the rear guard had betrayed them. Ehrenberg had been one of them, but he probably saved himself with the Greys by being the only member of the rear guard not to run off like the cowards they were. Saved himself to become a Mexican prisoner, just like Voss himself had been at Bexar.

Voss looked up over the Greys and other Texans and scanned the prairie grass outside their perimeter. During the negotiations, the Mexicans were taking advantage of the cease-fire to retrieve their wounded. He couldn't make a head count, but it was obvious they had a lot of casualties—far more than the Texans. And Voss knew from his talks with the soldiers as a prisoner at Bexar that the Mexican army was chronically short of medical staff.

Suddenly his thoughts were interrupted by a shout from one of the Texans on the backside of the circle. He was pointing at Fannin and yelling that the talks had broken up. The Texan negotiators made their way back to the formation, slowed by the fact Fannin required help walking because of his wounds. Voss had to also admire Fannin's courage—all the Greys had been impressed with their leader once the fighting had begun. The man might be a fool, but he was no coward.

As the Texan negotiators reached the perimeter of their formation, the Greys stepped aside making an opening for Fannin and his assistants to enter. He was helped over to the wagon where Voss was perched and assisted as he sat on a wooden water cask—one of several they had emptied yesterday to lighten their load as they had marched. Fannin whispered something to one of his officers and the man yelled out, "Your attention, men, we have agreed to surrender our arms, and General Urrea has agreed to treat us as prisoners of war, attend our wounded, and arrange our parole back to the United States."

The formation by this time had collapsed in around the wagon. There was an immediate murmur of voices, and Voss detected several loud protests. "Quiet, men!" the officer continued. "Stack your arms in piles and form two lines. Gentlemen, we're going home!"

This time, the mob erupted into loud protest, but Voss noticed that around the fringe of the group, several men were starting to stack their rifles and line up where the perimeter had been the day before. Slowly, all the men did the same, but the Greys were the last to comply, and several made obscene gestures at Fannin and his contingent and yelled insults. Quietly, very quietly, Johann George Andreas Voss slipped off the wagon and crept over among the wounded to a soldier stretched out near Dr. Shackleford. Kneeling beside the man, "Doctor" Voss began unwinding his field dressing and pretending to change it.

ψψψψψψ

*T*he morning of March 19 dawned with heavy fog completely hiding the San Antonio River and extending up the fifty-foot slope to the north wall of the presidio.

Much of the previous night had been spent blasting the walls with the remaining unspiked cannon. Anything wooden was set afire and foodstuffs to be denied the Mexicans were stacked against the rear of the chapel and also burned. The thick stone walls and bastions of the presidio were destroyed by cannon fire. Amazingly, in the confusion, nobody thought to pack any food for the evacuating army.

Supplies that were packed were overloaded in the carts that Horton's men had brought, and the hungry and unruly oxen were harnessed to them. Fannin finally decided to take nine pieces of brass field artillery and these, too, were hitched to oxen.

Considering the urgency that Houston had conveyed in his letter to Fannin and the fact that the Texans knew local spies were reporting their every move to Urrea, it is amazing that the Greys and other volunteers took the time that morning to cook and eat breakfast. Cooking, packing supplies, and spiking cannon took up so much of the morning that by the time they actually did depart, much of the element of surprise and the cover of fog had disappeared. Sometime in mid-morning, the Greys and other volunteers exited through the sally port on the south wall and headed below the fort to the fording point on the river.

The Alabama Red Rovers were leading the column with the Kentucky Mustangs serving as rear guard and the New Orleans Greys interspersed in the middle of the approximately 250 soldiers leaving Goliad that morning. Scouting ahead for the army were Horton's mounted men.

As the day—and the journey—progressed, reports would differ considerably concerning distances and time frames, but virtually every report describes problems immediately outside the fort as the army crossed the lower ford of the San Antonio River. Shackelford reported that the Red Rovers had to help pull the cannon up the bank once they had crossed the river.

Ehrenberg later wrote that the Texans almost immediately began discarding supplies, then the carts themselves, in an effort to hurry up the pace of the march, but Shackelford claimed that this part of the evacuation "moved briskly and in good order for about six miles." Part of the disparity may have been due to the fact that Shackelford and the Red Rovers were at the front of the Texan column, while Ehrenberg and several others were serving as "rear guard"—posted behind even Duval's Mustangs.

As such, Shackelford might not have been aware of the problems behind his unit, while Ehrenberg, bringing up the very end of the column, would have been witness to discarded and broken equipment.

After eight or nine miles, the fatigued oxen were becoming increasingly unruly and difficult to handle, so Fannin made the decision to stop and rest the animals. Against the vehement advice of his officers, including Shackelford and Duval, Fannin chose not to continue on to the nearby timber along Coleto Creek—a distance of less than four miles.

For about an hour, the army and the oxen rested while Horton's scouts reported no signs of the Mexicans. As the column started up again, yet another cart broke, and the army had to wait while the supplies were loaded to a different cart. During this time, Fannin dispatched a four-man guard to watch for Urrea's soldiers. One of those men was New Orleans Grey Herman Ehrenberg.

Once the army had started moving again—reports vary from two to four miles—the Texans began noticing troubling signs initially from the west, then from two other directions.

Captain Shackelford, with the Red Rovers who were leading the column, recorded later that the first Mexican cavalry were observed about two miles to the west. Dr. Barnard later wrote that two companies of cavalry and one infantry company were seen advancing in the rear of their column. Duval would later recall that two mounted Mexicans had been observed to the right in the timber, on the eastern flank, during the rest break but that after resuming their march, the Texans saw a line of cavalry on the left.

So the Texans, from various points within the column, observed Mexican soldiers from every side except the area into which they were marching. Goliad was a known center for local sympathizers with the Mexican Centralists, so it would have been expected that some spies would be shadowing the army. If these reports were accurate, however, it would appear that General Urrea had the Greys and other volunteers nearly surrounded by the time the Mexicans were detected.

How—and why—Fannin, the Greys, and other volunteers were taken by surprise by a Mexican military force at least three companies in size without being detected by Ehrenberg's rear-guard party remains a mystery.

Ehrenberg wrote years later in Germany that the four-man unit had been trailing Fannin and the volunteers from a distance of approximately two miles while watching for enemy activity on the left and had noticed a single rider. According to the Grey, the guard party had stopped to again graze their horses when they noticed "a long black streak."[1]

Ironically, Duval would later also write that, from within the main column, the Mexicans first appeared as a "long dark line on the left."[2] Upon detection of the Mexican cavalry, the Texans positioned a six-pounder and fired three shots.

According to Ehrenberg, his party immediately mounted and started racing toward their comrades after the "dark streak" was determined to be quickly advancing Mexican soldiers. He does not mention the three rounds fired by the main column.

Eight days later Barnard accused the rear guard of sleeping as the Mexicans caught up with and surrounded the Texans. "It appears that four horsemen had been left in the rear and that they, instead of keeping a lookout, had, under a false sense of security, laid down, and were only aroused by the close approach of the Mexicans."[3] Or perhaps aroused by the firing of the cannon.

Ehrenberg and his three fellow guards raced to cover the approximately two miles distance between themselves and the main army. By the time they reached the Greys and Fannin's other soldiers, the Mexicans were starting to close in on the column, and according to Barnard:

> They [the rear guards] now came up at full speed, one of them, and one only (a German by the name of Ehrenburg) joined us. The other three, in the greatest apparent terror, passed about a hundred yards on our right, without even stopping to look at us, and under the strongest appliance of whip and spur, followed by a few hearty curses from our men.[4]

Ehrenberg deserves credit for at least rejoining his fellow Greys when the three other members of this party rode off towards Victoria and personal safety. Less than twenty years old, Ehrenberg was the youngest member of the Greys and possibly the youngest of Fannin's command. Still, he was a soldier and an experienced veteran of the battle for Bexar. It would have been expected that he resume his post with the main army.

His reunion with the Greys on that grassy plain near Coleto Creek that afternoon, however, was a prelude to the appearance of even more Mexican troops.

At the sound of the six-pounder, Horton's scouts returned to the main force only to be driven off by the overwhelming numbers of Urrea's cavalry. Almost immediately after detection, Urrea's companies had succeeded in surrounding Fannin's group. There was speculation among the Greys and others that Horton's men would ride to Victoria and return with the local militia there—erroneously thought by some to be as large as six hundred men.

After the initial detection, Fannin ordered his column forward at a normal pace until the Mexicans surrounded them and opened fire with small arms. By then all chance of reaching the banks of Coleto Creek with its protective trees and crucial water source was lost to the Greys.

Instead, they found themselves trapped with the other Texans in a recessed plain nearly four miles from any water and with Mexican cavalry and infantry completely surrounding them from positions elevated six or seven feet above their formation. It was, in terms of military strategy, one of the worst positions from which to make a stand against an enemy superior in numbers and supplies.

What Fannin could not have known prior to this situation was that Urrea had been reinforced by Morales' Battalion of Alamo veterans and that the combined force now numbered nearly one thousand men.

Another critical miscalculation on the Texas leader's part was the stop for rest prior to observing the first Mexican soldiers. Despite the folly of the morning departure from La Bahia, he had somehow caught Urrea's spies and advance scouts by surprise. They had observed neither the fording of the San Antonio River nor the rising clouds of smoke from the burning buildings, provisions, and equipment. It was not until Fannin was at least an hour on his way that the scouts reported the fort to be empty and the Texans gone.[5]

Fannin, who never missed an opportunity to point out his West Point background, should have learned in his abbreviated coursework there that his choice and time of stopping was tactically unsound. Even worse, he should have at least counseled with his senior officers, like Shackleford, who were adamantly opposed to halting. With the equipment failures and unruly oxen, he should have known to drive to the nearest protective cover before stopping his army.

Had he not stopped for the hour, or perhaps as long as two hours, it is probable that the army would have reached Coleto Creek before Urrea's pursuing army could have caught up with them. Even with the late start from the fort, he had an hour's start on the Mexicans plus whatever time he spent grazing the oxen.

With regards to his posting of scouts and guards of his own, Fannin appears to have done what was possible given his limited means. Horton's mounted volunteers were the closest thing to cavalry forces the Texans had that day, and Fannin wisely posted them between the army and their objective of Victoria.

Horton's men also correctly surmised that if confronted by Mexican cavalry, they would be outnumbered and outmaneuvered, so they remained in a group, which limited their ability to scout the countryside in any considerable range. This also resulted in their being separated from Fannin's main force until too late to rejoin them.

Fannin should never have left the presidio that morning without first posting a guard unit to protect his rear. With the countryside controlled by Mexican sentries, Horton had been unable to adequately scout around the fort; Fannin, therefore, had no idea where Urrea was or what kind of army he was leading.

It has been suggested that Fannin simply underestimated the will and ability of the Mexicans to confront and attack him. But Fannin, on the morning of March 19, was also aware that Morris, Johnson, and King had fallen victim to that line of reasoning, and he knew that a large force of Mexican soldiers was shadowing him somewhere close by. Waiting until the rest stop to post a rear-guard that morning was not just a tactical error, it bordered on negligence.

That he posted the rear-guard during the rest break indicates that he was at least aware that Urrea might be in pursuit. But the size of the party was far too small for the task they were given. True, the Texans were chronically short of horses—Grant and Johnson had been on corralling missions when surprised by the Mexicans—and that may have played into his decision to only post Ehrenberg and three others.

But with nearly 300 troops including the battle-experienced Greys, he should have chosen a better detail than a teenage boy and three of his friends. And more importantly, they should have been given specific posted orders while they were in the field.

Whether Ehrenberg was correct in suggesting they were merely grazing their horses or Barnard in charging that they had stopped and gone to sleep, the rear guard was disastrously derelict in protecting the rear flank of the army. Fannin should clearly have ordered them to keep moving, keep scanning the timberlines to the east and west, and to relay messages to him in tandem regarding the sighting or lack of observance of Mexicans.

Had Ehrenberg or any of the other three rear guards been scouting the ridgelines and reported the first sight of Mexican spies or soldiers, Fannin and the rest of the Texans might well have had time to traverse the three or four miles to Coleto Creek.

Still, later reports suggest that even after the main column observed Mexican soldiers, they continued to march at a normal—even leisurely—pace without apparent concern or alarm.

Thermopylae may have had her messenger of defeat and the Alamo none,[6] but the New Orleans Greys and other Texans at Coleto that morning would later have survivors to recount their story, and although the versions often differed radically, each messenger after the battle suggests Fannin intentionally stopped where he did against the advice of his officers and men.

And now they were surrounded and outnumbered three to one. Given the field positions of Fannin and Urrea's troops, the Battle of Coleto would probably have ended before the smoke from the first rounds had cleared except for one factor: Urrea had no artillery. Once he had confirmed that Fannin and the Texans had left the presidio, Urrea ordered Colonel Garay to send the Mexican artillery and extra ammunition on after his pursuit group, then to move in and take Presidio la Bahia over.[7]

By the time Fannin had formed his soldiers into a square that afternoon, Urrea had surrounded him with cavalry and infantry, but his artillery pieces had yet to catch up with him. They would not arrive until later that night.

This lack of Mexican artillery gave the Texans the one advantage they could utilize in this situation: superior firepower. The nine pieces of artillery were manned by the Polish artillerymen under the command of Francis Petrusseweiz, but others in the army including many of the Greys were familiar with the pieces and the firing drill. The Greys, after all, had been apprentice artillerymen during the siege of Bexar as they dueled with Deaf Smith in cannonading the north wall of the Alamo compound and the chapel front.

The formation was textbook for the situation: three ranks deep behind what little barricade could be hastily thrown up—mostly supply carts and equipment. The Greys were generally posted in two areas: Pettus' Greys formed the front line with the Alabama Red Rovers, and the Mobile Greys were stationed on the right flank. Westover's troops formed the left flank while Duval's Mustangs and Frazer's Refugio militia deployed to the rear of the square. The artillery was positioned on each corner with a disabled cart placed in the center and used as a hospital center.

The Greys were well armed in the front line—ammunition and weapons had been much of the problem on the overloaded carts. Each man received three or four muskets. Bayonets, rifles, more than forty pairs of pistols, and abundant ammunition complimented this arsenal.[8] The artillery pieces were positioned on the four corners of the formation.

No sooner had the Greys managed to form their lines when Urrea immediately attacked. Rifle companies advanced to the front and on the left, while cavalry attacked on the rear flank. Urrea's grenadiers directed their assault on the right side of the square directly opposite the Greys assigned to the Mobile unit. The remaining Greys were scattered around the perimeter except for the extreme right of the outside line that was manned by the Alabama Red Rovers.

The fighting began in early afternoon and lasted until dark, which at that time of year would have been around 6:15 P.M.

Fannin was fielding an army that afternoon that was, except for the New Orleans Greys, basically untested in combat. There had been some skirmishing around the area of Goliad, and a few of the volunteers who had been with Johnson and Grant had escaped fighting to return to La Bahia, but only the Greys were truly battle-tested on the Coleto plains that day.

The Greys' baptism of fire had been in San Antonio de Bexar three months earlier, and that campaign had stalled and become room-to-room fighting for which the Greys, with superior physical size and weapons, had been at an advantage so long as they had protective cover from which to launch their assaults.

On the plains of Coleto that afternoon on March 19, however, the Greys had no such cover, and their superior weapons and firepower were negated by the poor field position from which they were defending themselves. Here, there were no heavy adobe *tufa* buildings in which to take refuge nor protective entrenchment for communication or water supply. The few supply carts positioned as barricades afforded little protection in this open, depressed plain.

The Greys during the days of garrisoning at La Bahia despised and even defied Fannin as a commander. On this afternoon, however, they followed his commands, and when the day's fighting was over even the cynical Ehrenberg praised his courage.[9]

As the Mexicans advanced on the square formation, Fannin issued orders from his command post on the right flank.

For perhaps the first time in his command since arriving in Texas at Copano, James Walker Fannin was decisive in his issuing of orders: No Texan was to fire until he made the command, and the first Texan volley would be at point blank range.

This meant that the outer line—where almost all the Greys were assigned—would take the brunt of any incoming fire until Fannin decided to respond. In an unflinching defense that probably would have collapsed if manned by other, more inexperienced soldiers, the Greys held fast that afternoon.

From about a quarter mile, the Mexican cavalry dismounted and opened fire on the Texans. But at that range, little damage was done. It would later be reported that many of the Texans were hit and bruised but not wounded by Mexican shot that day.

The Mexicans continued to advance from all sides, and the second round of fire also flew over the heads of the Greys but close enough this time that Fannin ordered them to sit down in the grass but continue to hold their fire.

Still the Mexicans continued to advance, and the third round wounded several of the Texans, and one shot destroyed the rifle Fannin was holding. At about one hundred yards, the Mexicans stopped to reload their weapons, and Fannin issued the command to fire.

Almost simultaneously, the Greys opened fire as the supporting artillery also discharged shot and canister with what Ehrenberg would later call "frightening effect."[10]

Despite the heavy Mexican losses, Urrea's infantry now charged the square with fixed bayonets as the cavalry charged with lances. Again, the canister from the Texan cannon pulverized the oncoming Mexicans, and many of Urrea's riflemen dropped into the tall grasses to begin sharpshooting into the square: the primary targets being the Texan artillerymen and draft animals.

This was the kind of warfare for which the American frontiersman was best suited. Although devoid of established breastworks, the Texans were able to rotate their muskets and maintain a steady field of fire, while others were able to single out and kill the Mexican sharpshooters. To the rear of the formation, the Mexican cavalry lancers suffered the same fate as their infantry comrades. Canister and heavy rifle fire thinned their ranks volley after volley. After the initial charge, most of the cavalrymen dismounted and stayed close to the ground for the rest of the afternoon.

The initial Mexican assault had been repulsed.

For about a half-hour, Urrea regrouped his companies. Despite overwhelming numbers, the Mexicans had suffered horrendous casualties. For the Mexican veterans of the Alamo assault, there must have been flashbacks of the initial carnage during the first assault there.

When the Mexicans did charge the square again, the killing began once more. By one later report,

> Their front ranks were so suddenly swept
> off as almost to form a breastwork sufficient in
> itself to shield our friends from their assaults.
> The scene was now dreadful to behold; killed
> and maimed men and horses were strewn over
> the plain, the wounded were rending the air
> with their distressing moans, while a great
> number of horses without riders were rushing
> to and from back upon the enemy's lines,
> increasing the confusion among them: they thus
> became so entangled, the one with the other,
> that their retreat resembled the headlong flight
> of a herd of buffaloes, rather than the retreat of
> a well-drilled regular army as they were. . . .[11]

Ehrenberg also later described a terrible battlefield scene during this stage of the fighting:

Herds of horses were running about without riders, while others were wallowing in blood and kicking about furiously...the countless bugles of the Mexicans from all directions sounded for the attack. The cavalry itself rapidly advanced from all sides at once, not in closed ranks but in broken formation and with yelling and constant firing....

...We were soon enveloped in such dense smoke that we were occasionally obliged to cease firing and to advance slightly on the enemy in order to see our sights. The whole prairie as far as one could see was covered with powder-smoke, and thousands of lightning flashes quivered through the dark masses accompanied with the incessant thunder of the artillery and the clear crack of our rifles. Among them sounded the scattered bugle calls of the Mexicans, encouraging the men to battle. From time to time our grapeshot hailed death into the ranks of the enemy under the majestic roll of thunder....

...Many of our people were either severely wounded or killed. All of our artillerymen with the exception of one Pole had fallen and formed a wall around the now silent cannon, which were no longer effective as the range was now too close.

The whole battleground was covered with dead men, horses, guns, and all kinds of objects....[12]

This assault-and-retreat fighting continued throughout the afternoon until nearly dusk, when the Mexicans withdrew and sent forth Campeachy Indians to snipe against the Texans from the tall prairie grass. In the last hour before darkness they were able to inflict about fifty casualties among the Greys and other Texans despite sporadic cannon fire spreading canister in the grass.

From the beginning of the fighting, the artillerymen and oxen had been primary targets of the Mexican sharpshooters, and by dusk Petrussewiez and the Polish cannoneers were all dead and the guns were manned by the Greys.[13]

But they found they were plagued by the severe shortage of water, not just to cool the barrels but also to suppress smoldering powder residue between packing charges—one of the most dangerous threats to nineteenth-century artillerymen. Clogged from several hours of firing without proper swabbing, the guns were becoming increasingly dangerous to fire or, in many cases, totally inoperable.

With darkness, the Indian snipers could no longer fire into the Texan formation, since the flash of their rifles gave away their positions and the return fire effectively drove them even further back out of range.

As they retreated, the fighting ended, and the prairie became silent again except for the cries of the wounded and the intermittent Mexican bugle calls designed to keep the Texans on edge throughout the night.

Although, in numbers of casualties, the Texans had inflicted far more damage to the Mexicans, they found that darkness exacerbated the misery of their own wounded since they were denied access to water and could not light fires to nurse the wounded. Campfires would only outline silhouettes for Mexican snipers, and the lack of water was particularly devastating for those who had been wounded by the newly developed and fever-inducing copper musket balls used by the Mexicans.

Among the Anglo Texans wounded that night was James Fannin. Although shot three times during the day's fighting, he continued to assume command and again conferred with his officers. Horton and his mounted men were effectively blocked, they realized, and the remnants of Ward's Georgia

Battalion—although still in the area—were unlikely to rejoin the main force. Ammunition was low, food and water nonexistent, and the cannon inoperable. Mexican snipers had targeted all horses and oxen inside the formation during the day's fighting, so there was no way to evacuate the wounded.

There were strong arguments in the command center that night for those able to slip through the lines and escape toward Victoria and Gonzales to do so. Among those advocating an escape—fighting their way out if necessary—were the Greys. Ehrenberg later indicated that the majority of the Greys "would rather sacrifice a part of their forces for the young Republic than to knowingly leave their whole force to the gruesomeness of the enemy, upon whose honor and humanity we could not rely."[14]

Faced with a growing rebellion within the ranks, and particularly from the Greys present that night, Fannin used the powerful argument against leaving the wounded to the mercy of the Mexicans. It was a particularly poignant argument: Virtually every solider that night had, among the wounded, friends or family.

And so the Greys reluctantly agreed to remain through the night. It was probably the only line of persuasion Fannin could have successfully employed with them. Despite the changes of leadership and division of forces after Bexar, the Greys still identified themselves as a cohesive unit. The previous month had, after all, been spent campaigning to return to San Antonio and relieve those Greys besieged in the Alamo.

Later reports from both sides indicate the night became a chorus of moaning and begging for water by the wounded of both sides. Light drizzle only teased the suffering but did not produce the needed water to bathe wounds or quench thirst, and worse yet, the temperatures dropped, leaving the Greys and other survivors even more miserable.

With the decision made to remain with their wounded comrades, the Greys began fortifying, although with lingering resentment, the perimeter in preparation for the coming morning's renewal of fighting. Dead animals were placed as barricades and Bowie knives were used to scrape shallow trenches in the dirt.

It was during this period of fortification that Ehrenberg stumbled upon a wounded Grey who was calling out in broken German. The fallen soldier was Conrad Eigenauer, one of Breece's men who had come to Texas with Ehrenberg through Nacogdoches.

In a passage of his diary, Ehrenberg recalls hearing the voice in the dark:

> "Friend," it said, "lay this carpet bag under my head for me!"
> I did so and asked in German the name of the unfortunate comrade.
> "I am—a German," was the answer. "Oh," he continued, "I would gladly—gladly—have fought—ten more battles for Texas—but it's over—with my labors—I'm done, my countryman—I am dying—my name—Eigenauer from—Lauterback—friend, if you ever get home again—think of me—my old mother still lives—write—I died—for Texas, write I died—for Texas, write her—my country—all—all"
> He had to be silent; death sat on his tongue. Three bullets had passed through him after he lay bleeding on the ground. I heard his last groan—and I went out—toward the enemy.[15]

Eigenauer, after coming to Texas from New Orleans with Breece, had gone to Goliad as part of Burke's Greys. One early muster roll for Breece's company lists an "_____ Eguior" from Germany as killed in the Alamo, however there is no name remotely similar to that on the final Alamo rolls. A muster roll for Captain David Burke's Mobile Greys lists a Conrad Egenour (Eigenauer) as a former member of Breece's

New Orleans Greys[16] and killed at the battle at Coleto. His name is today engraved at the base of the memorial located at La Bahia in Goliad.

Another Grey seriously wounded that day was Captain Samuel Overton Pettus, leader of the San Antonio Greys. His wounds were so serious that he was unable to walk or be moved without a wagon.

As morning dawned, the Greys and others were able to survey the battlefield. During the night the Mexicans had retrieved some but not all of their own wounded and dead. But more ominously, Urrea had received reinforcements overnight and with them the artillery pieces he had been lacking during the battle the day before. Now, the barricades of dead animals and discarded wagons were nearly useless: The Mexicans could simply lob canister and shot from their elevated positions into the depressed formation of the Texans.

There had been considerable discussion among the Texans about the merits of making a bold charge against the Mexican line and attempting to fight their way out. Again, as had been the case the night before, the question of the wounded prevented any consensus for an escape. There was also some discussion about surrender—but only if such a capitulation could be achieved under honorable terms guaranteeing the Texans treatment as prisoners of war instead of pirates or mercenaries.

Urrea's strategy that morning was to make a display of firepower proving beyond doubt how vulnerable the Texans were. After two or three Mexican rounds had been fired into the Texan formation, Fannin called for a conference with his officers. Unquestionably, the Texans were not in a position to hold out in their current formation, and the wounded could not be evacuated during an escape. The Greys and most of the Red Rovers remained adamantly against surrender, but the majority of Texans favored it if under honorable terms that would assure their parole back to the United States.

Fannin ordered a white flag raised, and immediately three Mexican officers appeared including the German colonel of artillery, Juan Holzinger, who spoke English. The final terms of the surrender document have been historically disputed, but it appears Fannin drafted a copy that guaranteed they would be considered prisoners of war, that their wounded would be given adequate medical care, and that all prisoners would be returned to the United States. These terms appear to be the document that Fannin presented to Holzinger, but Urrea refused to ratify it, insisting instead that the Texans surrender unconditionally.

Conditions existed for confusion about the wording: Discussions were conducted in English, German, and Spanish, and the final documents were written in both Spanish and English. But the final wording appears to be consistent and clear:

> Art. 1st. The Mexican troops having placed their artillery at a distance of one hundred and seventy paces and having opened fire, we raised a white flag at once. Colonel Juan Morales Mariano Salas came in company with Lieutenant Colonel Juan José Holsinger of the Engineers, and we proposed to them to surrender ourselves at descretion, to which they agreed.
>
> Art. 2nd. That the wounded and their commander Fannin should be treated with all consideration possible, since we propose to surrender all our arms.
>
> Art. 3rd. All the detachment shall be treated as prisoners of war and placed at the disposal of the Supreme Government.
>
> Camp on the Coleto between Guadalupe and La Bahia, March 20, 1836
>
> B.C. WALLACE, Major
> J.M. CHADWICK
> J.W. FANNIN, Commander

(Added by Urrea): When the white flag was raised by the enemy, I ordered their leader to be informed that I could have no other agreement than that they should surrender at Discretion, without any other condition, and this was agreed to by the persons stated above; the other petitions, which the subscribers of this surrender make will not be granted. I told them this, and they agreed to it, for I must not, nor can I, grant anything else.[17]

The key phrase in this document can be found in Article 1: "we proposed to them to surrender ourselves *at descretion*, to which they agreed." Fannin may have decided to accept these terms, in part, because Urrea assured him there was no known instance where a prisoner of war who had trusted to the clemency of the Mexican government had lost his life; that he would recommend to General Santa Anna acceptance of the terms proposed by Fannin's men; that he was confident of obtaining Santa Anna's acceptance of the terms proposed by Fannin's men; and that he was confident of obtaining Santa Anna's approval within a period of eight days.[18]

Further bolstering Texan support for signing the document was the fact that Colonel Holzinger was telling the men, "In eight days, home and liberty!"—a statement later recalled by almost every survivor.

Whether Fannin purposely kept this from his men to protect the needs of the wounded, many of whom had been suffering for over twelve hours, or he honestly misunderstood the translation and reported to the men that a capitulation would be *on terms*, including parole, will never be known. But he did not clearly relate the terms to the Greys and others since the survivors, to a man, would later insist that Urrea had reneged on his word.

1   Ornish, *Ehrenberg*, pg. 221.
2   Duval, *Early Times in Texas*, pg. 63.
3   Pruett, *Goliad Massacre*, pg. 79.
4   *Ibid.*
5   *Ibid.*, pg. 78.
6   Quote attributed to General Thomas Jefferson Green in 1841.
7   Pruett, *Goliad Massacre*, pg. 78.
8   Craig H. Roell, "Coleto, Battle of" *New Handbook of Texas.*
9   Ornish, *Ehrenberg*, pg. 221.
10 *Ibid.*, pg. 225.
11 Pruett, *Goliad Massacre*, pg. 82.
12 Ornish, *Ehrenberg*, pp. 222-4.
13 *Ibid.*, pg. 225.
14 Ornish, *Ehrenberg*, pg. 225.
15 *Ibid.*, pp. 227-8.
16 Texas General Land Office Archives, [A2, Section C][list][tran][note][A3; T1 p36-37].
17 Kathryn Stoner O'Connor, *The Presidio La Bahia del Espiritu Santo de Zuniga, 1721 to 1846* (Austin: Von-Boeckmann-Jones Co., 1966), pp. 177-8; and Pruett, *Goliad Massacre*, pp. 89-90.
18 Harbert Davenport, and Craig H. Roell, "Goliad Massacre" *New Handbook of Texas.*

Chapter 10

Surrender and Captivity

Our Lady of Loreto Chapel, Goliad, Texas, March 20, 1835: The slow-moving waters of the San Antonio River looked green in the late afternoon sun as the Greys crossed over at the lower ford. Herman Ehrenberg, like the others, entered the water and crossed against the current toward the other side. Up to his armpits, the water felt cold but wonderful. Cupping his hands, he filled them with the water and drank as he slowly made his way to the south bank.

From the sounds around him, he knew that Peter Mattern was doing the same thing in front of him and George Court-man directly behind him. It had been nearly thirty hours since they'd had anything to drink, and many of the men—suffering from fever—were gulping as much as they could before exiting the other side.

The bank was muddy and slippery from the others in front of him and he stumbled but caught himself and regained his footing. The Mexican lancer nearby growled something at him, and Ehrenberg muttered in German and heard Courtman behind him echo the sentiment.

They had made the eight or nine mile march from the battleground without a break, and now, clothes heavy with water, they were prodded toward the fort.

The refreshing coolness of the water as they entered the river now became chilling coldness as they marched the half-mile up the hill to the presidio. Ehrenberg was aware of heavy smoke in the air and knew it was the still-smoldering *jacales* they had set afire two days earlier before they had departed the fort.

Now as they marched around the east wall of the fort, the whole scene took on an eerie look as the campfires threw orange and yellow flames against the walls at irregular intervals in the semidarkness. Urrea's cavalry had escorted them across the prairie back to the fort, but now as they neared the sally port they marched through two solid lines of bayoneted infantrymen. The methodic pounding of the snare drums added a sense of melancholy and foreboding.

Since the Greys were at the forefront of the long column of Texan prisoners, only about fifteen or twenty men were ahead of Ehrenberg as they reached the arched sally port and were ordered to halt. He could see two cannon positioned at the entrance. Beside each piece was an artillery crew with burning torches at the ready to ignite the canister on a moment's notice. Around the gate itself several large fires illuminated the entrance.

Mexican officers started shouting orders in Spanish, and there was a flurry of activity around the gate before several soldiers started motioning with their bayonets that Ehrenberg and the Greys in front should enter the gate and spread out. Then it became clear: The Mexicans were afraid the Greys had left the fort trapped and were using them as human shields.

Our Lady of Loreto chapel was nestled against the north wall of the fort with the doors of the church facing west. Inside the walled presidio the area in front of the church formed a smaller, square courtyard within the larger parade ground. The Mexican guards signaled for Ehrenberg's group to stop walking and move to one side. The Greys mumbled to each other in low voices but, when overheard by the guards, were ordered to shut up with the threat of a jabbing bayonet.

Then, amid grunting and groaning, the Mexicans hauled two more cannon past them into the inner courtyard and positioned them aiming directly into the doors of the church with crews manning burning torches stationed behind each piece. The air was filled with the putrid smoke from the torches, but Ehrenberg also became aware of another smell—of burning flesh and hair. It was the beef and other food they had stacked against the outside rear wall of the chapel and set afire. As rancid as the smell of burnt flesh and seared hides was, it also reminded him of how hungry he was and how it had been nearly two days since they had eaten.

The other Greys were herded in behind Ehrenberg's group, and the rest of the prisoners marched in through the sally port. Ehrenberg and those in front were stripped of their torches and motioned to pass through the inner courtyard and enter the chapel. The fires from the artillery torches illuminated the entrance, but only a few steps inside the chapel was dark. "At least" he mumbled in German to Mattern and Courtman, "we'll be out of the weather."

"Wonder where they'll put the other units," Mattern answered in full voice now that they had reached the back of the chapel and there were no Mexicans near them.

The chapel was about eighty-five feet long and there were no pews or other furniture. Even the altar at the rear of the church had been removed—probably salvaged for firewood.

Glancing over their shoulders as they reached the back wall, they could see prisoners filing in through the illuminated doors. "How many are they going to put in here?" Courtman asked. By now they were against the wall, and the crowd was beginning to push up against them. The sick and the walking wounded were also pushing in towards the rear of the chapel and trying to lie down on the dirt floor to relieve their pain. The prisoners continued to file in through the entrance of the church even after it had filled up.

Ehrenberg realized it at the same moment as Courtman and Mattern: The Mexicans were going to pack all prisoners— some two hundred fifty men—into the tiny chapel. Finally, after some yelling at the front, the doors slammed shut and the church was enveloped in almost total darkness.

Many had been suffering cramps on the forced march back, and now the water of the San Antonio River was making them nauseous. Others had been suffering diarrhea for days, and the chapel immediately began to stink. The roar of voices slowly began to grow quiet and dissolved into occasional bursts of profanity. Elsewhere in the darkness, voices urged people to move around to accommodate those who by necessity had to lie down.

After a while, somebody in front began beating on the doors and shouting for water and food. The church became filled with voices shouting, complaining, cursing, and threatening those standing guard outside. But the two doors remained closed. In one corner, somebody was advocating they make a mass breakout, but someone else responded that the canister from the two cannon would kill them all. Yet another Grey claimed that if just a few could get outside the church, they could sneak down to the river in the covered trench leading from the water gate. But the cannon blocked the water gate as well, and the church doors remained closed.

Despite the coldness outside, the body heat of the men in the chapel made conditions even more difficult, and the prisoners finally assumed the most comfortable positions and stopped talking in order to expend as little energy as possible. As the heat increased, the stench made breathing difficult. Since Ehrenberg hadn't been wounded in the fighting, he was one of those forced to stand, and now he was trying to sleep as he leaned one shoulder against the wall.

Looking up at the roof, he could make out the dim silhouettes of the three small octagonal windows. If it weren't for them, he thought to himself, they'd all suffocate before morning. After the conversations and cursing had finally stopped, the church was strangely silent for a short period. Then the cries began.

At first, they were pleas for water. Even in the darkness, the voices could be identified as those of the seriously wounded. When the group had been marched back to Goliad, rumors had circulated that the Mexicans were going to execute those left behind. As a result, many with serious wounds had found a way to remain with the main group. Now, feverish, they were suffering the symptoms of infection and begging for water— anything to drink.

Ehrenberg continued to stare up at the windows nearly forty feet above them and tried to ignore the cries. He thought about Eigenauer and wondered if he himself would ever have a chance to tell the German's mother how her son had died on the battlefield. He thought about Captain Pettus, too wounded to return to Goliad even with support from his men. He wondered, too, about John Noland lying in the grassy field.

Then he thought about Voss, the other Grey from Germany, who was like a chameleon—changing himself to adapt to whatever suited his personal needs. Last time Ehrenberg had seen him, George Voss was pretending to be a doctor back on the battlefield.

The Germans among the Greys had remained a tight knit group, but Voss had been somewhat of an outsider. He would make a good medic, Ehrenberg admitted to himself, and would have been useful here in the church this night.

Suddenly, somewhere very near, a prisoner screamed at the top of his lungs, and immediately a flurry of movement erupted not far from where Ehrenberg was leaning against the wall. Someone was trying to tear his bandages off, begging to be allowed to bleed to death.

"The copper bullets," he thought to himself. He and the other Greys had heard that the Mexicans were using these new forms of ammunition—designed specifically to induce copper poisoning in their victims. Especially with intestinal wounds, the copper quickly got into the blood system and caused severe vomiting, cramps, and convulsions. And that was what was happening near him now.

The men near the delirious victim managed to calm and silence him only to have a similar incident occur in another area of the church. The tiny chapel had a vaulted roof, and as the fever of the wounded continued to build, the screaming and begging to die began filling the church in a chorus of agony.

Herman Ehrenberg tilted his head upward toward the windows again and covered his mouth with a cloth he had been using as a bandanna, but the stench and acrid taste of the air he was breathing continued to choke him. The screams became a blurred noise. He shut his eyes, but he knew there would be no sleep for anyone in the church this night.

CBCBCBEOEOEO

*T*he capitulation was met with hostility by the Greys and many of the Red Rovers, but unable to fight on alone, they joined the other Texans in surrendering their weapons.

As the Greys stacked their guns, the Mexicans began entering the Texan encampment to survey the spoils of war. Ehrenberg reported that "group after group of Mexicans crowded over into our camp to see the pretty guns that we had surrendered."[1] Those guns almost certainly included some of the fifty issued by Adolphus Sterne at Bank's Arcade only five months earlier. Other rifles probably had been provided to Morris' men by McKinney and Williams at Quintana.

During the course of the fighting, the area around the ammunition cart had become strewn with unspent cartridges that then became trampled into the dirt and grass. As the Mexican soldiers inspected the camp, many of them discarded their cigars on the ground causing small fires that set off the unspent cartridges.

Ehrenberg's account of the post-surrender camp—written years later—differs from those of other survivors. Ehrenberg claims that one of the Texans, in a suicide mission, purposefully set off the ammunition wagon by throwing his cigar into it.[2] Other reports claim that the wagon did not blow up but became surrounded by small fires and sporadic cartridge explosions.[3]

By either account, the atmosphere surrounding the camp, especially with regards to the hostility of the Greys toward both Fannin and the Mexicans, was tense, and the exploding cartridges seemed to unnerve and infuriate the already distrustful Mexicans.

In the midst of this potential disaster, Colonel Horton appeared on the ridgeline with the much-awaited militia from Victoria: not a force of six hundred men but a pitiful nucleus of maybe forty citizen-volunteers. Ehrenberg speculated that their arrival even a half hour earlier might have swayed the Texans to fight on rather than surrender. But the Greys had been anticipating a militia force of at least battalion size, and Horton's small group could have made no significant impact in future fighting. Under the circumstances that morning, Horton did the only thing he and his men could do—they turned and galloped back toward Victoria.

Prior to the evacuation of the prisoners, it was agreed that the wounded would be left at the surrender site until carts and wagons could be dispatched to carry them back to Goliad. This caused a great deal of concern among the Greys, who, after the fighting at Bexar, had no trust for the Mexicans.

The Greys were lined up in early afternoon and marched back to Goliad. Ehrenberg claims they were the first group of prisoners to arrive back at the fort. Crossing the San Antonio River in water up to their armpits, they were able to drink their first water in over thirty hours.

From the river they were marched up the south bank about a quarter mile to the still-smoldering ruins of the old Spanish fort they had abandoned less than two days earlier.

The Mexicans, fearful of traps, had waited outside the walls until the Greys and other Texans were marched in through the arched sally port and across the three-acre parade ground to the small chapel located near the northwest bastion and the water gate.

Our Lady of Loreto chapel had been built by the Franciscans for the Spanish garrison nearly a hundred years earlier and was now in ruins. It had served as an observation post armed with cannon when Dimitt had taken command of the presidio.

It had been in this small chapel that Dimitt and his men had written and issued their unilateral declaration of independence from Mexico. On this night, however, the bloody severed-arm flag had disappeared and was replaced by the Mexican Centralist tri-color.

The chapel itself consisted of *tufa* construction and measured roughly thirty by eighty-five feet with the longer walls facing north and south. Inside, the church had a forty-foot vaulted ceiling with two octagonal windows on the south side and one octagonal window above the front doors on the west side.

Also along the south wall was a small sacristy measuring perhaps fifteen by twenty feet. This small room had been previously used by the Texans as a powder magazine but was now empty. With a dirt floor, the chapel had no furnishings except for a few wooden Stations of the Cross on the walls. Prior to Dimitt's, and later Fannin's, occupation the chapel had been, despite its poor condition, regularly used by the local Mexicans in Goliad as a place of worship.

The night of March 20, 1836, it was used as a prison. The Greys joined the other approximately 250 Texan prisoners who were packed into the small building. The conditions inside were so crowded that the men could only stand packed against each other and only a few of the prisoners were able to sit on the floor at any given time.

Outside the doors several cannon were positioned with the guards manning burning torches ready to discharge canister into the chapel interior.

The prisoners had been through two long marches, a six-hour battle, a night of misery on the plains, and without bathing or other sanitary measures, were now packed inside the chapel. Many of them had minor but messy and often infected wounds, and the doctors who later survived all wrote of the nausea and diarrhea that was rampant among the volunteers. After gulping the waters of the San Antonio River as they had crossed, the Texans now had to relieve themselves on the dirt floor.

The first night was spent without any additional water being provided, and in the early morning hours the Mexican soldiers began confiscating blankets from the wounded under the threat of bayonets.[4] No food was provided nor was there any to be scavenged inside the church.

As the morning of Monday, March 21 dawned, the prisoners had become so parched with thirst that they threatened—despite the danger of artillery canister—to revolt. A few men were allowed out through the water gate under guard to obtain river water. A total of three trips to the river provided the only water during the day.[5]

Almost two days without food now, the Greys continued to protest until Holzinger finally appeared and assured them that beef would be provided as soon as possible. That evening some meat was produced as promised—but only a small, unsalted serving for each prisoner. To cook the raw meat, some of the prisoners burned the remaining wooden Stations of the Cross. Without water, the meat could not be boiled nor could a broth be made, and given the cramped quarters and lack of wood, only those closest to the fires could roast their portions. The rest ate their ration raw and suffered from the additional heat and smoke the small fires caused inside the building. Later the Mexicans would lament the barbaric actions of the Texans in burning the wooden religious symbols.

Had it not been for the high vaulted ceiling and three windows, there probably would have been casualties due to suffocation, since conditions inside the church became even more cramped during the day as the first of the battlefield wounded started arriving. In the midst of all this misery, there were reports of flute music being heard from inside the chapel: music thought to be from one of the Greys, Charles Sargent from Massachusetts.[6]

Among those wounded brought in by oxcart and wagon was Irishman John Noland, a New Orleans Grey private who had come to Texas with Morris' company. The extent of Noland's injuries are not known. He had also been listed as one of the wounded at Bexar.

Monday night, the second evening inside the church, was later described by several survivors as the worst period of the captivity. Air inside the chapel became stifling from odor and body heat. The Greys and others, who were still near starving, had received no additional food and only a limited amount of water retrieved from the river by canteens.

With seriously wounded among them inside the chapel, the volunteers now had to stand back-to-chest in order to make room for the wounded to be placed on the filthy ground. What sleeping did occur that second night was done while standing in an upright position.

Tuesday morning, March 22, began with only water being provided as breakfast. During the day the last of the wounded were brought in to the church. Five Texans including New Orleans Grey Captain Samuel Overton Pettus joined the cramped quarters. Pettus, who had been so severely wounded that he could not travel with the other Greys on

Sunday, had remained on the ground at the battlefield three days with no medical attention, little water, and no food.

The third night inside the chapel was again spent with those able to stand jamming against each other upright so the wounded, numbering about fifty-five, could rest on the ground.

Wednesday, the twenty-third brought a light rain that had little effect on the hot, stuffy conditions of the Greys. During the day, however, they were removed from the church into the parade area along the west wall. At first Pettus and the other wounded remained in the church while the Mexican wounded were brought in, and the casualties of the two armies were divided on each side of the chapel. With the large number of Mexican wounded, however, the chapel was still too crowded, and the Texan wounded were relocated into one of the stone rooms along the west wall barracks.

The other Texan prisoners were placed under guard along the wall of the barracks. Though they were exposed to the elements—the intermittent rain—without decent clothing or blankets, most of them felt their plight was improved over the unsanitary, cramped conditions of the church.

A ring of Mexican infantrymen formed a solid human wall around the prisoners while cannon stood at the ready: filled with canister and manned by artillerymen holding burning torches. As the day progressed, the Greys began to identify some of the Mexican officers. Captain Pedro Balderas and Captain Antonio Ramirez were seen inspecting and issuing orders to the infantrymen. Two of the *Tres Villas* battalion officers from the Alamo campaign, Adjutant Agustin Alcerrica and Captain Carolino Huerta, were also active around the perimeter of their guards.

Mexican soldiers and some of the local citizens who were returning to Goliad came into the presidio to sell tidbits of food at exorbitant prices. These same peasants had only weeks and days earlier been driven from their homes or subjected to harassment and robbery by Duval's men as well as some of the Greys. Now they were extracting their revenge on the starving Texans who had been their antagonists.

Ehrenberg, in a passage that seems naïve for a prisoner of war, complained about losing a poncho that he had obtained earlier under questionable circumstances:

> From me they stole one of those large, pretty, woolen blankets which are made in the mountain lands of Mexico and are completely waterproof. But they also had an enormous price. Mine, that I had bought for ten dollars twelve to fourteen days ago from a Mexican spy that we had captured, was probably worth from forty to fifty dollars. . . .
>
> Besides that, they are light and warm. In vain I asked Holsinger to have mine sent back to me. He answered that was not possible because I as a prisoner would have to put up with many things. During the afternoon I had the pleasure of seeing my poncho wrapped over the body of the same villain to whom I had paid ten dollars when he was our prisoner.[7]

More serious losses were the surgical tools of the Texan doctors and blankets and dressings that could have been used to dress the injuries and wounds. When the Greys refused to part with an item one of the soldiers desired, it was often simply appropriated by the threat of a bayonet.

A fire was built outside the building and water boiled in a copper pot for sanitizing dressings and boiling any food that could be found. On one occasion, a Mexican gave the Texan physicians a quarter cut of a calf to boil in the pot for soup. When they later threw the severed hooves over near the fire, several of the men roasted them over the fire and ate them "hide and all."[8]

By Thursday, March 24, some of the wounded had not had their field dressings changed since the Saturday battle—some five days—and almost all the open wounds were now infested with fly larvae. The Anglo Texan physicians had still not been allowed to treat their own but were being kept apart and forced to tend to the Mexican wounded.

The medical situation improved somewhat when during the day another seventy men arrived. They were, the Greys learned, a Nashville battalion under the command of Major William C. Miller. Although kept separate from the Greys and other prisoners, some of Miller's men were allowed to tend to the medical needs of the wounded.

Through the volunteer medics, the Greys learned that Miller and his men had landed aboard a chartered ship at Copano a few days earlier and had disembarked to discover the port had been occupied by the Mexican army under the command of Rafael de la Vara.

Anxious to reach land after a rough sea voyage, the Nashville volunteers had quickly come ashore only to be placed under arrest even before their guns and ammunition had been unloaded. After being imprisoned at Copano, Miller's men had been force-marched to Goliad as prisoners of war but were being billeted outside the fort in separate quarters and instructed to wear white armbands. Through their Mexican captors, they had been told the armbands identified them as noncombatants unlike the Greys, who had been captured under arms.

To the Greys this confirmed their worst fears: The Greys at the Alamo were dead, Victoria was now under Urrea's control, the Mexicans controlled the ports and access to the sea, and nearly 400 Texas volunteers were now held prisoner at Goliad.

Still, Urrea had promised to intercede with Santa Anna on behalf of their being paroled, and Holzinger had told them they'd be home in eight days. Now, from Miller's men they also learned that Fannin had gone to Copano with Holzinger to charter the ship these most recent prisoners had arrived on.

This was Thursday, the fifth day after the surrender and Holzinger's promise. The coming Sunday would be Palm Sunday—and the eighth day. There was speculation that maybe the end of this nightmarish captivity really was in sight.

During this day, George Voss was assigned to assist the Anglo Texan physicians serving the Mexican wounded. Pretending to be a doctor, Voss was able to gain a measure of freedom of movement around the fort. This was Voss' second captivity in the short revolution—he had also been imprisoned by General Cos at the Alamo prior to the Bexar campaign. At that time, he had gained Cos' confidence by swearing to be a good Catholic and cigarmaker. Now, in Goliad, he was pretending to be a medical doctor. Voss, who had the advantage of speaking Spanish, was becoming adept at finding ways in which to ingratiate himself with his captors—a point not missed by some of the other Greys.

Another New Orleans Grey who spoke and understood Spanish was the Louisiana Creole Joseph Spohn. Spohn, who had previously been taken prisoner outside Bexar, was now being utilized by the Mexicans as an interpreter—a position that gave him access to discussions between the leaders of both sides. It was also an assignment that would connect him closely to Colonel Fannin in the coming days.

The prisoners were given small rations of beef that day and allowed to roast it over small fires, but the portions were very limited and water still severely rationed.

Friday morning March 25 brought little change in their incarceration until the arrival of Colonel Ward and approximately eighty of his Georgia Battalion. Unlike Miller's men, the Georgia Battalion was housed inside the fort with the Greys and other prisoners since they had been "armed" against Mexico when captured.

Through the new prisoners, the Greys learned that Ward and his men had succeeded in relieving Amon King's surrounded men at Refugio, but because of internal squabbling over command, the forces had divided again. While King's men had been captured, Ward and most of the Georgia Battalion had managed to escape on March 15.

The next day, wandering lost on the prairie, Ward had detailed seven men including New Orleans Grey John Bright to find and retrieve water. They never returned, and it was not known if they were ambushed, lost, or simply took off on their own escape.

On the nineteenth they had been close enough to the Coleto battlefield to hear the sounds of the fighting but had little ammunition, so they continued on toward Victoria. Disoriented, short of rations and ammunition, and weary from fleeing Urrea's cavalry, they had been within ten miles of the battle but unable to assist.

On Monday they had entered Victoria and found Urrea's forces in control of the town. After a brief firefight with the Mexicans, the Georgia Battalion had become scattered, with some more men taking off on their own. The rest had regrouped and tried to find their way back to Dimitt's Landing on Lavaca Bay but were surrounded and forced to surrender. Like Fannin's men, they felt they had capitulated on honorable terms. And now, like Fannin's men, they were imprisoned at Goliad. Counting Miller's noncombatants and Ward's prisoners, the total Anglo Texans incarcerated in La Bahia now totaled nearly 450.

Also on Friday Holzinger singled out several of the Texan volunteers, including some of the Greys, and demanded an audience with them. As the group assembled in front of the Mexican artillery commander from Germany, it was apparent they had been selected because they were all Germans.

Holzinger had separated them to offer them freedom, but only at a price. They would be released from the Goliad prison and given positions in the Mexican army as artillery-men and the privilege to return to Mexico and live as citizens when the war was over.

If in fact all the Germans in the Texan camp were called out, four New Orleans Greys would have been present: Ehrenberg, Peter Mattern, George Courtman, and George Voss. Ehrenberg recalls his own personal dislike for the Mexican-German officer and claims fellow Grey Peter Mattern told Holzinger that he would rather "slave in the mines among criminals" than live as a free Mexican.[9]

George Courtman, whose brother had just died as a New Orleans Grey in the Alamo, was unmoved by the offer as well. No mention is made of Voss at the meeting, but he did not choose to join the Mexican army, and several references would be made about him in the coming days as he treated the Mexican wounded under the guise of being a physician.

James Fannin arrived back at Goliad on Saturday, March 26 and was quickly quarantined in the chapel—ostensibly because of his wounds. The Greys soon learned that the mission to Copano to secure a ship had failed. The captain, fearing a Mexican conspiracy to capture the vessel with its arms and ammunition aboard, sailed out of the port before any negotiations could take place. While this was a setback, the Greys knew that there were other ships and even other ports.

Optimism ran high on this seventh day after the battle and sixth day of captivity. Despite missing the ship, Fannin felt assured that Holzinger was making progress in obtaining their release. He spoke to the physicians attending him about the courtesy the Mexicans and Holzinger had shown him on the trip to Copano. Another indication that they might parole soon was the increased demand for their private possessions by the Mexican civilians and soldiers. To some of the Greys, this simply indicated that the Mexicans wanted to get what they could before the Texans left for New Orleans.

There were probably very few remnants of the distinctive gray uniforms that had been issued from the warehouses in New Orleans only five months earlier. In the short history of the New Orleans Greys, some had marched to Texas from Nachitoches and others had marched to San Antonio from Velasco. Prairie ashes had darkened the uniforms of Breece's men. Morris and his company had fought storms, rain, and mud through to Bexar. Many of the men had shed their coats in the first minutes of the Bexar fighting, and by now what uniform pieces remained were worn and tattered. Even Ehrenberg had resorted to wearing a Mexican poncho for warmth.

Few possessions of any value remained at this point, and the townspeople and soldiers were starting to make comments to the effect that the Greys wouldn't be needing them anymore since they were all going to be killed anyway. These threats were in themselves nothing new, and few, if any, of the Greys let them dampen the optimism of the moment. Ehrenberg does not mention if the Greys were aware of any other changes in the behavior or attitudes of their guards, but other later reports indicate that during this time the fort commandant, Colonel José Nicolas de la Portilla, had begun acting nervous and withdrawn. Neither Voss nor Spohn, who had considerable freedom of movement around the post compound, reported any strange or unusual behavior among the Mexican officers.

Peter Griffin, a Louisianian who had been in Breece's company, was now helping Voss and the physicians treat the Mexican wounded in their quarters as this sixth day of captivity ended. Joseph Spohn, the interpreter, was also housed in the chapel that evening. As darkness set in, word was passed that a ship was now available at Copano and that a part of the prisoners would be marched down to the port in the morning, to embark. The others would be sent on working parties, then would return to the fort to await their time to make the trip.[10]

Chapter 10

Spirits were high that night. Charles Sargent took out his flute and began playing. Soon a few other flutists joined in, and the prison area of the old Spanish presidio was enveloped in music. The popular tune of the day "Home, Sweet Home" was the favorite, but the Greys also sang and joked to other songs.[11]

As the fires burned down and the music died, the prisoners bedded down in what grass and scraps of cloth they could find. Hungry to the point of starving, sick, wounded, and physically and mentally exhausted, they prepared for sleep that night with the promise of leaving for the United States the following morning.

The next morning would be Palm Sunday, and some of them probably offered a prayer that night.

---

1   Ornish, *Ehrenberg*, pg. 232.
2   *Ibid.,* pp. 232-3.
3   O'Connor, *The Presidio La Bahia del Espiritu Santo de Zuniga, 1721 to 1846*, pg. 209.
4   Pruett, *Goliad Massacre*, pg. 109.
5   Ornish, *Ehrenberg*, pg. 237.
6   Notation to a list titled "CAPTAIN SAMUEL OVERTON PETTUS' COMPANY SAN ANTONIO GREYS" compiled by Kevin R. Young at Presidio La Bahia, August 7, 1985.
7   Ornish, *Ehrenberg*, pp. 242-3.
8   O'Connor, *The Presidio La Bahia del Espiritu Santo de Zuniga, 1721 to 1846*, pg. 210.
9   Ornish, *Ehrenberg*, pp. 241-2.
10 Pruett, *Goliad Massacre*, pg. 108.
11 *Ibid.,* and Ernest Wallace, ed., *Documents of Texas History* (Austin, Texas, Steck Co., 1994), pg. 109.

Chapter 11

Palm Sunday Massacre

Margaret Wright Ranch, East of Goliad, Texas, April 10, 1836: William Lockhart Hunter pulled his arms from the salt brine solution and inspected the cuts. There was still some scabbing, but the wounds were beginning to scar and there were no signs of infection. Drying himself with the fresh, clean rags, he began to gently massage the salve into the cut areas. The wounds on his neck were also healing nicely, but the hole in his shoulder continued to weep. Margaret Wright had warned him it might continue to ooze for the rest of his life.

After wrapping his arms with fresh dressings, he tied them down—using his teeth to hold one end of the string. Then he craned his neck and inspected the hole in his shoulder. It was an ugly triangular hole, and although not infected, it was red and puffy and filled with a clear puss. The sulfa powder seemed to have stopped the earlier infection, and he tenderly worked some of the salve over the open hole. With the tip of his finger he rubbed the gel over all three sides of the opening—the result of a Mexican bayonet and French ingenuity. Hunter had once heard how the French had perfected the triangular bayonet blade to prevent wounds from healing cleanly and increasing the chance of deadly infection.

He folded a clean pad and clumsily tied it into place with the strips of rags lying on the table. Finished, he made a visual inspection of his dressings and nodded in satisfaction. The bruises and cuts on his face were nearly healed now, and as soon as his shoulder was better he could head east toward Harrisburg.

He lay down on the bed of Spanish moss and glanced around the crude hut where he was hiding. It was only about four feet by seven feet, barely big enough to lie down in, but it was comfortable and dry when it rained. It was also well hidden. Last night he had heard Mexican lancers down by the Manahuilla Creek bank calling to each other in Spanish as they rode on patrol toward Victoria. They had ridden within twenty feet and never knew he was hidden here. Nor could they find him in daylight; the entrance required crawling through a thicket of bushes.

Only Margaret Wright knew where he was hiding, and she never visited unless she was driving some cattle in front of her. Any footprints the Mexican lancers might have detected would have been those of her herding her livestock to the nearby creek for water. Hunter himself never left the hut except to relieve himself among the thicket where the Mexicans wouldn't detect his presence. Mrs. Wright dropped off food and medicine late in the afternoon every third day and picked up his three water gourds. After watering her cattle, she would come back by and drop off the freshly filled canteens. On dark nights when there was no moonlight she would stop to talk. A couple of times she had crawled back into his hut to inspect the cuts on his back that he had trouble dressing.

On those occasions, William Hunter learned the latest rumors about the revolution. The Greys and other Texans had been massacred at Goliad. He had somehow survived the killing of the Greys, but Mrs. Wright now told him that the other groups suffered similar fates. Some estimates were that almost three hundred fifty Texans were killed that morning. She didn't know of any other Greys who had survived.

The Mexicans completely controlled this area now, and Santa Anna was reportedly chasing Sam Houston and the remnants of the Texan army toward the Louisiana border. Hunter wondered if the United States would enter into the war now that so many Americans had been killed at San Antonio and Goliad. The Anglo colonists, Mrs. Wright had told him, were now in a panic and abandoning their homes and plantations across Texas and following Sam Houston's army.

Hunter knew that Margaret Wright would never abandon her league of land here on the west bank of the Guadalupe River between Goliad and Victoria. She cherished her land and worked it—improving and expanding it—until it was now as much part of her as she was of it. She belonged here, and Hunter doubted that even Santa Anna could drive her off of it.

But Texas would eventually be free. If not in this war, another would follow soon until Mexico had to let go. And then people like Margaret Wright would be the foundation of a new nation—or maybe a new American state. Hunter knew she would never be part of a "proper" society. The woman, by her own admission, didn't fit the "high society" mold that the ladies in Victoria liked to project.

While Hunter had been in charge of supplying the commissary at La Bahia, he had traveled around the area making purchases and had become acquainted with many of the settlers—Tejano and Anglo.

William Hunter was by nature a fair man. He had studied law and intended to one day be a judge. As commissary officer for Fannin he had treated all the settlers around Goliad with respect and fairness in stark contrast to the usual Texan practice of impressing whatever was needed with no compensation to the locals. In the conduct of his duties, William Hunter had become a relatively well known and well liked man around Goliad. And he had heard the rumors of Mrs. Wright's background.

Originally from New Orleans, she had outlived one husband only to bear two "illegitimate" children in a common-law relationship. In her late forties, she had been homesteading in Texas for fifteen years and was now married to another husband from whom she was separated. That, of course, was the source of many other rumors—the main staple of which was that she very much liked men.

And a damned good thing, Hunter thought to himself, since he knew that in addition to himself she was harboring and tending several hidden Texan refugees at various locations around her large ranch. She had told him that some of them were also wounded and that they had devised a system by which they left notes for her in a hollow tree. She conveyed food and medicine to them, like she did for him, during her visits to the river.

Hunter, who was twenty years her junior, knew that she had saved his life—the second woman to do so since the massacre. For hours on Palm Sunday he had feigned death after being shot at only to later be bayoneted, clubbed, and have his throat cut. After lying among the victims all day, he had waited until darkness and literally crawled over the dead bodies of the other Greys to make his way to the San Antonio River.

After regaining some strength from the loss of so much blood, he had stumbled naked toward Victoria until he had met Nicholas Fagan, whom he had known at Fort Defiance. Fagan had tried to help him but was unfamiliar with the countryside, and Hunter had suggested that they go to the home of a nearby Mexican family from whom he had previously purchased grain.

The Mexican woman had taken him in and also had hidden him in the woods. Despite their language differences, Hunter had recognized her compassion immediately. Afraid to tell her own husband because of the threats against local Tejanos who aided Texans, she secretly tended him as he had hovered on the edge of death for several days. Collecting spider webs to pack in his wounds, she dressed his cuts and fed him broth from beef she had boiled and spoon-fed him soup made of cornmeal tortillas. Slowly he had recovered enough to leave. Recognizing the danger he was placing her in, he had asked her to help him get to Margaret Wright's ranch. Taking clothes from her family, she had dressed him and had brought Mrs. Wright to retrieve him.

Hunter stretched his legs and reflected that he had grown to like this area of Texas. At first, like the rest of the Greys, he had found Goliad to be dirty and backwards—especially compared with San Antonio. But returning a second time after the fighting at Bexar, he had come to know the people and appreciate the stark beauty of the land. He liked the character of people like Margaret Wright and the Mexican family who had saved his life. He planned to remain here after the revolution and practice law—maybe even become a judge. He figured this area, with its proximity to the sea, would play a prominent role in the development of a free Texas in the future. And now, if he lived, he wanted to be a part of it.

ᏻᏻᏻᏸᏸᏸ

*P*alm Sunday dawned warm and muggy under overcast and cloudy skies. The Greys awoke that morning at the command of the guards, and they found the Mexicans had been preparing overnight for their departure. The cannon inside the fort had been repositioned to cover their prison compound, and the Mexican soldiers had been stationed around them dressed in parade uniforms.

They were ordered to pack what few belongings they still retained quickly and line up for a head count. Assembled inside the fort, the Greys and others responded as the Mexican officers walked around the encampment calling out names from prepared lists.

From within their ranks, the Greys speculated what the day's march would have in store for them. Some thought they would go to Copano; others even suggested they might march to Matamoros to be shipped out. There was some dark speculation that they might be marched to Mexico and worked as slaves in the mines until the war was over.

But for the most part the mood was spirited and optimistic. After all, today was Holzinger's promised "eight days, home and liberty!" Since few of the Greys or any other Texan volunteers had any personal possessions left, packing required no time and the head counts began immediately.

Shortly after daylight, probably around 8:00 A.M., the orders were issued to move out through the sally port. The Greys were the first to leave the compound at the head of approximately three hundred tired, dirty, and starving Texan volunteers. It was noted that Fannin and the medical personnel including George Voss and Peter Griffin were missing from the ranks. Their interpreter, Joseph Spohn, had joined their line inside the presidio, but just outside the sally port he was recalled and sent back to the church. Inside, with the wounded, Captain Pettus and Private James Noland remained under medical care.

As the Greys led the long double column out through the south entrance of the fort, they were met by even more Mexican soldiers who then formed a single-line escort on each side of them. They turned to the northeast, past the burned shanties they had destroyed prior to their departure to Coleto. Marching down the gently sloping incline outside the fort, they were herded suddenly northward—away from Copano. The Greys found this unusual but justified it as a move toward the eastern ports—perhaps even Velasco and Quintana—if Urrea's forces had marched that far north.

Ehrenberg recalled looking back and noticing that neither Fannin's men nor the Georgia Battalion continued to follow them. The Greys and a few colonists were the only Texans in their column now. Ehrenberg and the other German Greys were marching together. They began to notice disturbing signs among the soldiers escorting them: no backpacks or rations and the lack of conversation among the soldiers. And then the cavalry, who had been patrolling the countryside in small tactical units, began to show up alongside the footsoldiers.

For about fifteen minutes the Greys marched northeast of the presidio toward the lower ford of the San Antonio River—the same crossing where they had once had to abandon their relief mission for their comrades in the Alamo. Only eight days earlier they had taken this same road when leaving La Bahia to cross the plains of Coleto. But before they reached the river, they were given a command to leave the road and march off to the left. Doing so, they realized the Mexican infantry ranks had formed into a double row about three steps away from their column.

During eight days with very little food and water, the Greys had been forced to live in a cramped church and later in an open exposed compound with no clothing or blankets. They were fatigued, starving, and many were sick. In this near delirious state, they finally realized what they were being led into. A command to halt was given, which confused them. They were then told in Spanish to "kneel down"—a command they didn't understand at first. Upon second issuance of the command, the Mexicans raised their rifles into firing position.

For a few seconds, everything seemed to freeze around them. Then they heard volleys of firing from two other areas around them. Just as they realized they were being ambushed, the order was given for their executioners to fire on them.

From a distance of only three steps, the first round killed nearly every New Orleans Grey in the formation that morning. Ehrenberg recalled a terrible cracking sound followed by silence and a thick smoke rolling toward the San Antonio River nearby. Peter Mattern, who had spurned Holzinger's offer of Mexican service only two days earlier, collapsed against the dead body of fellow German George Courtman.

In the smoke of the burnt powder also lay dead on the ground W. B. Wood, who had traveled to Texas from New Jersey with Captain Breece. Virginians Nathaniel Brister, the regimental adjutant, and Allen Kinney fell that muggy warm morning as did New Yorkers Stuart Hill, John S. Smith, and Stephen Winship. Charles Sargent took the blast of that first volley and with him died the flute music that had consoled in the crowded chapel and rejoiced the night before in celebrating parole. Fellow Massachusetts volunteer Edenezer Smith Heath joined him among the ranks of the fallen Greys.

Pennsylvania lost five native sons that morning: George M. Gilland, Joseph P. Riddle, John Scott, James West, and Mandaret Wood. Irishmen William Harper and Dennis Mahoney perished as did Englishman George Green and Scotsman Francis H. Gray. Noah Dickinson Jr. had traveled south from upper Canada and now lay dead in the land claimed by Mexico and Texas. Closer to their natural homes, South Carolinians Charles J. Carrine and John Wood fell near the banks of the San Antonio River that morning as did Louisiana's Charles Clark and William G. Preusch. Tennessean William James Gatlin had escaped death with Dr. James Grant less than a month earlier, but this Palm Sunday morning he fell with the other mortally wounded New Orleans Greys.

At least one other Grey died that morning: William (John) Stephens. No home is listed for him, no heirs identified, no citations during the Grey's short history—but he had come to Texas with Breece, and he died with the Greys that overcast Sunday morning. The muster rolls simply state "With Fannin-killed."

Not all Greys died with the first volley. Some, wounded and trying to crawl away, were bayoneted or had their heads crushed by rifle butts. In the confusion, smoke, screaming, and yelling five Greys did manage to reach the banks of the San Antonio River and jump into the water. One of those was Herman Ehrenberg who, despite being slashed by a sword across the head and one forearm, did manage to cross the river and escape a hail of bullets while swimming to the other side. In doing so, he claimed, he lost his diary—resulting in his having to reconstruct it years later from memory.

Another New Orleans Grey, William L. Hunter, also managed to escape into the river. His story, as retold years later by Dr. John Washington Lockhart, is one of amazing survival. At the time of the massacre, Hunter was a second sergeant with Pettus' company of the Greys, but Lockhart refers to him by his later title of "judge":

> . . . took his place with the others and at the crack of the musketry fell with the others, though not wounded. He lay as he fell. After the murderous affair had taken place the Mexicans commenced to strip the dead bodies of the Texans. They succeeded in getting the outer clothing off the judge, but thinking him not quite dead, they picked up a musket and stuck the bayonet through his shoulder. The bayonet fortunately struck the shoulder blade and did not enter the vital parts. The brute left the bayonet sticking in his shoulder, and the heft of the musket as it fell turned the judge's face and upper portion of his body over. In this painful position he had to lie for some time, for the least movement on his part would have been noticed, and that would have been followed by instant death. The judge had on a nice knit striped undershirt which struck the eye of a Mexican, who proceeded to possess himself of it by taking out the bayonet and pulling it off the dead judge, as he thought. The judge said the garment fit pretty tight and he reckoned he must have helped the Mexican in some way to get it off, for when he had stripped him the Mexican commenced to curse him, and pulling out an old, dull knife, such as every Mexican

carries, proceeded to cut his throat. To prevent this the judge threw up his hand and protected his neck as much as possible. After he had made several attempts to cut the judge's throat and having drawn blood freely both from his neck and fingers, the Mexican desisted without serious harm. The judge had only to be thankful for the dullness of the knife for the preservation of his life. In this condition the judge lay until night had drawn her dark curtain over the ghastly scene. The sun had hidden her face behind the western hills, the stars peeping down on the merciless act as if too horrid for their steady gaze, gave only twinkling lights, and as all nature seemed stilled in death over the field where the brave soldiers lay, Judge Hunter crawled over the dead bodies of his comrades, nearly exhausted by the loss of blood, to the river, and there slaked his thirst and washed his wounds as best he could. After bathing his already fevered body he slowly crawled off into the brush, not knowing whether he would ever be restored to his friends or not. . . .[1]

Another New Orleans Grey who managed to reach the river and escape was John Rees, a twenty-five-year-old volunteer born in Wales who had come to Texas with Morris. The details of his escape are unknown, but he, like Englishman Thomas Kemp and William Brennan, did manage to cross the San Antonio River and elude the Mexicans in the period immediately following the massacre. Brennan also has no home listed nor any personal information on the muster rolls except the notation "Escaped."

After the initial killing, the Mexicans attacked the wounded and chased down those trying to escape. The attack itself was basically one simultaneous volley fired into the Greys formation, followed by about an hour of chasing, clubbing, stabbing, and shooting the wounded survivors. It was a scene repeated against Ward's Georgia Battalion and Duval's company near the river on the Bexar road with a few survivors crossing the upper ford of the river. To the south, the Alabama Red Rovers and Ira Westover's men were ambushed on the San Patricio Road, and without the cover of water, only four were known survivors.

Back in the fort at La Bahia, Captain Carolino Huerta of the Tres Villas Battalion had been left in charge of the remaining wounded Texans. In their quarters for the wounded along the south wall, Pettus and Noland first heard the volley of shots from different directions, then a protracted period of scattered shooting. They were aware that the Greys had left the presidio only about fifteen minutes earlier, so it is fairly certain that they were aware of the events going on outside when they heard the shots.

Joseph Spohn, the interpreter, was quartered in the church with the Anglo Texan physicians. Like George Voss and Peter Griffin who were working as medics, he had been awakened before daylight just as the Greys outside were being lined up. Spohn, being the only nonmedical person in the group, was instructed to go outside and form at the end of the line of the Greys outside. In an interview published in the *New York Evening Star* a few months later, Spohn gave his version of the morning's events:

> On Palm Sunday, being the 27th of March, the prisoners were formed into a line, and Mr. Spohn, who was then sleeping in the church, (the hospital) being about 6 o'clock in the morning, was called out and told to form into line; being the last, he fell at the end. They were then marched out of the fort and ranged before the gate, when an officer stepped up and asked Spohn what he was doing there, and ordered him to go back to the hospital where

he was wanted, and when on his way was
stopped by another officer, who told him to
order the assistants to have the wounded
brought into the yard: such as could not walk
were to be carried out. Being astonished at
these preparations, he asked why, when the
officer said "Carts were coming to convey them
to Copano, the nearest seaport." The orders of
the officers were obeyed, and the wounded
brought into the yard, and they were full of
hope that they were to be shipped to the United
States, which had been promised; but their
hopes were cruelly blasted when they heard a
sudden continued roar of musketry on the outside of the fort, and observed the soldiers' wives
leap upon the walls and look towards the spot
where the report came from.[2]

Ehrenberg, who was at that moment struggling towards
the San Antonio River and had no idea what was going on
inside the fort, later wrote that in the church, "...nothing
could induce them to bring their dying or raging comrades to
the place of murder, and only the attendant Voss, who had
hopes of not being shot, helped the brown murderers carry
out the dying ones, several of whom died before they
reached the fateful spot."[3]

Ehrenberg gives no reference for which he based this
claim that Voss was once again too willing to act as an agent
for the Mexican enemy. Spohn did not mention Voss in his
interview with the *New York Evening Star* but did indicate he
had been "employed in helping them (the wounded) out." As
the newspaper article continued:

The wounded were then conscious of what
was passing, and one of them asked Spohn if he
did not think that their time was come; and
when they became convinced from the

> movements about the fort that they were to be
> shot, greater part of them sat down calmly on
> their blankets, resolutely awaiting their miser-
> able fate; some turned pale, but not one
> displayed the least fear or quivering.[4]

And so, as the Greys near the lower ford of the San Antonio River were being slaughtered, Captain Samuel Overton
Pettus and Private James Noland were placed against the
western rock wall of the barracks in the La Bahia courtyard
and summarily executed with the other Texan wounded.

As the wounded were being shot, one of the injured
Mexican officers whom Peter Griffin had been treating took
the opportunity in the confusion to hide the young Grey
under his blankets.[5] Elsewhere, George Voss managed to slip
out of the church and cross the three-acre parade ground to
the sally port where he found his way into the calaboose
(jail) and hid himself under a pile of boards stored there.[6]

Meanwhile, Spohn's difficult role in this massacre was
not finished. After the killing of the wounded, only Fannin
remained alive, and his execution has probably been the
most chronicled death outside the walls of the Alamo. What
is not as well known is that a New Orleans Grey—Joseph
Spohn—prepared Fannin and comforted him until the
moment of his death.

Spohn's version, as reported in the *New York Evening Star*
article describes the emotional, difficult role Spohn had to
perform that deadly morning:

> ... a Mexican captain of the battalion,
> called Tres Villas, with six soldiers, came up to
> Spohn, and told him to call Col. Fannin, at the
> same time pointing to a certain part of the
> yard, where he wished him to be taken Spohn
> asked him if he was going to shoot him, and he
> coolly replied, "Yes."—When Spohn approached
> Fannin, the Colonel asked what was that firing,

and when he told him the facts he made no
observation, but appeared resolute and firm, no
visible impression on Colonel Fannin, who
firmly walked to the place pointed out by the
Mexican captain, placing his arm upon the
shoulder of Spohn for support, being wounded
in the right thigh, from which he was very
lame.[7]

Fannin was not well liked by the Greys. Ehrenberg's
account of the colonel's command emphasizes the dislike and
distrust the New Orleans Greys felt towards the commander.
And other survivors also have pointed out that, especially at
Coleto, the Greys were openly hostile to Fannin. The reason
may have been that they held him personally responsible for
preventing them from going to San Antonio and relieving
those Greys in the Alamo. This was a situation unique to the
Greys, since no other unit in Fannin's command had been
veterans of the Bexar fighting.

Given the hostility by the Greys toward the commander,
it is ironic that it was one of their members—Spohn—who
attended him at the moment of his death. In a humane, gra-
cious manner Spohn notified Fannin that the men of his
command were all dead. It was Spohn who served as a
crutch to assist him to the chair in which he was to be shot.
As he later recalled:

When Colonel Fannin reached the spot
required, the N.W. corner of the fort (in front of
the chapel doors and near the water gate),
Spohn was ordered to interpret the following
sentence: "That for having come with an armed
band to commit depredations and revolutionize
Texas, the Mexican Government were about to
chastise him." As soon as the sentence was
interpreted to Fannin, he asked if he could not
see the commandant. The officer said he could

not, and asked why he wished it. Colonel Fannin then pulled forth a valuable gold watch, he said belonged to his wife, and he wished to present it to the commandant. The captain then said he could not see the commandant, but if he would give him the watch he would thank him—and he repeated in broken English, "tank you—me tank you." Colonel Fannin told him he might have the watch if he would have him buried after he was shot, which the captain said should be done—"con todas las formalidades necessarias" (with all necessary formalities)—at the same time smiling and bowing. Col. Fannin then handed him the watch, and pulled out of his right pocket a small bead purse containing doubloons, the clasp of which was bent; he gave this to the officer, at the same time saying that it had saved his life, as the ball that wounded him had lost part of its force by striking the clasp, which it bent and carried with it into the wound; a part of a silk handkerchief which he had in his pocket, and which on drawing out drew forth with it the ball. Out of the left pocket of his overcoat, (being cold weather he had on one of India rubber) he took a piece of canvass containing a double handful of dollars, which he also gave to the officer.[8]

At this point, Spohn had been Fannin's interpreter in conveying his last wishes to the Mexican officer. He was then ordered to take Fannin's handkerchief, fold it, and tie it over his eyes. He tried, but in nervousness, he had problems folding it, and the Mexican captain snatched it from his hands and ordered Fannin to sit down on a chair that had been placed there. After he had been seated, the captain tied the blindfold over Fannin's eyes himself.

As the captain returned to face Fannin, the Georgian made one last request of Spohn:

> . . . tell them not to place their muskets so near as to scorch his face with the powder. The officer standing behind them after seeing their muskets were brought within two feet of his body, drew forth his handkerchief as a signal, when they fired, and poor Fannin fell dead on his right side of the chair, and from thence rolled into a dry ditch, about three feet deep, close by the wall.[9]

Fannin had made three last requests: his watch be properly placed, he be given a Christian burial, and that he be shot in the chest. His executioner pocketed his watch, he was shot in the head, and his body was dumped in a pile with those of his men.

Spohn was then led to the gate and placed in a room with a guard. At one point another Mexican officer entered the room and nearly ran him through with his sword before being stopped by the guard. After a while, Spohn was led back into the fort where he observed the dead being loaded onto a wagon.

As the sun set on Presidio La Bahia and Goliad that Palm Sunday evening, approximately 342 Texan volunteers had been shot down at close range and then stabbed, clubbed, and lanced. Later reports would tell that the Mexican soldiers, attempting to wash the blood from confiscated Texan clothing, turned the San Antonio River red for a brief period.

As darkness settled over the tiny Our Lady of Loreto chapel in the fort that night, the shooting had stopped. Charles Sargent's flute lay silent somewhere. The New Orleans Greys had ceased—on March 27, 1836—to exist as a military unit. The Greys at Goliad had joined their brethren from the Alamo in silent death. The youthful toasts made at Nacogdoches and Brazoria were barely five months old, but the ambitious men who had made them no longer existed. There would be no more roll calls, no more muster rolls scribed, and no more talk of journeys to Bexar or Matamoros.

Palm Sunday and the Lenten season are a period of Christian contemplation and forgiveness. But the Palm Sunday this day at Goliad would not spawn forgiveness. To the contrary, this Palm Sunday would spawn the challenge that became the rallying cry for revenge: "Remember the Alamo. Remember Goliad!"

---

1   Dr. John Washington Lockhart, *Sixty Years on the Brazos*, pg. 63.
2   O'Connor, *The Presidio La Bahia del Espiritu Santo de Zuniga, 1721 to 1846*, pg. 142.
3   Ornish, *Ehrenberg*, pg. 255.
4   O'Connor, pg. 142.
5   *Ibid.*, pg. 145.
6   *Ibid.*, pg. 212.
7   *Ibid.*, pg. 143.
8   *Ibid.*
9   *Ibid.*, pg. 144.

Chapter 12

To the Scattered Winds

General Land Office, Austin, Texas, Christmas Day, 1847: Thomas William Ward sat behind his desk in the General Land Office building and pondered how to word the letter he had to send. Governor George T. Wood, who had just been in office four days, had been considerate and waited until Christmas dinner was finished to send the messenger over to Ward's house. The news had caught Ward by surprise: An old colleague and political enemy had died from tuberculosis the day before.

Ward had never liked William Gordon Cooke, but the two men's lives had been intertwined closely for over a decade now. Cooke's death was not devastating to Ward—the two men had nearly fought duels on two occasions. No, Ward neither gloated nor grieved as he looked at the note from Governor Wood.

But after receiving it, he'd had to retire to his office to collect his thoughts. Unexplainably, something had died inside him, too, as he had read that note—something his wife Susan nor anybody else would understand. Nobody except for perhaps Judge Hunter down in Goliad. And as soon as he collected his thoughts, he was going to send a letter to the kindly magistrate to inform him of Cooke's death.

Leaning back in his office chair, he recalled the first time he had met William Cooke. They had both been seasick and miserable on the choppy waves of the Texas Gulf Coast during the autumn of 1835. Both men were still trying to become accustomed to the new gray uniforms they were then wearing as volunteer soldiers. The two men had taken an immediate dislike for each other on that sea voyage, but in the excitement and adventure of their mission they had generally ignored each other until they arrived at Bexar. Then, as the fighting started, Cooke had become a commanding officer of the New Orleans Greys.

In combat, both men had been involved in heavy fighting and proven themselves courageous and capable—forming a bond that could never be transcended by their other differences and feuds. Whether they liked each other or not, Ward and Cooke would always be New Orleans Grey combat veterans who had fought side by side. And for that reason, something had died inside Thomas Ward when he had read the message from the governor.

The Battle of Bexar had bonded the two men together while also sending them in different directions with their lives. Cooke had gone on to military acclaim and advancement after Bexar, and Ward had been furloughed back to New Orleans to recover from an amputated leg—the casualty of a Mexican cannonball.

But Ward was back in Texas within a few months, fitted with an artificial limb, and had been recommissioned back into the army after San Jacinto. By then Cooke was also a senior officer in the regular Texas army, and the two men crossed paths several times before they had both discharged and moved to the new community of Houston.

Ward had been granted a contract to construct the new Republic of Texas capitol in the swampy settlement, and Cooke had opened a druggist business there. Ward had even consulted Cooke's drugstore for medicine to treat the lingering pain of his lost leg, but the two men never became friends. It was in Houston that they had nearly dueled the first time.

By 1841 Ward had followed the government to the new capitol in Austin and had served as mayor before becoming the head of the General Land Office. Those were exciting times in Texas. The new government was just getting established, and there was talk of becoming annexed by the United States. Meanwhile Mexico was still threatening to reinvade and reclaim Texas as part of Mexico.

He had run into an old friend and another New Orleans Grey during that period—William Lockhart Hunter, who had survived the Goliad massacre and remained there after the war. Hunter had been elected a representative in Austin, and the two had been elated to see each other again. In February of 1841 a grand military ball had been held in the Senate chamber to honor Cooke's military exploits in developing central Texas for settlement while establishing a military presence to ensure the safety of the settlers. Ward and Hunter had attended the ball, and the three old New Orleans Greys had shared stories and memories in a moment of camaraderie.

Within two months, however, Cooke had been reassigned duties preparing for a punitive action against Mexican incursions into Texas, and Ward was attending a San Jacinto Day celebration when the ceremonial cannon exploded and blew off his right arm.

With the loss of one leg and now one arm, Ward had dedicated the remainder of his life to public service and concentrated on his duties as land commissioner, while Cooke had continued his military career. From his Austin office, Ward had followed Cooke's fortunes as a prisoner in Mexico and as a naval pirate on the high seas with the Texas navy. In 1846 Cooke had retired from the army and become adjutant general—giving the two men occasion to work together at times. Ward had known Cooke was in poor health, but the news today had still caught him by surprise.

He leaned back in his chair and closed his eyes. He and Cooke, for better or worse, had been co-conspirators in the revolution and evolution of Texas. And now he missed his old enemy.

Over the years, as an Austin politician and public servant, Ward had followed the few remaining Greys after San Jacinto whenever possible. Martin Kingsley Snell had sought him out after Stephen Austin's funeral in 1836, but the two had now lost contact. Through the General Land Office muster rolls, he knew that several former Greys had reorganized a new unit for duty with General Greene after San Jacinto, but he knew nothing of their present whereabouts. George Voss was a Texas Ranger somewhere, and John Rees had discharged to return to Europe.

He still occasionally ran into Michael Cronican, who was now a newspaper editor sometimes working in Austin. Someone had told him that Thomas Lubbock was involved with one of the many secret societies that had sprung up around Texas, and Albert Levy, the surgeon who had traveled to Texas with them on the *Columbus,* had retired from the Texas navy and was now practicing medicine in Matagorda. Ward had heard he was suffering bouts of severe melancholy.

The remaining New Orleans Greys had truly become scattered in the winds blowing across Texas since the revolution. Though he couldn't explain it—even to himself—his relationship to Cooke over the years had been the most binding tie he still felt with the group of young men that night in Bank's Arcade during another era.

He opened his eyes and pulled the rope next to his desk to summon an aide. With his good arm missing, he now needed help writing letters. And, although he was sure the governor had also sent a note to Goliad, Thomas Ward felt he needed to write Judge Hunter.

CRCRCREOEOEO

*T*he Alamo had no messengers of defeat, but Goliad did: A small group of Greys survived to tell their stories. A few others departed earlier, after the victory at Bexar, and some of them remained in Texas and became part of the new republic. A "third" company of former New Orleans Greys even re-entered Texas after San Jacinto and once more pursued an invasion of Matamoros.

But it is the Goliad survivors who give us the most detailed—and graphic—details of the fate of the Greys as a military force.

William Hunter, who had feigned death at the massacre only to be stabbed by a bayonet, have his throat slit, and be stripped of his clothing, did eventually manage to reach the San Antonio River that night. One account of his escape reveals:

> . . . he lay until nightfall, when he dragged
> himself to the river and crossed over and
> walked to Manahuila (Manawea) Creek, two
> miles away, where he wandered into a Mexican
> ranch. He met a woman, who concealed him in
> the woods, and for a week she came each night
> and brought him food and water until he was
> able to move on. She robbed the wardrobe of
> some of her men folk and provided him with
> clothes and prepared such food as he could
> carry. He trudged on for weeks and finally
> reached the Texas army.[1]

Another version suggests that Nicholas Fagan, Fannin's blacksmith spared by the Mexicans at Goliad, also escaped and found Hunter badly wounded. Fagan then carried him to a nearby Mexican family living on Manahuilla Creek. They hid and nursed him until he could proceed to Mrs. Margaret Wright's nearby ranch house on the Guadalupe River above Victoria, where he recovered from his wounds.[2]

In his later years Hunter avoided speaking of the subject of his escape and rarely mentioned it. He did, in fact, remain in Goliad after the revolution and took a prominent part in the development of the area and the republic both as a lawyer and a politician. He served as chief justice of Refugio and Goliad Counties and was elected to the Republic of Texas House in 1839 where he served in three legislative sessions before being elected senator and representing Goliad at the annexation convention of 1845.

In 1850 he married Eunice Fedelia Cook and remained in Goliad until his death on October 25, 1886. His remains are interred in the Texas State Cemetery at Austin.

Herman Ehrenberg also survived the massacre by swimming the San Antonio River that day. Ehrenberg had many mysteries in his life—a fact enhanced by his unabashed self-promotion. There is much confusion about him and his life. He was born in either Thuringia, Germany, or Steuden, Prussia, between 1816 and 1818, which would make him as young as seventeen years old at Bexar.

Some reports indicate he was Jewish, others claim he was Lutheran. One source even states he once claimed to be "Pastor Ehrenberg" and traveled around baptizing children[3]—a claim that could not have been true in post-revolutionary Texas, since he had returned to Germany during that period.

He was one of the youngest New Orleans Greys and had been the third to sign up at Bank's Arcade, therefore he probably received one of Stearne's prized new rifles.

Ehrenberg joined Dr. James Grant, a leader he deeply admired, but like the other Greys ended up in Goliad under Fannin's command. Ehrenberg later wrote so vehemently against Fannin that many historians question his objectivity on the events occurring at Coleto and Goliad.

After crossing the San Antonio River the day of the massacre, he wandered lost across the south Texas prairie for nearly a week—wounded, infected, and feverish. He eventually discovered an abandoned plantation—probably that of Sylvanus Hatch—and ate some raw eggs. There he found written in charcoal, on the door, the name of Thomas Camp whom Ehrenberg had known at Goliad, so he knew he was not the only survivor.

He had some close calls around Mexican military encampments but was becoming too weak to even steal food, so he approached the soldiers and claimed to be a German traveler who had become lost. He was taken to Urrea's tent and confronted by Holzinger, but the artillery colonel didn't recognize him in his tattered, sickly state. Paraded before several Texan prisoners, none of them gave away his true identity.

Holzinger took him to Matagorda where he helped other prisoners build a boat. After the defeat at San Jacinto, Holzinger left for Mexico on the boat, and Ehrenberg again slipped away to wander along the coast with another escapee. They wandered for several days, eating at the deserted plantations they came across, until they met a third escapee at the home of Thomas Kelly. While there, Kelly returned to inform them of the victory at San Jacinto, and they walked to Matagorda, which was by then occupied by Texan troops.

On June 1, 1836, in an ironic twist of fate, a captured Holzinger was brought into camp, and Ehrenberg convinced the Texans not to kill him. The next day Ehrenberg received an honorable discharge from the army, a worthless draft for $130, and title to one-third league of land, which he never claimed.

After discharge he returned to Germany and studied mining and taught English at a university there. He reconstructed his diary, which was lost in the San Antonio River, from memory while in Germany and published copies under different titles in 1843, 1844, and 1845. After seven years and geographical separation from other Goliad veterans, he claimed to have written an accurate account of the Greys and the revolution. His book, however, covered periods—Fannin's execution for example—where he was not present, and he never returned to Texas so he could not have consulted with other survivors.

He did later return to the United States, however, and crossed the country—probably on the Oregon Trail—with a fur-trapping party. From Oregon, he sailed to Hawaii and worked as a mapmaker while visiting a number of Polynesian islands.

In 1846 he was back in California and took part in the "Bear Flag Rebellion" against Mexico. In March 1848 he joined the First New York Regiment on an armed incursion to Baja, Mexico, to rescue American prisoners during the Mexican War. The mission succeeded, and Ehrenberg and the recovered prisoners retreated an amazing 130 miles of rugged Baja territory in just thirty hours.

During the California Gold Rush in 1848 he became heavily involved in mining operations, and in 1853 he made the first map of the recent Gadsen Purchase. By 1856 he was an engineer and surveyor for the Sonora Exploring and Mining Company. He gained a degree of wealth and distinction in territorial surveying, cartography, and mining during which he filed over one hundred mine claims.

In the 1860s he was an Indian agent for the Mohaves on the Colorado River Reservation. Early in the morning of October 9, 1866, he was shot and killed after he had stopped overnight at a desert stage station at Dos Palmas. Some reports claim he was killed by Indians for his mule; others speculate the stationmaster killed him for money he was carrying. He was buried in Mineral City, Arizona, and the town was renamed Ehrenberg in his honor.

Ehrenberg, largely due to his writings and maps, was a well-known name outside Texas at the time of his death. Inside Texas, due to three translations of his diary, his name is often synonymous with the New Orleans Greys.

But for a man who claims he jumped, wounded, into the San Antonio River yelling "Republic of Texas forever!," he never returned to his "adopted homeland" nor did he have any known contact with other veterans afterward. There is no question his diary serves as a valuable reference for the Greys and the revolution, but the issue remains that he was one of the guards who possibly slept on the plain of Coleto while Urrea's forces surrounded Fannin. This is a fact he does not directly address in his diary, and the other survivors' accounts—except for Dr. Barnard who condemned him—hardly mention Ehrenberg at all. Whether or not he was held responsible by the other Greys for their predicament that day, he was in fact grossly negligent in his guard duty.

William Brennan was another Grey who made it to the San Antonio River and escaped during the massacre. Little is known about him after that. Two weeks later Doctors Barnard and Shackleford, who had been paroled at Bexar, rode into deserted Goliad where they found Brennan wandering about as if in a dream.[4]

Jonathan Rees escaped the river on March 27 only to be recaptured and held prisoner until after the Mexican defeat at San Jacinto. In April or May of 1836 he was paroled back to New Orleans where he met former New Orleans Grey William Graham, who was organizing another volunteer group to go to Texas and march on Matamoros once again. Rees signed up and joined five former Greys during the summer of 1836 but discharged the army honorably on October 10.

After cashiering out of the army, he sold all his land bounties and returned across the Atlantic and worked for a time in Manchester and London before returning to his native Wales.[5]

By 1839 he was employed in the Welch village of Tredegar as a mason in the local ironworks, and his name began appearing in literature involving the workers' rights rebellion against the local wealthy industrialists. Unionism of the workers had largely failed, and the radical insurrectionary leaders had promoted labor unrest under the name of Chartism.

Chartism was based upon a manifesto printed in 1838 titled *The People's Charter* and advocating six specific reforms including universal male suffrage. Throughout the isolated villages around Tredegar, the Chartist movement was attracting large numbers of impoverished miners and ironworkers. In the aftermath of the British government's refusal to recognize the Chartist demands, several of the leaders began advocating violent rebellion against the Queen's government.

One of those leaders was John Rees, the former New Orleans Grey and veteran of the battle of Bexar and a survivor of the Goliad massacre. In his native Wales, Rees was known as "Jack the Fifer" to differentiate him from another Chartist leader by the name of John Rees.

Revolutionary rhetoric and mass demonstrations during the summer of 1839 led to a high state of tension in the region and the dispatch of British troops to the larger towns. By November the Chartist leaders, including John Rees, were advocating an armed rebellion to militarily drive the British soldiers and police back and establish a "worker's commonwealth."

On November 3 nearly five thousand armed workers advanced upon the town of Newport in three columns. Former Grey John Rees was selected to command the column from Tredegar and was designated to direct the attack on Newport.[6]

By 7:00 P.M. that evening, the several thousand workers began entering the town from the surrounding countryside with Rees leading his column and, in torrential rain, establishing a position in front of the Westgate Hotel where the mayor and British army had assembled their defenses in the center of Newport.

The attack on the Westgate Hotel was begun around 9:00 on the morning of November 4, 1839, by several hundred workers. John Rees directed the attack from the front of the hotel. Forced back by the soldier's fire and himself wounded in the hand, Rees made some attempt to rally his men.[7] The fighting lasted fifteen or twenty minutes and resulted in a rout of the workers with at least nine dead in and around the Westgate and at least twenty other rebels dead in other areas of Newport. The rebel leaders were either captured or forced to flee to avoid arrest. John Rees was among those able to escape.

Rewards were posted for the capture of Rees and the other leaders—all but two of whom were arrested in various points around Wales. Rees, however, was able to successfully avoid apprehension. In December he was charged with treason in "levying war against the Queen in her realm." The following month he was tried *in absentia* and found guilty of treason and sentenced to hanging and quartering with his body to be thrown on the town's rubbish dump.

Although his death sentence was later reduced to life imprisonment, British authorities never succeeded in arresting Rees or obtaining his extradition for imprisonment. With treason charges pending and a warrant for his arrest issued, he returned to Texas and obtained yet another Republic of Texas army commission. By 1853 he had claimed additional land and was homesteading it.[8]

During his life, John Rees joined the New Orleans Greys in Texas to fight against Mexican suspension of civil liberties and survived Bexar and Goliad. He then joined the Welch Chartists to fight for workers' rights against the British military and mine owners and survived being wounded in the attack on Newport. By the time he returned to Texas, both General Santa Anna and Queen Victoria had issued him death warrants.

During the short Texas revolution a great deal was written about and spoken of revolutionary ideals. For the most part, however, the rhetoric of civil liberties quickly faded after the fighting had started. Of all the New Orleans Greys—enlisted and officers—who subscribed to the Texan cause in 1835 and 1836, John Rees was probably the only real revolutionary in the true sense of the word.

Another New Orleans Grey, Thomas Kemp, is also listed as having escaped the massacre, but there are no further records of him. It is unknown if he died of wounds that day somewhere on the south Texas prairie or if he escaped and left Texas for his native England or elsewhere.

The three Greys who survived the massacre by virtue of their job assignments had far different experiences and stories to tell afterwards.

Joseph Spohn, after witnessing Fannin's execution, was held captive at Goliad briefly with Miller's men from the Copano capture. The distinguishing white armbands were designed to separate them from the men being massacred.

Urrea took a liking to Spohn and sent him to Matamoros where Spohn joined the Mexican navy and enlisted on the *Correo* long enough to jump ship and escape at Vera Cruz.[9]

New Orleans Grey Peter Griffin had survived the massacre when one of the wounded Mexican officers in the church hid him under his blankets. Griffin, who has also erroneously been listed as a Refugio colonist, was a Louisianian who had come to Texas with Breece's Company. He spoke a little Spanish, which increased his usefulness as a medic, and this probably saved his life after the massacre.

In the days after March 27 he helped save another Anglo Texan doctor by interpreting. Able Morgan had treated a Mexican patient for colic by rubbing camphor on the sick man's stomach. When the man lost consciousness the Mexicans thought Morgan had poisoned him, and only Griffin's intercession saved Morgan's life.[10]

Griffin evidently had a short temper, and the conditions he was subjected to as a prisoner medic became so bad that he finally rebelled. According to Morgan:

> He had all the labor of washing bandages to perform, except what little help he received from Shirlock, who sometimes aided him when he was not otherwise engaged. They worried Pete and made him so mad that he cursed the whole of the Mexican officers and soldiers for a set of blood-thirsty savages, to their faces, in the Spanish language. They took him with the avowed intention of shooting him. Pete defied them, for he felt that his condition could not be made worse. This is what Pete told us afterwards, for neither Shirlock nor myself understood three words of Spanish at that time. They put him into the Calaboose three or four days and then took him out again and set him at his old task of washing the bandages. At the time of the massacre they took all of our clothes from us.
>
> The interpreter told us that the Mexican Physicians had said that if we could find any of our clothes we should have them. I went to searching and found one of my shirts and one blanket. I do not think that any of the rest got any thing at all. Mine were marked. Pete had not change of clothes and his employment caused him to be very offensive, as he was careless about keeping himself clean.[11]

When the Mexican wounded were transported to Copano for evacuation to Mexico, Morgan later recalled:

> The wounded were hurried off in carts and sent down to the Copino, and placed on board of a vessel. When we were about to leave

Goliad the interpreter told us that Hale, Shir-
lock, Pete and myself could have our choice to
go on with the wounded and their guard and
remain loose, or we might be tied two and two
together and walked to Matamoros with Miller's
men. We four agreed to by sea.[12]

George Voss, at the beginning of the massacre, hid himself
under some lumber in the fort's jail. Some time later Able
Morgan was escorted to the jail and found Voss. He recalled
that Voss came out and the Mexicans cursed him awhile, then
brought him over and seated him with the other physicians.[13]

Since the Mexicans had been duped into believing Voss
was a real doctor, they spared him and used him to continue
assisting their wounded. In this capacity he worked closely
with Dr. Joseph Field, who recalled: "At length a German by
the name of Vose, whose impatience under repeated insults
had subjected him to many mortifying punishments, came to
an understanding with me. . . ."[14]

It appears the long, exhausting filthy work of changing
infected bandages and washing dressings had brought Voss,
like Peter Griffin, to the point of insubordination. The
"understanding" with Dr. Field was an escape plan that they
successfully executed.

Voss and Field crossed the San Antonio River and headed
north across the Guadalupe and Colorado Rivers. Because
Voss could not swim, Field had to pull him across the rivers
on handmade rafts. Eleven days and 150 miles later they met
a San Jacinto veteran and learned of Santa Anna's defeat.
They arrived at Velasco in mid-May, and Voss received his
military discharge on May 30.

Based upon various reports concerning Voss during the
revolution, it would be easy to view him as an opportunist,
slacker, and even as a coward. However in the following
years he remained in Texas and become deeply involved in
the evolution of the Republic of Texas.

By 1842 he was a veteran Indian fighter and had served a six-month duty assignment with famed Texas Ranger Captain John C. Hays. Voss' service with the elite Hays' Rangers is documented, therefore it can be safely assumed he was neither a slacker nor a coward.

Voss was working in San Antonio when the Mexicans reinvaded the city in 1842 and was captured with sixty-one other Texans. Taken to Mexico, he was imprisoned in Perote prison until 1844. It was his third imprisonment by the Mexicans: Bexar, Goliad, and Perote.

After his release, he returned to San Antonio and died a few years later. Like fellow German Herman Ehrenberg, he never married and left no family. His career and service to Texas has been eulogized: "As a survivor of both the Goliad Massacre and captivity in Perote prison, and a former Texas Ranger, George Voss was one of the most experienced veterans of the Texas struggle to gain independence from Mexico and to civilize the frontier."[15]

After Bexar, several Greys discharged or furloughed for personal or medical reasons. Since the revolution would end four months later at San Jacinto, these furloughs effectively ended the participation of these men in the conflict; however, they did not end the military careers of the men in the post-revolution military of the Republic of Texas.

A West Point graduate who was already involved in land speculation arrived in Texas shortly after San Jacinto. Enlisting in the Texan cause, Thomas Jefferson Green abandoned his land business and was commissioned a brigadier general with the mission of returning to New Orleans and recruiting soldiers for Texas.

On July 25, 1836, a company of volunteers under General Green's command was assembled near Victoria. The roster from the General Land Office Archives Office titled "Company [of Volunteers], Brig. Gen. Green Command" reveals that the company of three-, six-, and nine-month enlistees was commanded by a Captain William Graham—formerly of "Cooks Orleans Greys" and staffed by New Orleans Greys veterans 2nd Corporal "John L Hall," 3rd Corporal "M McKeevor," and 4th Corporal "Wm D Durham." The roster also includes Private "Jno Rees," of Wales—also a former New Orleans Grey.[16]

While the terms of enlistment for these volunteers ranges from three to nine months, the roster also includes an enlistment dated from October 12, 1835—the date of the Bank's Arcade meeting in which the Greys were formed. It is not clear if this enlistment date was chosen so that veterans like the Greys could have their service backdated to allow credit for the storming of Bexar when they made future land grant claims.

The archive records show that Graham joined the company on April 15—the very day his furlough ended—and was elected captain on the sixteenth. Durham's participation is more difficult to trace. According to the *New Handbook of Texas*, he "marched to the east and fought at the battle of San Jacinto. His name is engraved (incorrectly, as William Daniel Durham) on the face of the San Jacinto monument."[17]

The roster for Graham's company included the notation for Durham: "Private in Cooks Orleans Greys. 17th Jany 1836 recd. an unlimited furlough. Joined this Co. at Orleans. 16th April Elected 2nd Sergt. 16th May resigned. Elected 4th Corpl. 26th June 1836."[18] Since he had joined this company at New Orleans on April 16—five days before the battle of San Jacinto—it is unlikely he could have participated in the fight there with Sam Houston. Also, Samuel Dixon and Louis Kemp, in their book *The Heroes of San Jacinto*, do not mention a William Durham being present at the battle.[19]

Durham was elected second sergeant of Graham's Company on May 16 and resigned but was elected fourth corporal on June 26. He was serving a three-month enlistment.

The *New Handbook of Texas* also states that William Davis Durham, the New Orleans Grey, resided in Houston after the revolution until 1838 when he died of yellow fever. He is buried in Old Founders Memorial Park, and his grave is identified with a marker placed by the state.[20]

John L. Hall, who had received an unlimited furlough, reenlisted in Graham's Company on the twenty-seventh of May 1836. Marshall McIvor (spelled "McKeever") also enlisted in the company on May 27, one month before his five-month furlough expired. He was elected third corporal on June 26.[21]

Jonathan Rees, one of the New Orleans Greys who made it across the San Antonio River on March 27, is listed on Graham's roster as "Jno Rees" who "escaped from the massacre at Labaoie (La Bahia), then in Cooks Greys." He joined Graham's company at Galveston on May 6 and was on furlough at the time of the July 25 roster report.[22]

Pennsylvanian Martin Kingsley Snell was a New Orleans Grey who would later fight at San Jacinto. A private with Morris' company, he was only twenty years old when he left Bexar. Three months later he was commissioned a second lieutenant in the Texas army marching toward Harrisburg. By April 21, 1835, he had been promoted to first lieutenant and fought at San Jacinto with the Regular Infantry Company A.[23]

San Jacinto would only be the beginning of a long military career for Snell. After the revolution, he remained with the regular Republic of Texas army and commanded the honor guard at Stephen Austin's funeral in 1836. A letter posted August 10, 1836, reveals he was struggling desperately to make ends meet as a quartermaster:

> Office of the Quarter Mr General
> Quintana August 10. 1836
> To Lieut. M. K. Snell
> Sir,
> I have just received a requisition from you
> for numerous articles most of which do not
> belong to this department for instance Medicins

cloathing &c There is but one article in your
requisition that is in store here, that is, soap.
There is a lot of cloathing expected soon.

You had better make your requisitions for
your stores in Bulk as you are situated so far
from here, unless there is stores at your place
Respectfully Yours &c
A. Huston
Qr Master General[24]

On December 11, 1836, he was promoted to the rank of
infantry captain. In March of 1837 he was assigned as company commander of regular army troops at Velasco when he
was called upon to arrest a soldier for being absent from his
post. On March 24, 1837, he and a small detail of men
approached Lieutenant J.T. Sproul—the soldier to be
arrested. Francis Lubbock later described the scene:

Captain Snell, commanding a company of
regulars on the post, came in. He accosted Lieutenant Sproul as to his absence from the post.
Hot words ensued, and the lieutenant was shot
down by his captain and killed. Snell was exon-
erated, as Sproul probably attempted to draw
his sword. He afterward had several unfortunate difficulties, and was himself many years
afterward killed in Hempstead. He was a member of my brother Tom Lubbock's company the
New Orleans Grays, and proved himself a brave
soldier.[25]

In 1840 Snell's name reappears in the midst of yet
another Mexican civil war—this time between the Centralists
and Federalists in the northern Mexico state of Coahuila.
Again, he was sided with the anti-Santa Anna Federalists,
only this time in the secessionist Republic of the Rio Grande.
He was one of ten Texan volunteers serving in the Federalist
army when they were surprised and captured.

He succeeded in escaping and was pursued and over-taken by a Mexican who had known him at San Antonio and was his friend. Hiding Snell under some canes, a Mexican family managed to save his life.[26]

He later fought in the Mexican War with the U.S. Army and in the Civil War as a Confederate major. Contrary to Francis Lubbock's report that he was later killed at Hemp-stead, at the end of the Civil War Snell returned to Houston where he died in 1865.[27]

Blaz Phillipe Despallier returned to his native Nachito-ches after the fighting for Bexar. He has been variously listed as wounded and sick. He did not return to Texas and died from cholera around 1839. His son, also named Blaz Phillipe, later fought for the Confederacy with the famed Louisiana Pelican Rangers.

Thomas Saltus Lubbock continued on a long military career, although he discharged from the Greys after Bexar and did not serve again until after the revolution.

Lubbock's brother Francis later wrote that at the time of the Texas revolution, the family was undergoing a difficult bankruptcy proceeding in South Carolina, and he had man-aged to obtain a position for Tom in the cotton business in New Orleans. Before the younger brother could get estab-lished, however, he announced he was volunteering for the military units organizing at Bank's Arcade and leaving soon for Texas. The older Lubbock, although disappointed, outfit-ted Thomas and sent him off to war knowing the family in South Carolina would disapprove.

Francis Lubbock described Thomas as: "...so young to go on such an expedition without a particular friend or coun-selor. Though well up in all manly sports, quite an athlete, very strong and muscular, and full of fire and determination, he was only seventeen years of age."[28] If this is true he—and not Herman Ehrenberg—may have been the youngest Grey.

Upon leaving Bexar and the Greys, Lubbock operated a steamer on the upper Brazos River and later claimed he was not aware that Santa Anna had reentered Texas until hearing of the Texan victory at San Jacinto. While this story seems difficult to believe given the state of Texas politics and social upheaval during the fall of the Alamo, Runaway Scrape, Goliad massacre, and battle at San Jacinto, Lubbock cannot be accused of hiding throughout the war due to cowardice.

He would later join the Texan Santa Fe expedition, be captured and imprisoned in Mexico, escape, and return to Texas. When the Mexican army recaptured San Antonio in 1842, Lubbock joined the Somervell forces in driving them back across the Rio Grande but stopped short of joining the disastrous Mier Expedition.

It is somewhat surprising that Dr. James Grant did not influence Lubbock in the days immediately after the battle for Bexar. In the years just before the Civil War he was a strong secessionist and characterized as a "very worthy and zealous Knight of the Golden Circle."[29]

Like Grant, the Knights of the Golden Circle advocated the annexation of Mexico—only to establish a slave empire controlling supplies of tobacco, sugar, rice, and coffee.

His high profile military career was aided in part by his political affiliations with Texans like Benjamin Terry, John Wharton, and his brother Francis R. Lubbock, who was the governor of Texas during the Civil War.

The Knights of the Golden Circle died out with the advent of the Civil War. Lubbock was active in the Confederate army and participated at the First Bull Run and later in Terry's Texas Rangers. Late in 1861 he became ill and died in December of 1862. He was characterized by one of his men as "small and affable, and made a favorable impression on us."[30] He and Snell are the only known Greys who were also Confederate veterans.

Thomas Breece, one of the two original Greys captains, had furloughed after Bexar to do recruiting work for Sam Houston. After the revolution, he received a bounty grant for 640 acres, which he later sold. A "Thomas H. Breeze" was elected justice of the peace of the Sixth District at Harrisburg on February 4, 1839. The 1840 census of the Republic of Texas listed Breece as a resident of Harris County and the possessor of one watch and one clock. By February 1, 1851, he had died, and a Henry J. Breece had been named executor of his estate.[31]

Thomas R. Stiff joined the New Orleans Greys at Bank's Arcade with a letter of high reference from A.R. McNair. He distinguished himself during the storming of Bexar and afterwards disappeared from the rolls and rosters of the Greys. After the Texas revolution, however, he reappeared in Fort Bend and wrote a letter to Vice President Lamar, warning him that a local newspaper had printed something with his name attached that he might object to. In that letter, dated March 3, 1838, he describes leaving a copy of the newspaper article in question with Mrs. (Jane) Long and concludes the correspondence by signing himself as "Your friend."[32]

By September 5, 1839, Stiff is no longer referring to himself as Lamar's friend. To the contrary, on that date he filed a lawsuit against Lamar, then president of the Republic of Texas, to recover $435 in debt he claimed Lamar owed him. In the suit, Stiff claimed:

> ... in the year 1838 and at divers times thereafter petitioner furnished and supplied the said M B La[mar] with board for himself and servants and others, also furnished and provided at sundry times the meats an[d] wines necessary for supplying Cabinet diners all of which doth more fully and at large appear by particular account hereunto annexed. And your petitioner in fact saith that all these things were

done and performed and supplies furnished at
the special instance and request of him the said
M B Lamar, and did specially assume and promise to pay the sum of money aforesaid
whenever thereafter requested. But notwith-
standing the promise and obligation of him the
said Lamar, he hath refused and still doth
refuse to pay his Just de[bt.]³³

It appears from the charges that Stiff, in 1838, was operating a hostelry in Houston that catered to government
officials near the republic's capitol. Among the charges were
two months board at $20 a month; fifteen days board for
Lamar's private secretary; $100 for a Cabinet dinner; $125
for a senatorial dinner; and $250 for a dinner catered for
Representatives. Stiff claims a total of $685 in owed debts
and credits Lamar $250 for "1 sorrel Horse," making a bal-
ance due of $435.³⁴

On October 26, 1839, Stiff wrote a letter from Richmond
and addressed it to Lamar in Austin. In that letter he accused
the president of slandering him and even of interfering in
Stiff's marital problems. In that correspondence he charged:

I beg pardin for obtruding my self upon
your notice, but under the existing circumstances I can not refrain from so doing. On my
arrival at Houston I was informed by many
respectable citizins of that place, that you had
taken an unwarrintable privilige of abusing me
in my absence, The first charge you brought
was that I had forged your signature on two
notes drawn by me in favor of Judge Scott in
Houston In the second place that you knew that
I had left my family never to return. In the
third place that I had sued you for three thousand dollars in good money, I do pronounce the
above charges to be false, and debace as the

author which I hope I shall be able to prove to
every honest citizin of this republic; I shall take
my family to Houston in some few days, where
I shall be happy to receive an answer to the
above

Respectfuly
T R Stiff

P S I am extreamly happy to here that you
have become so sympathetic of late, that when
ever you saw my wife that your heart bled &
that you would do every thing in your power to
obtain a divorce for her. Permite me to
reckomind the affair of the government to your
charge as I percieve them to be in a much
worse state, than my own[35]

By December 2, 1839, the feud had evidently involved
the already legendary "Mother of Texas" Jane Long, who also
wrote Lamar from Richmond: "From what I can learn Mr
Stiff is decidedly hostile in his feelings toward you & threat-
ens to sue you for slander I have not seen him since his
return—"[36]

By September 21, 1840, the lawsuit must have been
resolved. Lamar received a letter from his attorney in Richmond suggesting Stiff had prevailed in at least part of the
final judgement. In that letter John V. Morton wrote Lamar:
"I have had an interview with Judge Scott in relation to the
Stiff Business and the following is what he will do. (To Wit)
he will take the $500, you pay the cost of the suit and his
attorney fee and leave to him the right of collecting of Stiff
the Balance of the Judgment, he transferring to you the
amount you pay, and exonerates you from further Liability"[37]

Private Michael Cronican, a printer and newspaperman
from Boston, was another Grey who had left Bexar for medical treatment. Returning to Texas in time to participate in the
battle of San Jacinto with the 2nd Regiment Volunteers, 3rd
Infantry Company, he remained in the service of the Texas

army as an express rider in the days after the revolution had ended. As a civilian, he managed the Fayetteville Hotel, located between Houston and San Felipe, briefly before returning to his trade as a printer. In 1842 he joined in the ill-fated Mier Expedition and escaped captivity to return to Texas. He then helped found and print newspapers in Galveston, Austin, and San Antonio.

It was in San Antonio—scene of his service as a New Orleans Grey at Bexar in 1835—where he died during a cholera epidemic in 1849. He was eulogized as a "warm-hearted man, a printer, and, in his late years a sprightly editor."[38]

Another New Orleans Grey who later pursued a career in journalism was Sidney S. Callender. Although he never published any known diary or journal of his time with the Greys, he was instrumental in maintaining the Greys' unit history. When the original muster roll was lost in the 1855 fire at the adjutant general's office, it was initially thought all records of the early Greys were lost. In 1886, however, historian John Henry Brown contacted Callender, who at that time was a retired printer and publisher in New Orleans, and discovered that the former Grey had maintained a copy of the original muster roll of Morris' company.[39] Brown also reports that the two had served together on the Rio Grande in 1842, although there is no record of Callender listed on the Army of the Republic or Republic of Texas militia rolls for 1836-1842.

New Orleans Grey Captain Thomas William Ward was also furloughed to New Orleans after the fighting. Serving with the artillery during the battle of Bexar, Ward lost his leg to a cannonball and was sent to Louisiana to be fitted with an artificial limb. Also like Cronican, he returned to Texas in the spring of 1836.

Born in Ireland in 1807, he had immigrated to Quebec in 1828 and later to New Orleans and had studied engineering and architecture. After the revolution, he worked briefly in construction in Houston and contracted the building of the

Republic's capitol there while serving in Harrisburg County politics.

When the capitol was moved to Waterloo, soon renamed Austin, Ward moved to that city and served as clerk of the House of Representatives. He was elected mayor of Austin on two occasions and appointed to the mayoral position one other time. He also served as the second commissioner of the General Land Office for seven years.

Nicknamed "Peg Leg" for the limb lost in the battle of Bexar, he suffered another cannon accident during a celebration in 1841. At a San Jacinto Day celebration in Austin, Ward, in his position as land commissioner, was preparing to light a cannon when it misfired and blew off his right arm and injured his right eye. The tough Irishman and ex-Grey did not let his injuries and loss of limbs deter him from public duty.

A year later he was fired upon with grapeshot, but not injured, in the so-called "Archives War" over removal of records from the state capitol. Ward apparently never let his physical limitations keep him far from the action of the moment throughout his lifetime.

He also served outside Texas politics: United States consul to Panama in 1853 and U.S. customs collector in Corpus Christi in 1865. He died in Corpus Christi during a typhoid fever epidemic in 1872.[40] In a fitting obituary, the *Austin Democrat Statesman* compared the former New Orleans Grey to an "oak, which had been shorn of its limbs. . . ." Like William Hunter, he is buried in the Texas State Cemetery in Austin.

One of the Greys' two physicians, Albert Moses Levy, also discharged the unit after Bexar but continued in a military capacity throughout the remainder of the revolution with the Texas navy.

Levy, the Dutch-born Virginian who had studied medicine in Pennsylvania, had been appointed surgeon in chief of the volunteer army prior to Bexar. Ten days after Cos' capitulation, Levy wrote a letter to his sister back in Richmond. In his letter, he wrote of his role in the fighting and his self-perceived importance in the events of the five-day battle. The letter was generally typical of soldier's correspondence home from afar except for one remarkable comment: Levy claimed it was he—and not Cooke—who joined Ben Milam in rallying and mobilizing the Greys for the assault on Bexar.

In the December 20, 1835 letter, the doctor wrote of the events leading to the assault on the city:

> ...Finally affairs became so bad that the
> army broke up in confusion, and desperate
> would have been the consequences for we
> would all have been cut by the enemy when I,
> *insignificant* I, and another individual citizen of
> Texas called Milam [Colonel Ben R. Milam],
> beat up for volunteers who would join us two
> in storming the town and fort that very night. (I
> should mention that from my mixing about a
> great deal with the soldiers and chatting and
> joking with them I had acquired some popular-
> ity among them). Our company, called the
> Grays, immediately and to a man signed their
> names and mounting one of the baggage wag-
> gons (for we, as I have observed, were just
> ready for a hasty retreat) I harangued them for
> a few minutes and thus succeeded in getting 3
> hundred men....[41]

This passage, if taken literally, would question the role of William G. Gooke and even the historical role of Ben Milam himself. In reality, Levy may have *helped* rally the troops, but it is almost certain he was not instrumental in "haranguing" the Greys and succeeding in signing up three hundred men. Of the four men actually present at Burleson's headquarters who later wrote accounts of the meeting—Cooke, Johnson,

W.T. Austin, and Dr. Field—not one even mentioned Levy's name in reporting the rallying call for troops that day.

Levy's letter continues to describe some of the street fighting and house-to-house combat during the five-day battle:

> Our men fought like devils, (even I fought). I worked in the ditches, I dressed the sick and wounded, I cheered the men, I assisted the officers in their counsels, for five days and nights I did not sleep that many hours, running about without a coat or hat, dirty and ragged but thank God escaped uninjured. I received a slight wound on the forehead the first day which was completely well before we took the town. I was much exposed to the fire of the enemy and all our men wondered how I escaped with my life. I have crossed a street when more than two hundred muskets were shot at me, our men begging me not to expose myself as I was a double man, being both soldier and surgeon.[42]

Levy's "head wound" must have been very slight since in their December 17 letter to the governor and General Council, surgeons Samuel Stivers and Amos Pollard did not list Levy among the Greys and other volunteers injured during the fighting.

Nevertheless, after the fighting at Bexar, Levy discharged the Greys and joined the Texas navy—enlisting to serve on the *Brutus*. In 1837 he transferred to the *Independence* and was aboard when Mexican ships captured it. Imprisoned in Matamoros briefly, he escaped with the help of a British subject serving in the Mexican army and returned to Matagorda where he settled.

While he succeeded in establishing a medical practice and starting a new family in Matagorda, he never managed to overcome his despondency over the death of his wife, Maria, and his separation from his daughter, Rachel. After the revolution he was unable to reestablish close ties with his father, who had opposed his leaving Rachel and traveling to Texas with the Greys in the first place. After settling in Matagorda, Levy—who was Jewish—married an Episcopalian woman, and they had five children, who were raised in the Episcopalian religion. This caused a further breech between Levy and his family in the United States, and they refused to respond to his requests for information about Rachel. His despondency increased, and he committed suicide in 1848.[43]

Second Lieutenant Charles B. Bannister discharged the Greys after Bexar and also joined Houston's regular army. His role in the remainder of the revolution is unknown until April 15, 1836—one week before San Jacinto—when he wrote the following letter to David Burnet:

> To His Excellency the President of the Republic of Texas
> I now hold a commission given by Col. Ed. A. Wharton as a Commissary at the Port of the Brazos; as that commission has, by necessity, been expired, I will either accept a Capt's. Commission to recruit or a regular Commission of Commissary. I have business in New Orleans and think with my acquaintance, I could recruit there to some extent.
> C.B. Banister
1st Lieut. N.O. Greys
Actg Comy. Galveston Island
> New Washington
> April 15th 1836[44]

Bannister, it appears, had been employed as a commissary officer and was now offering his services to Texas as a recruiter.

Private Adam Mosier, a private with Morris' company who served with Cooke at Bexar, disappeared from the Grey's rosters after the San Antonio fighting but appeared at San Jacinto with Captain Fisher's Infantry Company I, 1ˢᵗ Regiment. He later enlisted in the Somervell Expedition and continued on with the Mier Expedition. He was captured and held in Perote Prison. He later retired and built a home in Gonzales County.[45]

John Belden, who had lost an eye spiking a cannon outside the Priest's House, had discharged the Greys with $40 mustering out pay on January 20. Three months later he was back at San Jacinto serving in Infantry Company B (Volunteers) under Captain Asama Turner.[46]

Bennett McNelly, a sergeant with Pettus' Greys at Goliad, was later listed as "absent because of illness or duty." His name reappears at San Jacinto as a sergeant major with Sidney Sherman's 2ⁿᵈ Regiment Texas Volunteers.[47] In 1840, with Martin Kingsley Snell, he reappears in the Federalist Mexican army during the Republic of the Rio Grande civil war. Captured during the same battle in which Snell managed to escape, McNelly was one of nine Texan volunteers who were captured and executed.[48]

Another Grey who disappears from the Bexar rolls is Pennsylvanian William Boyle, who came to Texas with Morris and served at San Antonio under Cooke. After Cos' surrender, Boyle is not mentioned in any further Greys' correspondence, but a "William Boyles" appeared at San Jacinto with the 2ⁿᵈ Regiment 5ᵗʰ Infantry Company under Captain Thomas McIntire.[49]

The New Orleans Grey to achieve the greatest post-revolution prominence was William Gordon Cooke. After leaving Goliad on February 14, he had transported two Mexican prisoners to Washington-on-the-Brazos where he was appointed assistant inspector general by Houston.

His heroism and success in the storming of the Priest's House during the Bexar fighting had launched what would become a distinguished military and political career in the republic and later, the State of Texas.

Cooke was at San Jacinto on April 21 when the Texans routed Santa Anna's forces and was in charge of Mexican prisoners when the Mexican general was brought into the Texan camp. Only Cooke's intervention prevented the angry Texan mob from lynching the Mexican president before the wounded Houston could meet with him.

In the process, he became a close friend and confidant of Sam Houston, and when Houston was sent to New Orleans to have his San Jacinto battle wounds treated, Cooke accompanied him. Later, in 1839, when Houston's injuries became disabling, he appointed Cooke to sign promissory notes for the Republic of Texas—an appointment based upon a great deal of personal trust.

Between San Jacinto and 1839 Cooke held military appointments and commissions as chief clerk of the War Department, stock commissioner, acting secretary of war, and inspector general.

Cooke, who had learned the druggist business with his family back in Fredericksburg, Virginia, and had been a druggist in New Orleans when he enlisted with the Greys, opened two drugstores in Houston in 1837.

A year later he reenlisted in the army and was commissioned quartermaster general of the republic and given responsibility for negotiating treaties with the Comanches. He was present in San Antonio in 1840 during treaty negotiations when Texan soldiers, in response to Comanche refusal to release prisoners, entered the Council House and attempted to take custody of the Indian leaders there. In the resulting melee, thirty-five Comanche were killed, resulting in a prolonged period of Indian warfare in Texas.

That summer he was promoted to colonel and given responsibility for constructing a road through central Texas and establishing military posts to deal with the Comanche backlash to the Council House incident. Despite Indian attacks and difficult engineering problems, the project was completed, and Cooke was offered the nomination for vice president of the Republic of Texas. Choosing at that time to concentrate on his military career, he refused the nomination, and President Lamar assigned him the duty of organizing the Santa Fe Expedition. Participating in it, Cooke was captured and interned in Santiago Prison in Mexico for six months. He returned to Texas in August 1842 and rejoined the Texan forces.

In September of that year he was wounded in action and shortly later appointed quartermaster general. In that capacity, he organized the punitive Snively Expedition to intercept and capture the property of Mexican traders passing through Texas on the Santa Fe Trail. He was also responsible for the organization of another punitive force, the Somervell Expedition, which he briefly joined himself.

In the spring of 1843 Cooke went to sea and joined Edwin Ward Moore on his raiding expeditions against Mexican shipping off the coast of Yucatan. Since Yucatan rebels funded the blockade and raids, this involved Cooke once again in internal Mexican politics against the Centralists under Santa Anna.

He also managed to become involved in British-Texan politics through his naval excursions. On the sloop-of-war *Austin,* Cooke participated in attacks against two Mexican ships, the *Montezuma* and *Guadalupe.* The ships had been a diplomatic sore point between Texas and Great Britain, since they had been constructed and armed in England in defiance of British neutrality laws. With Moore, Cooke participated in attacks that severely damaged the *Montezuma* and nearly disabled the *Guadalupe* in April of 1843.

Although Sam Houston had initially commissioned Moore to blockade the Mexican coast, funds had been withheld and the orders rescinded. Still, Moore continued his raids financed by rebel Yucatan money, and by June he controlled the entire Gulf. Aboard the *Independencia*, Cooke twice participated in attacks against Mexican ships—military actions which led Houston to suspend Moore from the Texas navy and accuse him of disobedience, mutiny, piracy, and murder. Upon his return to Texas, a trial was held in which Cooke defended Moore in court; all but a few minor charges were dismissed and Moore's commission was reestablished. After the trial, General Sidney Sherman appointed Cooke adjutant general of the Texas militia.

In August 1844 Cooke married Angela Maria de Jesus Blasa Navarro, niece of Jose Antonio Navarro—signer of the Texas Declaration of Independence. At this point in his life, he had risen to the higher echelons of Texas elite—politically and socially.

The following month Cooke was elected to the legislature as a representative from San Antonio. His defense of Moore had earned the admiration of President Jones, who appointed him as secretary of war, a post he held until running unsuccessfully for the U.S. Congress in 1846. After his defeat he was appointed adjutant general of the State of Texas by Governor Henderson—a post he held until his death from tuberculosis while visiting his father-in-law's ranch in Seguin on December 24, 1847.[50]

During his later years he frequently came into contact with another former New Orleans Grey, Thomas William Ward, with whom he feuded and nearly dueled on two occasions.[51] Like Ward and William Hunter, Cooke is interred in the Texas State Cemetery in Austin—the last of three Greys so honored.

---

1   Wharton, *Remember Goliad*, pg. 51.

2   Craig H. Roell, "Hunter, William Lockhart" *New Handbook of Texas*.

3   O'Connor, *The Presidio La Bahia del Espiritu Santo de Zuniga, 1721 to 1846*, pg. 192 (footnote).

4   Wharton, *Remember Goliad*, pg. 45.

5   Ivor Wilks, *South Wales and the Rising of 1839* (Urbana: University of Illinois Press, 1984), pg. 139.

6   *Ibid.*, pg. 186.

7   *Ibid.*, pg. 200.

8   Ivor G.H. Wilks, "Rees, John" *New Handbook of Texas.*

9   O'Connor, *The Presidio La Bahia del Espiritu Santo de Zuniga, 1721 to 1846*, pp. 144-5.

10 *Ibid.*, pg. 216.

11 *Ibid.*, pp. 216-7.

12 *Ibid.*, pg. 219.

13 *Ibid.*, pg. 212.

14 Jenkins, *The Papers of the Texas Revolution* Vol. 9, pg. 221

15 Louis E. Brister, "Voss, Johann George Andreas" *New Handbook of Texas.*

16 Texas General Land Office Archives, [A10][tran, pg. 2].

17 Charles Durham Gouldie, "Durham, William Davis" *New Handbook of Texas.*

18 Texas General Land Office Archives, [A10]tran].

19 Samuel Dixon and Louis Kemp, *The Heroes of San Jacinto* (Houston: Anson Jones Press, 1932).

20 Gouldie, *Ibid.*

21 Texas General Land Office Archives, [A10]tran].

22 *Ibid.*

23 Dixon, *The Heroes of San Jacinto.*

24 Jenkins, *The Papers of the Texas Revolution* Vol. 8, pg. 195.

25 Francis Richard Lubbock, *Six decades in Texas; or, Memoirs of Francis Richard Lubbock, governor of Texas in war time, 1861-63* (Austin: B. C. Jones & Co., 1900), pg. 28.

26 *Lamar Papers*, Vol. 6, pg. 105.

27 Thomas W. Cutrer, "Snell, Martin Kingsley" *New Handbook of Texas.*

28 Lubbock, *Six decades in Texas*, pg. 35.

29 Thomas W. Cutrer, "Lubbock, Thomas Saltus" *New Handbook of Texas.*

30 *Ibid.*

31 Thomas W. Cutrer, "Breece, Thomas H." *New Handbook of Texas.*

32 *Lamar Papers*, Vol. 5, pg. 177.

33 *Ibid.*, Vol. 3, pp. 99-100.

34 *Ibid.*, pg. 100.

35 *Ibid.*, pp. 146-7.

36   *Ibid.*, Vol. 5, pp. 328-9.

37   *Ibid.*, Vol. 3 pp. 450-1.

38   Helen B. Frantz, "Cronican, Michael" *New Handbook of Texas.*

39   John Henry Brown, *History of Texas From 1685 to 1892 in Two Volumes* (Austin: Jenkins Publishing Company, 1970), Vol. 1, pp. 404-5.

40   Sara May Meriwether, "Ward, Thomas William" *New Handbook of Texas.*

41   Saul Viener, "Surgeon Moses Albert Levy," *American Jewish Historical Quarterly*, December 1956, pp. 101-13.

42   *Ibid.*

43   Natalie Ornish, "Levy, Albert Moses" *New Handbook of Texas.*

44   Jenkins, *The Papers of the Texas Revolution* Vol. 5, pg. 479.

45   Dixon, *The Heroes of San Jacinto.*

46   *Ibid.*

47   *Ibid.*

48   Nance, *After San Jacinto—The Texas-Mexican Frontier, 1836-1841*, pg. 261.

49   Dixon, *The Heroes of San Jacinto.*

50   Steven A. Brownrigg, "Cooke, William Gordon" *New Handbook of Texas.*

51   Barr, *Texans in Revolt*, pg. 65.

Epilogue

Sam Houston never really knew the New Orleans Greys. He rode beside them and talked with them as individuals and in groups on the San Patricio Road to Refugio. He even convinced them to abandon Dr. Grant's Matamoros folly. But he never saw them in action. As his detractors liked to point out, Sam Houston was not at Bexar, the Alamo, or Coleto. Had they gotten to know each other better, they probably wouldn't have liked each other.

The New Orleans Greys were the types of soldiers Houston would have scorned for their lack of discipline and, at the same time, admired for their courage and fighting skills.

One can easily imagine the Greys riding along at the head of the Runaway Scrape, complaining about Houston's indecision and threatening "to go their own way." One can also imagine them leading the eighteen-minute assault on the Mexican breastworks at San Jacinto. But it was not to happen.

Overall, Sam Houston probably wouldn't have disliked them any more than the other volunteer units he often disdained. And they probably wouldn't have liked him simply because he wasn't one of their own.

The Greys were highly effective when serving under their own leaders: Morris, Breece, and Cooke at Bexar; Blazeby in the Alamo; and Pettus at Coleto. They did not serve well under leaders they had not chosen. They liked Ben Milam and had genuinely mourned his loss at Bexar, but Milam had not exercised direct leadership over them. Despite Ehrenberg's glowing praise of Dr. James Grant, the Greys quickly abandoned him at Refugio. They were critical of Travis in the Alamo—voting unanimously for the drunken Bowie as their leader. With regards to Fannin, they were openly defiant to the point of insubordination and hostile to his command.

But under the command of Cooke at Bexar, the Greys led the final deadly assault on the Priest's House that was the turning point in the battle. Two Greys officers, Cooke and Morris, accepted Cos' surrender. Inside the Alamo compound, it was a New Orleans Grey, John Baugh, who sounded the alert in the early morning hours of March 6, and it was also Baugh who—after Travis' death early in the assault—was the commandant of the Texan forces throughout the Alamo battle. It was yet another New Orleans Grey, Joseph Spohn, who attended Fannin until the moment of his execution and gave us a firsthand account of the final terrible moments in that courtyard on March 27, 1836.

Led by their own, the New Orleans Greys were the most effective fighting force to serve in Texas during the seven-month revolution. They are the only Anglo Texan unit to have served at Bexar, the Alamo, San Patricio, Agua Dulce, Refugio, Coleto, and Goliad. A few survivors even served at San Jacinto.

Santa Anna claimed the New Orleans Greys were mercenaries and pirates, and technically he was correct. The Greys entered Texas at Gaine's Ferry and Velasco as military units. There is no indication any of them brought along wives or families. They carried American-manufactured guns and Dupont powder and wore uniforms made in the United States. They were non-Mexican, non-Catholic, and English-speaking. They did not stop at Nacogdoches or Brazoria and become Mexican citizens nor did they even pretend to convert to Catholicism as had the earlier settlers including Sam Houston. They had no intention of adopting the Spanish language: a fact brought home at Goliad when only one Grey, Spohn, could translate.

They were military mercenaries, not pioneers or settlers, and they came to Texas for adventure and material gain—

not constitutional freedoms. Initially buoyed by the boisterous and generous welcomes from the Anglo Texan settlers as they advanced on San Antonio, the Greys eventually became disillusioned at their role as revolutionaries when the colonists failed to take up arms and join them once the fighting had begun.

At Bexar, they had shared the combat with Mississippi volunteers and a handful of colonists from Brazoria. At the Alamo, the total force of nearly two hundred men included only thirty-two Anglo settlers from Gonzales and a sprinkling of other colonists. Muster rolls at Goliad are even more revealing: *New Orleans* Greys, *Kentucky* Mustangs, *Mobile* Greys, *Louisville* Volunteers, *Alabama* Red Rovers, *Nashville* Volunteers.... Only a few Irish colonists from around Refugio and San Patricio were present at Coleto or the later Goliad massacre.

They served without pay and certainly without adequate supplies. For some, the adventure of war was enough, but most wanted free land—whether to settle on or to sell will remain unknown.

They drank, smoked, and gambled. Reports after Bexar indicate they freely took part in the vices of the city. They were very young men, far from home, and recent combat veterans. Almost certainly some of the Greys joined Bowie's drunken rampage through town to free jailed prisoners. Records from Goliad show that large quantities of brandy and corn liquor were consumed by the volunteers there. Some of the Greys took part in appropriating—robbing— horses and other supplies from the Mexican locals there. Harassment and abuse of the townspeople remaining in Goliad were rampant.

But the New Orleans Greys were not a barbaric horde sweeping through Mexican Texas in 1835 and 1836. They also revealed acts of compassion as well as bravery. After the Mexican woman was shot retrieving water during the battle of Bexar, the Greys rushed to her aid despite enemy fire. Rather than execute Mexican prisoners during the fighting, they adopted the practice of drawing crosses on walls and making their prisoners "swear" not to pick up arms again. Some of those same parolees returned to massacre Greys in the Alamo and at Goliad. After Cos' surrender, the retreating Mexicans were even given enough arms and ammunition to protect themselves from Indian attacks.

When Ehrenberg and other Greys found hidden grain in storage at the ruins of Mission San Jose, they did not steal it from the impoverished families living there but negotiated a payment and assured enough would be left behind to feed them.

The Greys were heroic and fierce in battle but compassionate in victory. Far more so than some of the other U.S. volunteer units—Duval's Mustangs for instance—and certainly far more humane in their conduct of war than Santa Anna with his "no quarter" policy.

Because the Greys were always at the forefront of the fighting, they were wounded and killed in disproportionate numbers. The muster rolls carved into granite monuments at the Alamo and Goliad are testimony to those numbers.

There are few other memorials to their service. In New Orleans, on 336 Magazine Street, part of the original Bank's Arcade building still stands. Partially destroyed by fire in 1851, it was rebuilt by Henry Howard and later renovated during the 1960s and 70s. Today the building serves as a retail outlet on the ground floor.

The waters of Toledo Bend Reservoir now hide Gaine's Ferry where Breece's company entered Texas. The blue silken flag that was presented to Captain Breece by "grateful young ladies" on the western bank of the Sabine River now hangs in display at the Chapultepec Castle national museum in Mexico City. Retrieved near the end of the Alamo battle by Lieutenant Jose Maria Torres of the Zapadores battalion, the banner was returned to Mexico where Santa Anna touted it as proof of "the true intention of the treacherous colonists, and of their abettors, who came from the ports of the United States of the North." In 1995 Texas Governor Bush signed into law a legislative bill that created a commission to negotiate the exchange of three Mexican flags captured at San Jacinto for the New Orleans Greys standard, but Mexico has indicated little interest in the trade.

In Nacogdoches, Sterne's house is now a museum and features the bivouac area where the Greys camped for the "Feast of Liberty."

In downtown San Antonio, all that remains of the Alamo compound is the reconstructed chapel, part of the Long Barracks, and the cavalry courtyard. The deadly eighteen-pounder cannon that Morris and the Greys brought to Texas was ordered thrown into a drainage ditch by Santa Anna. It was later recovered and is on display in the Alamo compound outside the Long Barracks.

The location of the remains of the Greys and other defenders who died in the Alamo remains in dispute. Santa Anna ordered at least two pyres built and the bodies burned, but the fires were not effective and only partially destroyed the bodies. Local Mexican residents individually buried remains in several unmarked spots. In November 1836 Colonel Juan Seguin reoccupied San Antonio on behalf of the Republic of Texas and discovered three separate heaps of ashes assumed to be the remains of the defenders. He purportedly ordered these remains buried in a wooden coffin near the altar of San Fernando church, which was later elevated to cathedral status. In 1936 these remains were discovered by workmen making repairs to the altar of the cathedral, and the "remains" were then placed in a new marble coffin and enshrined near the entrance of the church. Many contemporary historians dispute the remains are those of the defenders.

La Villita has been restored as an art colony with only the house where General Cos signed the surrender papers still intact. Mission San Jose, where Ehrenberg and the others found the hidden supplies, has been restored.

After the revolution, the town of Goliad was rebuilt on the north side of the San Antonio River about two miles from the fort. Mission Espritu Santo, where the Greys camped before entering the presidio from San Antonio, is now a state park, and the mission is also restored. Across the river, Presidio La Bahia has also been reconstructed and restored with its massive stone walls and bastions.

Even after the fort had been abandoned and fallen into ruins, the Our Lady of Loreto chapel continued to serve as a Catholic church—as it does today. It too, has had massive restoration, but one can sit in the pews and imagine those nights when nearly three hundred starving men were packed inside and the sound of Charles Sargent's flute was the only respite from their misery. The small sacristy where Fannin was held is now a flag museum, and on the outside of the chapel, in the rear, there is a huge bleached area on the stones. It was here that the Greys and other volunteers stacked and burned their food supplies before leaving for the plains of Coleto. Across the parade ground on the west side of the sally port is the calaboose where George Voss hid under lumber during the massacre.

The massacre site is now on private land and closed to the public, but one can cross the river and take the road inside Goliad State Park. About a quarter mile down from the presidio one can look across the San Antonio River at the location where the Greys were shot down. The river has changed little and it is easy to imagine that morning when black smoke drifted through the trees and Jonathan Rees, William Brennan, George Kemp, and Herman Ehrenberg stumbled down the dirt banks into the green waters and swam for their lives.

About a quarter mile from the presidio, a large mound of dirt covers the resting place of the Greys and other Texans who were slaughtered at Goliad that Palm Sunday morning. In front of the mass grave, a huge granite monument bears the names of all the victims.

The most touching monument, however, is located nine miles north of Goliad at the Fannin Battleground State Historical Site. Located on a rural road, the isolated site has very few visitors. The small area has only a picnic shelter and a small museum, otherwise it is just another depression in the Coleto plains. At the center of a circular hedge there is a granite obelisk that stands on the assumed surrender site. I feel it is the heart and soul of the New Orleans Greys.

Here it is easy to wonder about those we cannot trace. Did Ehrenberg fulfill his promise to notify Eigenauer's mother when he returned to Germany? Was Vincent Druillard, Christy's nephew, able to obtain an apothecary position in the regular army? What happened to Nicholas Kelly, the printer from Nachitoches, and why didn't he write the story of the Greys afterward?

Perhaps the inscription on the obelisk says it best. Dedicated to all the volunteers who fought and died at Coleto and Goliad, it seems, however, to speak directly to the New Orleans Greys:

> Victims of treacherys
> Brutal stroke
> They died to break the
> Tyrants yoke.
> Also
> On fame's etternal camping ground
> Their silent tents are spread,
> And glory guards with hallowed Round
> The bivouac of these dead.

Muster roll. New Orleans Greys, Capt. Wm G Cooke in the army before Bexar. 1835. — Siege of Bexar

Names	Rank	From	Names	Rank	From
Robert C Morris (appointed Major)		Louis	McLeod John D	Private	Engd
Wm G Cooke	Capt	Virga	McNeil John D		Scotld
Chas. B Bannister	Lieut	Louis	McEver Marshall		Kenty
Albert M Levey	Surgeon	Virga	Mahony Dennis		Ireland
Maunsel Wood	Ensign & 2d M		Koshin Adam		Kenty
Nathan R Brister	1st Sergt	Va	Noland James		Ireland
H.S. Smith	2d do	N.Y.	O'Brian Christopher		do
Geo Stephens	3d do	Eng	Proctor F		Louis
Edward Wrentham	4th do	Engd	French Wm G		do
Richd Ross	1st Corpl	Ill	Russell Hiram MC		Tenn
J.P. Riddle	2d do	Pa	Russ John		Wales
Lewis S Ameling	3d do	Louis	Sergeant Charles		Mass
J.S. Hall	4th do	Ireland	Snell Martin K		Penn
Abrahams, Alex	Private	Ohio	Stiff Thomas K		Virga
Addison J.G.		Maryd	Stringer C.A.		Louis
Blewer William		Engd	Vose Geo		Genoa
Boyle William		Penna	Walker Hartwell		N Ham
Beldin John		N.Y.	Ward Shot W		Ireland
Carravis Chas S		S.C.	West James		Penna
Cony S		Vert	Wood John		S Carol
Callender Sidney S		Miss			
Chamberlain Willard		Ohio			
Connor Charles A		Tenn			
Cornell John		do			
Cass James M		Connct			
Croniaan Michael		Mass			
Dickerson Noah Jr		Up Cand			
Durham Wm D		Engd			
Donaldson W		Louis			
Gilland Geo M		Connt			
Graham W		Nova Scotia			
Gray Francis M		Scotland			
Lanis Geo		Engd			
Hardy Julian		S.C.			
Harper W		Ireland			
Aaron Nicholas		Virga			
Hill Stuart		N. York			
Holton Mathew		Mass			
Hunter Wm D		Virga			
Huyth C.L.		Mass			

New Orleans Greys roster taken prior to storming of Bexar.

290

Appendix A

New Orleans Greys' Roster

The following is a combined roster of the two companies of the New Orleans Greys formed at Bank's Arcade on October 13, 1835. This revised muster roll is the result of combining the information available from the Texas General Land Office archives, the Daughters of the Republic of Texas *Muster Rolls of the Texas Revolution*, Jenkins' *The Papers of the Texas Revolution 1835-1836 in Ten Volumes*, the Mirebeau B. Lamar Papers in the Texas State Library, *The New Handbook of Texas*, and various other sources listed in the bibliography.

The original handwritten muster rolls contained various spelling discrepancies, and the names listed below are cited by the most commonly used references. The unit commander of each individual is listed in parentheses based upon their assignment when they enlisted in the New Orleans Greys. While the names of the enlistees are fairly well documented, much of the information about the individuals remains a mystery. As Karl Baker wrote of his work in 1937, this appendix is to be taken as an attempt only—an invitation to future inquirers to amend and complete.

જીજીજીજ્ઞ ૭૭ ૭૭

Abrams, Alexander (Morris)

Private from Ohio who was wounded at Bexar. Does not appear on rosters after the battle.

Addison, G.L. (Morris)

Private from Massachusetts. No reference after enlistment.

Amelung, Lewis F. (Morris)

Third corporal from Louisiana. No reference after enlistment.

Andrews, George (Breece)

Sergeant with no listed home state. Fought at Bexar and later killed in the Alamo.

Bannister, Charles B. (Morris)

Second lieutenant from Louisiana who fought at Bexar and later discharged the Greys to serve in the Texas regular army. Registered as a commissary officer in the Texan army at Galveston after San Jacinto.

Baugh, John (Breece)

First lieutenant from Virginia who fought at Bexar and remained at the Alamo. Thought to have alerted the defenders when the attack began and became the *de facto* commandant when Travis was killed. Ordered the final retreat to the Long Barracks in the final moments of the fighting.

Belden, John (Morris)

Private from New York who lost an eye trying to spike a Mexican cannon during the fighting at Bexar. Mustered out to New Orleans for medical treatment but returned and fought at San Jacinto.

Blazeby, William (Breece)

Second lieutenant from Great Britain who fought at Bexar and was then assigned to command the Greys remaining in San Antonio. Died in defense of the Alamo.

Blown, William (Morris)

Private from Great Britain. No reference after enlistment.

Boyle, William (Morris)
Private from Pennsylvania who fought at Bexar and discharged the Greys to later fight in the regular Texas army at San Jacinto.

Breece, Thomas H. (Commanding)
Louisianian who was elected captain of the unit that traveled overland to Texas. Fought with distinction as a unit commander at Bexar and later discharged at Sam Houston's request to serve as a recruiter for the Texas army. He died in Houston around 1851.

Brennan, William (Pettus)
Name first appears on Pettus' roster during the Matamoros Expedition. Fought at Coleto and survived the Goliad massacre. Two weeks later he was found wandering "in shock" in the streets of Goliad. No further reference.

Bright, John (Breece)
Private from North Carolina who fought at Bexar and joined the Matamoros Expedition. Was on assignment with Ward to protect colonists when attacked and managed to escape. Was outside Victoria serving on a water detail when they were again attacked; was able to escape (one record indicates he was "lost") and was one of the very few to avoid capture and execution. No further references.

Brister, Nathaniel B. (Morris)
First sergeant from Virginia who fought at Bexar and Coleto and was later massacred at Goliad.

Brugnickse, John (Breece)
Private from South Carolina. No reference after enlistment.

Callender, Sidney S. (Morris)
Private from Mississippi who had previously been a newspaper printer and editor for the *Lafayette Gazette* in Louisiana. No reference after enlistment.

Canter, Joshua (Breece)

Private from South Carolina. No reference after enlistment.

Carrine, Charles J. (Morris)

Private from South Carolina. Fought at Bexar and Coleto and massacred at Goliad.

Cary, Seth (Morris)

Private from Vermont. No reference after enlistment.

Casey, John (Breece)

Private from Ireland who was later listed as "expelled" from the Greys with no reason listed.

Cass, James M. (Morris)

Private from Connecticut who was wounded during the Bexar assault and was later killed with Morris at Agua Dulce.

Chamberlain, Willard (Morris)

Private from Ohio. No reference after enlistment.

Clark, Charles (Breece)

Private from Louisiana. One of several Charles Clarks serving during the Texas revolution and sometimes erroneously listed as having died in the Alamo. Fought at Bexar and Coleto and was massacred at Goliad.

Coffee, John (Breece)

Private from Ireland who was later listed as "expelled" from the Greys with no reason listed.

Connell, John (Morris)

Private from Pennsylvania. No reference after enlistment.

Connor, Charles W. (Morris)

Private from Pennsylvania who became separated from unit as they approached Bexar and was later found murdered by Mexican soldiers. First New Orleans Grey casualty of the Texas revolution.

Cook, John (Breece)
Private from Great Britain who was a veteran British naval artilleryman. Killed during the storming of Bexar.

Cooke, William G. (Morris)
First lieutenant from Virginia who was promoted to captain and led company in the assault on Bexar. Considered one of the heroes of that battle. His heroism and success in the storming of the Priest's House during the Bexar fighting launched a distinguished military and political career in the republic and later, the State of Texas. Cooke was at San Jacinto on April 21; his intervention prevented the angry Texan mob from lynching Santa Anna. A druggist by trade, he reenlisted in the army and was responsible for negotiating treaties with the Comanches. He was present at the Council House incident and later given responsibility for establishing military posts to deal with the Comanches. Responsible for organizing the Santa Fe Expedition, he was captured and interned in Santiago Prison in Mexico. He organized the Snively and Somervell Expeditions, which he briefly joined. He also served with the Texas navy before retiring to private life where he held numerous governmental posts, including legislative representative, secretary of war, and adjutant general of the State of Texas. He died in Seguin on December 24, 1847, and is interred in the Texas State Cemetery.

Corine, Charles M. (Morris)
Listed Pennsylvania as his home when he enlisted at Bank's Arcade. No reference after enlistment.

Courtman, George F. (Pettus)
George Courtman (also listed as Curtman) was a German who does not appear on the Bank's Arcade muster rolls but was listed as a Grey at Coleto and was killed in the Goliad massacre. The brother of Henry Courtman.

Courtman, Henry (Breece)

Private from Germany who enlisted in New Orleans, fought at Bexar, and was later killed in the Alamo.

Cronican, Michael (Morris)

Printer and newspaperman from Boston who left after Bexar for medical treatment. Returned to Texas to participate in the Battle of San Jacinto and remained in the Texas army. In 1842 he joined the Mier Expedition and escaped captivity to return to Texas where he founded and printed newspapers in Galveston, Austin, and San Antonio. He died during a cholera epidemic in 1849.

Crossman, Robert (Breece)

Private from Pennsylvania who fought at Bexar and was later killed in the Alamo.

Dabney, Lewis (Breece)

Private from Tennessee. No reference after enlistment.

Dennison, Stephen (Breece)

Private from Great Britain who fought at Bexar and later was killed in the Alamo.

Despallier, Blaz Phillipe (Breece)

Joined Breece's unit as they traveled through Louisiana and participated in the assault on Bexar but furloughed home after the fighting. His brother Charles then came to Texas and died in defense of the Alamo.

Dickinson, Noah Jr. (Morris)

Listed citizenship as "Upper Canada" upon enlistment. Fought at Bexar and Coleto and was massacred at Goliad.

Dimpkins, James R. (Breece)

Private from Great Britain who fought at Bexar and was later killed in defense of the Alamo.

Druillard, Vincent (Morris)

Joined Greys as a runaway in New Orleans. Trained as a pharmacist, he was the nephew of New Orleans Greys organizer and sponsor William Christy. No reference after arrival in Texas.

Durham, William D. (Morris)

Englishman who fought at Bexar and then furloughed to New Orleans where he rejoined a military unit involved in border skirmishes in the Republic of Texas era.

Ehrenberg, Herman (Breece)

German who fought at Bexar and Coleto and later escaped the Goliad massacre to return to Germany and write a diary of his experiences with the Greys. Returned to the United States and traveled to Oregon and sailed to Hawaii and other Pacific locations as a surveyor and mapmaker. Joined the Mexican War and participated in the Bear Flag Revolt. Killed at a stagecoach stop in Arizona on October 9, 1866. Because of his diary, he is the most famous of the New Orleans Greys.

Eigenauer, Conrad (Breece)

German who fought at Bexar and joined the Matamoros Expedition. Killed during the Battle of Coleto and buried with the massacre victims at Goliad.

Fitzgerald, James (Breece)

Private from Louisiana who is listed as "Deserted" on later muster rolls without further reference.

Garrett, James Girard (Breece)

Louisiana native who enlisted as a private, fought at Bexar, and was killed in the Alamo.

Gatlin, William Jones (Breece)

Private from Tennessee who fought at Bexar and joined the Matamoros Expedition. Joined Grant and escaped the battle at Agua Dulce to return to the Greys at La Bahia. Fought at Coleto and was massacred at Goliad.

Gilland, George M. (Morris)

Private from Pennsylvania who fought at Bexar and Coleto and was later massacred at Goliad.

Graham, William (Morris)

Private from Nova Scotia who distinguished himself during the storming of Bexar and was mentioned for bravery at Zambrano Row. Furloughed to New Orleans after the fighting and later organized another volunteer unit consisting of at least five other New Orleans Greys veterans to participate in the Republic of Texas border wars with Mexico.

Gray, Francis H. (Morris)

Private from Scotland who participated in the battle for Bexar, fought at Coleto, and was later massacred at Goliad.

Green, George (Morris)

Englishman who joined as a private, fought at Bexar and Coleto, and was massacred at Goliad.

Greer, Andrew (Breece)

Private from Tennessee. No reference after enlistment, however his brother Thomas N.B. (who was not a Grey) later manned one of the "twin sisters" cannon at the Battle of San Jacinto.

Griffin, Peter (Breece)

Private from Louisiana who participated in the assault on Bexar and the Battle of Coleto. Spared from the Goliad massacre by a wounded Mexican officer to whom he had been administering aid. He was later held captive and forced to work as a medic until he escaped with Dr. Joseph Field.

Hall, J.L. (Morris)

Fourth corporal from Ireland who was wounded on the rooftops with Deaf Smith during the assault on Bexar. Given medical furlough to New Orleans but later joined Graham's company of Greys veterans and returned to Texas in the Republic of Texas border skirmishes.

Harby, Julian (Morris)

Private from South Carolina whose father, Isaac, was already considered the founder of Reform Judaism in the United States. There is no further reference after his enlistment.

Harpen, William (Morris)

Private from Ireland who fought at Bexar and Coleto and was later massacred at Goliad.

Heath, Edenezer Smith (Morris)

Massachusetts private who participated in the Bexar assault and the Battle of Coleto and was later massacred at Goliad.

Herron, Nicholas (Morris)

Private from Virginia. No reference after enlistment.

Hersee, Daniel (Breece)

Private from Great Britain who fought at Bexar and later was killed in defense of the Alamo.

Hill, Stuart (Morris)

New York private who fought at Bexar and Coleto and was massacred at Goliad.

Holbrook, Nathan (Morris)

Private from Massachusetts. No reference after enlistment.

Holloway, Samuel (Breece)

Tennessee private who fought at Bexar and was later killed defending the Alamo.

Howell, William D. (Breece)

A medical doctor from New York, Howell's name on the early roster lists him simply as a "private." He participated in the assault on Bexar and remained behind with the Greys in the Alamo. He died on March 6, 1836, with the other defenders.

Hunter, William Lockhart (Morris)

From Virginia, Hunter was a lawyer when he enlisted in the Greys as a private. He participated in Bexar and Coleto and escaped the Goliad massacre despite being bayoneted and having his throat cut. Hidden by a Mexican family and later by Margaret Wright, he survived and after the revolution became a Goliad resident involved in political affairs as a lawyer and elected official. He served as chief justice of Refugio and Goliad Counties and was elected to the Republic of Texas House in 1839 where he served in three legislative sessions before being elected senator. He remained in Goliad until his death on October 25, 1886, and is interred in the Texas State Cemetery at Austin.

Hutchinson, T.P. (Breece)

Private from Tennessee, he fought at Bexar and was later killed in the Alamo.

Jackson, F.W. (Breece)

Private from Great Britain. No references after enlistment.

Johnson, Francis (Morris)

Listed his home as Maine. No reference after enlistment.

Jones, John (Breece)

Sergeant from New York. Fought at Bexar and was later killed in the Alamo.

Kelly, Nicholas (Breece)

Irishman who enlisted at Nachitoches, Kelly was a printer by trade. He was immediately appointed quartermaster, but there are no references after his joining the unit.

Kemp, Thomas (Breece)

A private from Great Britain, Kemp fought at Bexar and Coleto and is listed as having escaped the massacre at

Goliad, but there are no further records of him after the revolution.

Kinney, Allen O. (Morris)

Private from Virginia. Fought at Bexar and Coleto and later massacred at Goliad.

Leonard, Francis White (Morris)

Louisiana native who fought at Bexar and joined the Matamoros Expedition. After Sam Houston's speech at Refugio convinced the Texans not to continue with Grant, a large number of dissatisfied men discharged the army, and Leonard also cashiered out at this time. No further reference after that time.

Levy, Albert Moses (Morris)

Born and raised in Holland and educated as a physician and surgeon in Virginia and Pennsylvania, Levy enlisted in the Greys after his wife had passed away. He participated in the assault on Bexar, then resigned the Greys to become a surgeon in the Texas navy. After the revolution he was captured and imprisoned in Matamoros briefly. Escaping, he returned to Matagorda where he remarried and began a medical practice. His personal life was plagued with tragedy and sorrow, and he committed suicide in 1848. He is buried near Matagorda.

Linn, William (Breece)

Private from Boston. Fought at Bexar and later died in defense of the Alamo.

Lubbock, Thomas Saltus (Morris)

After suffering family financial problems in South Carolina, Lubbock enlisted as a private in the Greys. He fought at Bexar then discharged the unit and became a steamboat operator on the upper Brazos River for the remainder of the revolution. He later joined the Santa Fe Expedition and was captured and imprisoned in Mexico but later escaped. When the Mexican army recaptured San Antonio in 1842 Lubbock joined the Somervell forces but did not join the disastrous Mier Expedition.

Prior to the Civil War he was a strong secessionist and member of the Knights of the Golden Circle, which advocated the annexation of Mexico to establish a slave empire. During the Civil War, Lubbock joined the Confederate army and participated at the First Bull Run and later in Terry's Texas Rangers. He died in December of 1862. He was the brother of Francis Lubbock, governor of Confederate Texas during the war.

Magee, James (Breece)

Private from Ireland. Was wounded in the assault on Bexar and later killed in defense of the Alamo.

Mahoney, Dennis (Morris)

Private from Ireland. Participated in the assault on Bexar and the Battle of Coleto and was massacred at Goliad.

Main, George Washington (Breece)

First lieutenant from Virginia. Wounded in the fighting at Bexar then remained behind with the Alamo garrison and was killed in the battle there.

Marshall, William (Breece)

Private from Tennessee. Participated in assault on Bexar and was later killed in defense of the Alamo.

Mason, George (Breece)

Private from Great Britain. No reference after enlistment.

Mattern, Peter (Breece)

German citizen who fought at Bexar and Coleto and was in formation with fellow Germans Ehrenberg and Courtman when he was massacred at Goliad.

McIvor, Marshall R. (Morris)

Private from Kentucky. No reference after enlistment.

McLeod, John C. (Morris)
Claimed British background when signing up at Bank's Arcade. No reference after enlistment.

McNeil, John D. (Morris)
Private from North Carolina. No reference after enlistment.

McNelly, Bennett (Breece)
Sergeant from Pennsylvania. Participated in attack on Bexar and joined Matamoros Expedition but was later listed "absent Goliad illness or duty." Reappeared on muster rolls as a master sergeant at the Battle of San Jacinto. In 1840 he joined the Federalist Mexican army during the Republic of the Rio Grande civil war and was captured and executed.

Mills, George (Breece)
Listed New York as state of origin. No reference after enlistment.

Moore, Robert B. (Breece)
Private from Kentucky. Fought at Bexar and remained after the battle where, at age 55, he was the oldest New Orleans Grey and probably the oldest Alamo defender to die there on March 6, 1836.

Mormon, John (Breece)
Irishman who served as a private during the battle for Bexar and was later killed in the Alamo.

Morris, Robert C. (Commanding)
Led unit to Texas by ship from New Orleans and across land through Victoria and Goliad to San Antonio de Bexar. Led company into the battle for Bexar and after Milam's death was promoted to major and placed second in command. Had already aligned himself with the Matamoros proponents prior to the battle and led the call to move south as soon as the Bexar fighting had ended. At Refugio, he left the Greys and accepted a commission in the Mexican Federalist army

and continued south with Grant only to be captured and executed at Agua Dulce.

Mosier, Adam (Morris)

Private from Kentucky. Fought at Bexar and discharged Greys afterward. Later fought at San Jacinto.

Mussleman, Robert (Breece)

Born in Ohio and raised in Pennsylvania. A U.S. Army veteran of the Seminole Wars. Took part in the siege and assault on Bexar and remained as a sergeant in Blazeby's infantry company of former New Orleans Greys. Died in defense of the Alamo.

Nelson, George (Breece)

Private from South Carolina. Wounded during the assault and fighting for Bexar and later killed defending the Alamo.

Noland, James (Morris)

Irishman who fought at Bexar and is sometimes erroneously listed at the Alamo but traveled south on the Matamoros Expedition and was wounded during the Battle of Coleto and later massacred at Goliad.

O'Brien, Christopher (Morris)

Private from Ireland. No reference after enlistment.

Pettus, Samuel Overton ((Morris)

Private from Virginia who participated in the battle for Bexar and later joined the Matamoros Expedition. With Cooke's departure at Refugio, he was promoted to captain and was severely wounded at the Battle of Coleto. Brought to La Bahia with the last of the wounded prisoners, he was later executed during the massacre.

Preusch, William G. (Morris)

Private from Louisiana. Fought at Bexar and Coleto and massacred at Goliad.

Proctor, Frederick (Morris)

Enlisted as private from Louisiana. No reference after enlistment.

Rees, John (Morris)

Native of Wales. Enlisted as private and fought at Bexar and Coleto. Escaped the Goliad massacre only to be recaptured and held prisoner until after the Mexican defeat at San Jacinto. Paroled to New Orleans and joined Graham's unit to return to Texas but quickly discharged. He returned to Wales and became involved in the workers' rights rebellion there. Because of his military experience with the Greys, he was selected to lead an attack on British military that resulted in his being wounded and a death sentence posted against him. Fleeing back to Texas, he obtained a Republic of Texas army commission, and by 1853 he was homesteading land.

Riddle, Joseph P. (Morris)

Second corporal from Pennsylvania. Fought at Bexar and Coleto and was later massacred at Goliad.

Ross, Richard (Morris)

First corporal from Illinois. No reference after enlistment.

Ross, William (Breece)

Private from Louisiana who was later listed as "expelled" from the Greys with no reason listed.

Russell, Hiram H. (Morris)

Tennessee volunteer who enlisted as a private. No reference after enlistment.

Sargeant, Charles (Morris)

Private from Massachusetts. Participated in assault on Bexar and in the Battle of Coleto. Thought to be the flute player referred to by several sources during the imprisonment in the Loreto chapel and the night before the massacre in which he was killed.

Scott, John (Breece)

Pennsylvanian who fought in the assault on Bexar and at the Battle of Coleto. Massacred at Goliad.

Shaw, John (Breece)

Private from Great Britain who is listed as "Deserted" on later muster rolls without further reference.

Smith, Henry S. (Morris)

Second sergeant from New York. Fought at Bexar and Coleto and was later massacred at Goliad.

Snell, Martin Kingsley (Morris)

Private from Pennsylvania, he was commissioned a second lieutenant in the Texas army after participating in the fighting for Bexar. He fought at San Jacinto and remained in the Republic of Texas army and commanded the honor guard at Stephen Austin's funeral in 1836. In 1840 Snell joined the Mexican Federalist army and was nearly captured in the civil war—escaping only when a Mexican family hid him from the Centralists. He later fought in the Mexican War with the U.S. Army and in the Civil War as a Confederate major. He died in Houston in 1865.

Spohn, Joseph H. (Breece)

Louisianian who enlisted as a private at Bank's Arcade. Fought at Bexar and Coleto and was spared at the Goliad massacre because of his ability to speak Spanish and translate. It was Spohn who prepared Fannin for his execution and provided us with the only Anglo eyewitness account. After the massacre, he was sent to Matamoros where he joined the Mexican navy long enough to jump ship and escape.

Spratt, John (Breece)

Private from Ireland. Fought at the battle for Bexar and was later killed in defense of the Alamo.

Starr, Richard (Breece)
Englishman who enlisted as a private and participated in the siege and assault on Bexar and later died in the Alamo.

Stephens, George (Morris)
Third sergeant from Great Britain. No reference after enlistment.

Stephens, William (Breece)
Private who traveled to Texas with Breece and listed no home state or country upon enlistment. Fought at Bexar and Coleto and was massacred at Goliad.

Stiff, Thomas R. (Morris)
Virginian who enlisted as a private. He distinguished himself during the storming of Bexar and afterwards disappeared from the rolls and rosters of the Greys. After the revolution, however, he filed a lawsuit against President Lamar for charges he claimed he was due for providing room and board for politicians.

Stringer, E.N. (Morris)
Private from Louisiana. No reference after enlistment.

Thomas, Henry (Breece)
Englishman who enlisted as a private and fought at Bexar and was later killed in defense of the Alamo.

Voss, Johann George Andreas (Morris)
German national who enlisted with the Greys as a private. He was captured just prior to the storming of Bexar and spent that period as a prisoner. He later rejoined the Greys and participated in the Battle of Coleto. He survived the Goliad massacre by hiding inside La Bahia and was later spared by pretending to be a doctor. He escaped and wandered around south Texas until he was found by a San Jacinto veteran. By 1842 he was an experienced Indian fighter and had served with the Texas Rangers. Captured

when the Mexicans re-invaded San Antonio in 1842, he was interned in Perote Prison until 1844, then returned to Texas and died a few years later. He was a prisoner of war at Bexar, Goliad, and Perote, and as a Goliad massacre survivor, Indian fighter, and Texas Ranger he was fully involved in the struggles against Mexico and the Indians throughout his lifetime.

Walker, Hartwell (Morris)
Private from New Hampshire. No reference after enlistment.

Ward, Thomas William (Morris)
Irish immigrant who had studied engineering and architecture. Fought at the battle for Bexar and lost a leg. Legend has it that his leg was buried in the same grave as Ben Milam. After Bexar he furloughed to New Orleans for medical treatment and returned quickly to Texas. After the revolution he supervised the construction of the Republic of Texas capitol in Houston. When it was relocated to Austin, he moved to that city and served as clerk of the House of Representatives and was elected mayor of Austin on two occasions and appointed to the mayoral position one other time. He then served as the second commissioner of the General Land Office for seven years. He lost an arm to a cannon accident at a San Jacinto Day celebration but continued in public life to serve as consul to Panama and U.S. customs collector. He died in Corpus Christi during a typhoid fever epidemic in 1872 and is buried in the Texas State Cemetery in Austin.

Waters, Thomas (Breece)
Private from Great Britain. Fought in the siege and battle for Bexar and remained behind where he was killed in defense of the Alamo.

West, James (Morris)
Private from Pennsylvania. Participated in the battle for Bexar and fought at Coleto and was later massacred at Goliad.

Williams, John (Breece)

New York native who enlisted as a private. No reference after enlistment.

Winship, Stephen (Breece)

Private from New York who fought in the battle for Bexar and later left for Matamoros. Fought at the Battle of Coleto and was later massacred at Goliad.

Wood, John (Morris)

Private from South Carolina. Participated in the siege and assault on Bexar. Fought at the Battle of Coleto and was later a massacre victim at Goliad.

Wood, Mandaret (Morris)

Pennsylvania native who enlisted as a private and fought at Bexar. Later joined the Matamoros Expedition and participated in the battle for Coleto and was massacred at Goliad.

Wood, W.B. (Breece)

Private from New Jersey. Fought at Bexar and Coleto and was later massacred at Goliad.

Wrentmire, Edward (Morris)

Fourth sergeant from Great Britain. No reference after enlistment.

Appendix B

Archive Photos and Documents

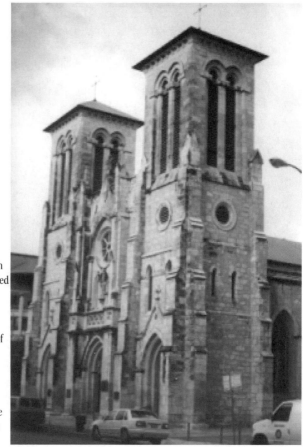

The San Fernando church from which the Mexicans shelled the New Orleans Greys with devastating effect during the Battle of Bexar is today a cathedral and contains a tomb thought by some historians to house the remains of the Alamo defenders.

The 18-pounder cannon was transported by Morris' company of the Greys from New Orleans to Velasco and later hauled overland to reach San Antonio shortly after the Battle of Bexar had concluded. It was later used by Travis and the Greys in the Alamo with deadly effect in defending the compound on March 6, 1836. It is displayed today in the Alamo complex.

This carronade cannon is a veteran of the Alamo siege and may have been the "twelve-pound gunnade" Ehrenberg later claimed Morris' company of Greys had transported to San Antonio.

This 6-pounder Spanish cannon was spiked and buried in the courtyard of La Bahia by the Greys prior to their departure in March of 1836. Excavated in 1936, it is now on display at the fort.

This large cannon was spiked and abandoned in Goliad prior to the Greys departure with the other Texans under Fannin. Hours later, they were surrounded on the plains of Coleto and after a fierce battle were forced to surrender.

The Mission Espiritu Santo lay in ruins when the New Orleans Greys camped here early in 1836 on their trip to Matamoros after the fighting in Bexar. At Sam Houston's urging, the Greys abandoned the Matamoros Expedition and later returned to the nearby La Bahia presidio at Goliad. The reconstructed mission is now part of Goliad State Historical Park.

Another view
of the Mission
Espiritu Santo.

The Our Lady of Loreto chapel inside La Bahia fort was used to imprison the Greys and other Texan prisoners after the Battle of Coleto. Sick, feverish, starving, and tending their wounded, nearly 250 Texan prisoners were packed into the tiny church for several days without food and very little water.

It was inside this tiny Our Lady of Loreto chapel that Herman Ehrenberg and the other Greys were imprisoned several days prior to the Palm Sunday Massacre in 1836.

Those Greys who did not remain at the Alamo after the Battle of Bexar eventually were bivouacked at the old Spanish fort La Bahia in Goliad under Fannin's command. It was from this fort they departed and later fought the Battle of Coleto, and it was here that they were returned as prisoners and massacred on Palm Sunday, 1836.

La Bahia

This granite obelisk, located in a depressed area on the Coleto plains north of Goliad, marks the assumed surrender site after the fierce battle in which the Greys and other Texans were forced to surrender in order to save their wounded.

After the Palm Sunday Massacre, the Greys and other Texans were partially burned and left to the elements until after the Revolution. Later, they were interred near the La Bahia presidio in this mass grave.

William Cooke, who assumed leadership of one of the Greys companies during the storming of Bexar, died near Seguin in 1847 and is today interred in the Texas State Cemetery in Austin.

The reverse of William Cook's monument in the Texas State Cemetery lists his membership in the New Orleans Greys.

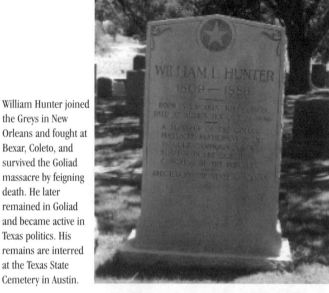

William Hunter joined the Greys in New Orleans and fought at Bexar, Coleto, and survived the Goliad massacre by feigning death. He later remained in Goliad and became active in Texas politics. His remains are interred at the Texas State Cemetery in Austin.

New Orleans Greys William Hunter and Thomas Ward (smaller marker) are interred together at the Texas State Cemetery. Both men became active in post-revolution Texas politics. Ward lost a leg at the Battle of Bexar, and legend claims his limb was buried in the coffin with Bexar hero Ben Milam.

William Lockhart
Hunter (Photo courtesy
of the Texas State Library,
Archives Division.)

Thomas William "Pegleg" Ward
(Photo courtesy of the Austin History Center,
Austin Public Library.)

William Gordon Cooke
(Photo courtesy of Z. T. Fulmore's "History and
Geography of Texas," The Texas Collection, at
The Center for American History, University of
Texas at Austin.)

Fannin Memorial, La Bahia

Battle of Coleto and Goliad Massacre marker

Fannin Memorial,
Coleto

The Alamo, San Antonio

Copy of the New Orleans Greys flag displayed in the flag room of the Alamo

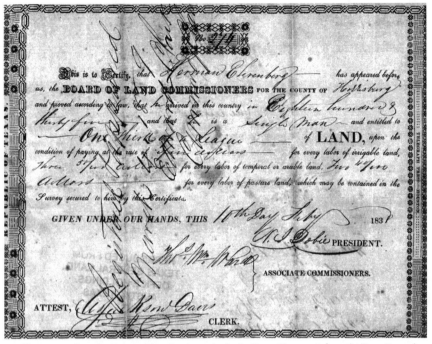

Land bounty certificate for Herman Ehrenberg's service in the Greys. The copy is from the Texas General Land Office.

Bibliography

Books

Asbury, Herbert. *The French Quarter—An Informal History of the New Orleans Underworld*. New York: Alfred A. Knopf, 1936.

Baker, D.W.C. *A Texas Scrap-Book*. Austin: Texas Historical Association, 1991.

Barr, Alwyn. *Texans in Revolt—The Battle for San Antonio, 1835*. Austin: University of Texas Press, 1990.

Biographical and Historical Memoirs of Northwest Louisiana. Chicago: John Morris Co., 1890.

Brown, John Henry. *History of Texas From 1685 to 1892 in Two Volumes*. Austin: Jenkins Publishing Company, 1970.

Chabot, Frederick C. *The Alamo Mission Fortress and Shrine*. Copyright Frederick C. Chabot: San Antonio, Texas, 1941, 3rd Edition: No publisher listed.

Chariton, Wallace O. *100 Days in Texas—the Alamo Letters*. Plano, Texas: Wordware Publishing, Inc., 1990.

Creighton, James A. *A Narrative History of Brazoria County, Texas*. Waco: Texian Press, 1975.

Deshields, James T. *Tall Men with Long Rifles*. San Antonio, TX: Naylor Co., 1935.

Dixon, Samuel, and Louis Kemp. *The Heroes of San Jacinto*. Houston: Anson Jones Press, 1932.

Duval, John C. *Early Times in Texas*. Austin: H.P.N. Gammel & Co., 1892. Reprint: Lincoln: University of Nebraska Press, 1986.

Field, Joseph E. *Three Years in Texas, Including a View of the Texas Revolution, and an Account of the Principal Battles,*

Together With Descriptions of the Soil, Commercial and Agricultural Advantages, etc., (1836); reprint. Austin: Steck Co., 1935.

Foote, Henry Stuart. *Texas and the Texans in Two Volumes.* Philadelphia: Thomas, Cowpertwiat & Co., 1841.

Groneman, Bill. *Alamo Defenders.* Austin: Eakin Press, 1990.

Hardin, Stephen L. *Texian Iliad—A Military History of the Texas Revolution.* Austin: University of Texas Press, 1994.

Haythornthwaite, Philip. *The Alamo and the War of Texan Independence 1835-36.* London: Osprey Publishing, 1986.

Jenkins, John H., Ed. *The Papers of the Texas Revolution 1835-1836 in Ten Volumes.* Austin: Presidial Press, 1973.

Johnson, Frank W. *A History of Texas and Texans in Five Volumes.* Chicago: American Historical Association, 1914.

Killion, Ronald and Charles Waller. *Slavery Time When I Was Chillun Down on Marster's Plantation—Interviews with Georgia Slaves.* Savannah: The Beehive Press, 1973.

Lack, Paul D. *The Texas Revolutionary Experience—A Political and Social History 1835-1836.* College Station: Texas A&M University Press, 1992.

Lockhart, Dr. John Washington. *Sixty Years on the Brazos.* Los Angles, CA: Privately Printed, 1930.

Lord, Walter. *A Time to Stand.* Lincoln: University of Nebraska Press, 1961.

Lubbock, Francis Richard. *Six decades in Texas; or, Memoirs of Francis Richard Lubbock, governor of Texas in war time, 1861-63.* Austin: B. C. Jones & Co., 1900.

O'Connor, Kathryn Stoner. *The Presidio La Bahia del Espiritu Santo de Zuniga, 1721 to 1846.* Austin: Von-Boeckmann-Jones Co., 1966.

Ornish, Natalie. *Ehrenberg: Goliad Survivor, Old West Explorer.* Dallas: Texas Heritage Press, 1997.

Pruett, Jakie and Everett B. Cole. *Goliad Massacre.* Austin: Eakin Press, 1985.

Tinkle, Lon. *13 Days to Glory: the Siege of the Alamo.* New York: McGraw-Hill, 1958.

Tyler, Ron et al editors. *New Handbook of Texas in Six Volumes.* Austin: The Texas State Historical Association, 1996.

Wallace, Ernest, ed. *Documents of Texas History.* Austin, Texas, Steck Co., 1994.

Wharton, Clarence. *Remember Goliad.* Glorieta, New Mexico: The Rio Grande Press, Inc., 1968.

Wilks, Ivor. *South Wales and the Rising of 1839.* Urbana: University of Illinois Press, 1984.

Williams, Amelia W. and Eugene C. Barker. *The Writings of Sam Houston 1813-1863.* Austin: Jenkins Publishing Company, 1970.

Wooten, Dudley G. *A Comprehensive History of Texas, 1685 to 1897 in Two Volumes,* 1898. reprint. Austin: Texas State Historical Association, 1986.

Yoakum, Henderson King. *History of Texas From its First Settlement in 1655 to its Annexation to the United States in 1846 in Two Volumes.* New York: Redfield, 1855.

Journals and Newspapers

Baker, Karl, "Trailing the New Orleans Greys," *Southwest Review,* Vol. XXII, No. 3, April 1937.

Carroll, Bess, "Help for Texans," October 17, 1935, in an unlisted San Antonio newspaper and part of the Daughters of the Texas Revolution Alamo library archives.

———, "Help from U.S.," November 21, 1935, in an unlisted San Antonio newspaper and part of the Daughters of the Texas Revolution Alamo library archives.

Davenport, Harbert, "The Men of Goliad," *The Southwestern Historical Quarterly,* Vol. XLVIII, No. 1, July 1939.

Houston Morning Star Newspaper, 1839-1844.

Koury, Mike, "Cannon for Texas Artillery in the Revolution and the Republic," *Military History of Texas and the Southwest*, Volume X, No. 2, 1972.

Lindley, Thomas Ricks, "Alamo Artillery—Number, Type, Caliber and Concussion," *The Alamo Journal*, Issue #82, July 1992.

Viener, Saul, "Surgeon Moses Albert Levy," *American Jewish Historical Quarterly*, December 1956.

Woolford, Sam, "Cooke Letter Coincides with Johnson's Report," *San Antonio Light*, April 21, 1940. Clipping from the archives of the Daughters of the Republic of Texas library.

Archives

Archives of the Adjutant General's Office (Louisiana), copy supplied by the Daughters of the Texas Revolution Alamo library archives.

Daughters of the Republic of Texas Library: MUSTER ROLLS OF THE TEXAS REVOLUTION, Austin, Texas, 1986.

Lamar Papers, Mirebeau B., Texas State Library.

Texas General Land Office:

[A1] Texas State Archives Online Index, Subseries: "Texas Revolution Military Rolls, 1835-1836" and "United States Volunteers Military Rolls, 1835-1837, 1842."

[A2] Texas General Land Office: MUSTER ROLLS #1 1850, Texas General Land Office, Archives and Records Division, Austin, Texas.

[A3] Texas General Land Office: MUSTER ROLLS #2 1856/1857, Texas General Land Office, Archives and Records Division.

[A10] Thomas Jefferson Green Papers (1801-1863), Southern Historical Collection, Univ. of North Carolina Library, Chapel Hill, NC.

Theses and Dissertations

Adams, Allen F., "The Leader of the Volunteer Grays: The Life of William G. Cooke, 1808-1847." M.A. thesis, Southwest Texas State Teachers College, 1939.

Young, Kevin, "CAPTAIN SAMUEL OVERTON PETTUS' COMPANY SAN ANTONIO GREYS" compiled at Presidio La Bahia, August 7, 1985.

Index